Eliza Calvert Hall

Eliza Calvert Hall

Kentucky Author and Suffragist

Lynn E. Niedermeier

To Tom:

Best regards,

Lynn Niederman

Nov. 2007.

The University Press of Kentucky

Frontispiece: Eliza Calvert Hall, after the publication of *A Book of Hand-Woven Coverlets.* The Colonial Coverlet Guild of America adopted the work as its official book. (Courtesy DuPage County Historical Museum, Wheaton, Ill.)

Publication of this volume was made possible in part by a grant from the National Endowment for the Humanities.

Scholarly publisher for the Commonwealth,
serving Bellarmine University, Berea College, Centre College of Kentucky, Eastern Kentucky University, The Filson Historical Society, Georgetown College, Kentucky Historical Society, Kentucky State University, Morehead State University, Murray State University, Northern Kentucky University, Transylvania University, University of Kentucky, University of Louisville, and Western Kentucky University.
All rights reserved.

Editorial and Sales Offices: The University Press of Kentucky
663 South Limestone Street, Lexington, Kentucky 40508-4008
www.kentuckypress.com

11 10 09 08 07   5 4 3 2 1

Library of Congress Cataloging-in-Publication Data

Niedermeier, Lynn E., 1956–
  Eliza Calvert Hall : Kentucky author and suffragist / Lynn E. Niedermeier.
     p. cm.
  Includes bibliographical references and index.
  ISBN 978-0-8131-2470-4 (alk. paper)
  1. Hall, Eliza Calvert. 2. Suffragists—United States—Biography. 3. Feminists—United States—Biography. I. Title.
  PS3515.A3168Z78 2007
  813'.52—dc22
  [B]   2007016756

This book is printed on acid-free recycled paper meeting the requirements of the American National Standard for Permanence in Paper for Printed Library Materials.

Manufactured in the United States of America.

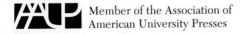 Member of the Association of
American University Presses

In memory of Emma Sailer and Agnes Crichton Young

Contents

Illustrations follow page 130

Acknowledgments

For their assistance in the preparation of this biography, sincere thanks are due to the following institutions and individuals: the Kentucky Library and Museum, Western Kentucky University; Jonathan Jeffrey, WKU Professor of Library Special Collections; Debra Day and Selina Langford, WKU Interlibrary Loan Librarians; Diane Kaufman, the Western College Memorial Archives; Kathleen Goodner Marine; Diane B. Jacob, Preston Library, Virginia Military Institute; Beth Burnett and Meg Meiman, University of Alabama Archives; Tim Tingle, Kentucky Department for Libraries and Archives; Sheila Biles, U.S. Military Academy Special Collections and Archives Division; Bob Glass, Grace Doherty Library, Centre College; Rachel Roberts, Dallas Historical Society; Josh Clough, University of Oklahoma Western History Collections; Van Pelt Library, University of Pennsylvania; Claire McCann, Special Collections Librarian and William J. Marshall Jr., Manuscripts Curator, Margaret I. King Library, University of Kentucky; William Bennett, for permission to use items from the Esther Bennett Deposit in the Laura Clay Papers; Eastern Kentucky University Library Special Collections; the Filson Historical Society; the DuPage County Historical Museum, Wheaton, Illinois, and its senior curator, Steph McGrath, for providing very helpful information on the Colonial Coverlet Guild of America; Dr. Morris A. Grubbs of Lindsey Wilson College and an anonymous reader for the University Press of Kentucky, for their thoughtful comments on the manuscript; and Cora Jane Spiller, for her generous gift of Lida's books.

Prologue

Lord, give me work, and strength enough to do it.

—Aunt Jane

"A HUMAN LIFE IS THE MOST interesting thing in the world," Eliza Calvert Hall once observed in reaction to the biography of a fellow author.[1] This book seeks to show—for what it tells us about the times of an ordinary Kentucky woman who resolved to be a writer and a feminist in the late nineteenth century—that no more interesting life can be chronicled than that of Eliza herself.

Eliza Calvert Hall was the pen name of Eliza "Lida" Calvert Obenchain, whose fame crested with her 1907 collection of stories, *Aunt Jane of Kentucky.* Appearing in at least thirty-three editions, the book endeared its principal narrator, the elderly, cheerful, plain-talking Aunt Jane, to perhaps a million readers.[2] Lida earned further acclaim with two more collections of stories, a novel, and a ground-breaking study of coverlet weaving. By the 1920s, however, she and other popular women writers such as Sarah Orne Jewett, Mary E. Wilkins Freeman, Charlotte Perkins Gilman, Ellen Glasgow, Kate Chopin, Alice Hegan Rice, and Annie Fellows Johnston had begun their slide into decades-long obscurity beneath a new wave of mostly male authors that included Theodore Dreiser, William Faulkner, Ernest Hemingway, F. Scott Fitzgerald, and in Kentucky, Jesse Stuart and Robert Penn Warren.[3]

The American women's movement of the 1960s initiated a rediscovery of Lida's generation of female storytellers. Aunt Jane's gentle,

1

homespun philosophy became newly quotable, particularly after feminists succeeded in elevating one of her domestic talents, quilt making, from an aesthetically trivial craft to the realm of legitimate art.[4] Although Lida remains largely ignored by anthologists of nineteenth- and twentieth-century American women writers, she too has been afforded some recent attention in scholarly journals, popular drama, and reissues of *Aunt Jane of Kentucky*.[5]

To know Aunt Jane, nevertheless, is to know little about Lida, her literary achievements, the sources of her creativity, or the challenges she confronted as both a woman and a writer. She was born into a family that was a microcosm of the stubborn principles, divided loyalties, and anguished choices that would soon ignite the Civil War. After the war, she suffered the economic dislocation common to many Kentuckians, but through circumstances that were uniquely catastrophic. Although the war abolished slavery in her state, Lida entered adulthood subject to laws that not only denied the vote to members of her sex but fixed their age of consent at twelve and, upon marriage, relieved them of most of their property and civil rights—all within a social framework of chivalrous, southern-style worship of the Kentucky woman's legendary beauty and charm. Of the few vocations open to respectable single women, Lida pursued two, teaching school and composing sentimental poetry, before becoming a wife and the mother of four children in eight years.

By the end of Lida's life, almost all of women's legal and political disabilities had vanished,[6] but she had hardly been a spectator to this transformation; indeed, the story of her contribution to Kentucky literature must be told alongside the story of her work with the Kentucky Equal Rights Association and its founder, Laura Clay. Lida's advocacy of simple justice for her sex—for every woman's right to vote, make a will, control her property, earn and keep her wages, develop her mind, and be accorded respect for her housekeeping and childrearing—was inseparable from her fiction writing. Even as these two passions competed for her time, she readily subordinated them to a third, the welfare of her family. As a consequence, Lida became starkly acquainted with the choices known to all women who take up the pen—between work and home, solitude and connection, dreams and duty, truth and propaganda, creativity and utility—in short, between the elusive prerequisites for art and the categorical demands of life.

Like many authors, Lida bristled at the notion that her fiction proceeded wholly from autobiography and that her own personality was identical to that of her Muse.[7] Her surviving letters to friends and family help to sustain her objection, even if they also trick Lida into exaggerating her flaws through personal missives that were never intended to be read cumulatively, much less by a stranger born one hundred years later. In contrast to the fictional Aunt Jane, a contented old woman who treasures her memories of a long and democratic marriage, accepts others' failings and believes that everything will work out for the best, Lida was more often troubled, pessimistic, quick both to judge and to regret, impatient with faith when it defied logic, and narrowed by assumptions—particularly about race—that marked her as a product of her time and place.

At the same time, Lida possessed not only talent but other strengths that proved critical to her success in literature and to her effectiveness as a champion of her sex: courage, loyalty, independence, robust intelligence, and the determination, despite significant obstacles, to keep her gaze fixed on things greater than herself. The life of Eliza Calvert Hall provides us with an opportunity to deepen our understanding of the battle for women's rights and women's writing—stories that, Aunt Jane would agree, are always worth telling.

1

Fighting and Preaching

> But there's so many ways o' beginning a story, and you never know
> which one leads straightest to the p'int. I wonder many a time how
> folks ever finds out where to begin when they set out to write a
> book.
>
> —Aunt Jane

THUS DOES AUNT JANE HESITATE, but only briefly. Remembering that two generations have passed through the "mills of God"— the men much more noisily than the women—to provide grist for her tale, she begins with them. Had she to tell the story of Lida Calvert Obenchain, Aunt Jane would settle happily upon the same starting point.[1]

The only grandparent still living at Lida's birth was her paternal grandmother, Eliza Caroline Hall Calvert. The oldest of nine children, Eliza was born in 1804 in Iredell County, North Carolina, where her father, Thomas James Hall, was a pastor and teacher. When Eliza was still a child the family moved to Rutherford County in middle Tennessee, and a few years later to Marshall County (then still a part of Bedford County) adjoining on the southwest; there, Thomas Hall took charge of Rock Creek Church and continued to teach.[2]

Samuel Wilson Calvert, Lida's future grandfather, was one of Rev. Hall's Latin scholars and an adopted member of his household. In her stories, Lida would portray Samuel as coming to study in Rock Creek only after first giving rein to his "wild streak." Born in Georgia in 1796, he was said to have spent a year in a Tennessee militia company during the War of 1812 and to have participated in several campaigns against the Indians, including Andrew Jackson's defeat of the Creeks at Horseshoe Bend. Having allowed the "fighting blood" in him "to have its day," Samuel had then turned to cultivation of his "preachin' blood" under the tutelage of Rev. Hall.[3]

Although deeply attached to the Hall family, Samuel decided to prepare himself more formally for service to his Lord. In 1821 he enrolled at Greeneville College, a small Presbyterian institution in east Tennessee. Under the presidency of Charles Coffin, a Harvard-educated minister, Greeneville College had weathered the storm at the turn of the nineteenth century when theological modifications—heresies, some would say—spread through the denomination. Commonly called the New Divinity, or sometimes "Hopkinsianism" after its leading proponent Samuel Hopkins, the doctrine reexamined Calvinism in the context of the Age of Enlightenment. While accepting the notion of humans' corrupt disposition, it questioned whether original sin, and not solely their own acts, predestined men and women to condemnation. Confirming the innate wickedness of humankind and not wishing to deny God's sovereignty, the New Divinity nevertheless suggested that men and women had some ability to contribute to the cause of their own redemption.[4]

After an uncomfortable journey to Greeneville, Samuel Calvert found lodging near the college and, fighting homesickness, waited anxiously for letters from Rock Creek. No sooner did he settle into his studies than a fire severely damaged his possessions. Samuel persevered, for by early 1823 he had assumed additional duties as an instructor at the college and moved into its new boardinghouse. There, he found himself in the middle of a serious breach of discipline when a group of students hung an effigy of a house steward whose cooking and manner they found unpalatable. Samuel was disturbed, not only by the retaliatory nature of the prank but by the students' unrepentant solidarity in the face of suspension—an example, perhaps, of men's innate disposition to wickedness. Only weeks earlier, his physical health had also suffered a blow. Attending chapel one morning, he began experiencing chest pain and coughing blood, first signs of the tuberculosis that would stalk him for the rest of his life.[5]

Samuel returned to Rock Creek early in 1824, but within six months departed again for east Tennessee to study divinity under the Presbytery at Maryville. Once more he regretted leaving the Hall home—my "earthly bliss," he called it—where he had grown ever fonder of Rev. Hall's daughter Eliza. Inching toward a formal courtship, Samuel sent her the journal he had kept during his trip to Maryville, with only the first page torn out. "There were some things on it which I wished no one to see but myself," he told her. "Indeed I never thought of any body but myself ever seeing a word of it, but it struck me this morning, that it might afford you some amusement." His other writing while at Maryville took a more serious tone. In his notebook "containing questions, notes & essays on important subjects in theology," Samuel carefully charted the Bible's clues to the mysteries of election, predestination, and God's grace. Despite the Hopkinsian atmosphere of Greeneville College, he had suspected the sinner to be incapable of attracting divine grace solely through his own change of heart; in fact, he wrote in his journal, the gift of grace was surely necessary to effect such a change in the first place. "I hope," he worried, "I have correct notions of the truth on this subject."[6]

On June 9, 1825, a month after the Presbytery of West Tennessee licensed Samuel as a minister of the Gospel, he and Eliza Caroline Hall married. The couple continued to live with Eliza's parents in Rock Creek while Samuel preached intermittently at a church in Maury County to the west. In January 1826, he secured a more regular appointment at Elk Ridge Church in Giles County, but he and Eliza did not take up permanent residence with the congregation until October, Samuel finding it "small and feeble" and ill-disposed to supporting a minister. It was there, nevertheless, on February 21, 1826, that their first child, Thomas Chalmers Hall Calvert, was born. A second son, John Griffin, was born July 1, 1827, and a third, Emmons Whitfield, on September 19, 1828. A daughter, Emma Hall, followed on October 12, 1829.[7]

Samuel and his family experienced five difficult years at Elk Ridge. The young preacher managed to convert some souls and to embarrass his flock into putting aside its Hopkinsian-inspired feuding, but he remained disappointed with the housing and other material comforts provided him. The Calverts' second son, John Griffin, sickened and died on February 26, 1829. Samuel's tubercular lungs drained him of strength, especially when he followed up a sermon at his own church with another at Marrs Hill, a few miles away.[8]

In early 1831 Samuel dutifully embarked upon a seven-week tour through Tennessee and Alabama to help raise funds for a regional school. Cold and rain, bad roads, and flooded creeks made the journey wearisome, but so did his own exacting standard of manners and Christian behavior. The good intentions of the hosts upon whom he depended for lodging along the way often fell short as Samuel found his social and intellectual tastes, so well nourished in the home of Rev. Hall, easily soured in the grip of his stern Presbyterianism. He became particularly anxious whenever the Sabbath drew near. Finding himself one Saturday evening in the company of a family with several young girls, he attempted to "relieve the tedium of their chit-chat about nothing, by engaging them in singing from a campmeeting Songbook." The next day was cold and gloomy, and carried no prospect of attending a service. "No society, because no religion here," he complained to his journal. Only after another of the family's girls rendered a song "with an air of becoming sobriety," and Samuel conversed at dinner with a reasonably well-schooled (though Methodist) visitor, was the evening somewhat redeemed. The next day found a high creek between him and his scheduled destination, but he was so desperate to leave that he took a fifteen-mile detour to Rev. Hall's, where he reflected upon his escape:

> How strangely is my mind affected by surrounding objects! My whole animal, intellectual & moral nature is susceptible of the most important changes from the mere change of circumstances. . . . However, with me, comfort depends more upon the society I am in than upon every thing else. . . . I felt this evening like I had exchanged the gloom of the dungeon for the cheering light of a cloudless sun.[9]

Before resuming his tour, Samuel also spent a week in Elk Ridge. While at home, his efforts to unite his principal parishioners with those at nearby Marrs Hill not only proved unsuccessful but raised his fear that the congregation itself was dissolving. Such a prospect may have prompted Samuel to make an exploratory visit the following October to Bowling Green, Kentucky, a town of about eight hundred people. After preaching several times over his ten-day stay, he accepted the offer to take charge of its Presbyterian church.[10]

The prospects there were no less daunting than what he had faced at Elk Ridge. Organized in 1819, the Bowling Green congregation had enjoyed promising beginnings under Rev. Joseph B. Lapsley, a Virginian who had also come to the post from Tennessee. Unfortunately, Lapsley had died in 1823, just before his forty-fourth birthday. Other deaths, removals, and temporary preachers had caused the church to wither, and by the summer of 1828 the pastorship was entirely vacant. Sometime in 1831 the church building was also lost to fire.[11]

With Eliza now pregnant for the fifth time, the Calverts began their journey north from Giles County on November 16, 1831. After a stop at the Hall home in Rock Creek they set out for Bowling Green, Samuel gripped by melancholy over his imminent separation from friends and kin. They arrived in Nashville intending to catch the stage to Bowling Green on Thursday, December 1, but missed it. Another was scheduled to leave that Sunday but Eliza elected to wait until the following Tuesday, her conscience forbidding her to travel on the Sabbath. Her husband, however, decided to continue ahead on horseback with their son Thomas, now almost six years old. Arriving at his new home late on Saturday night, Samuel preached his first sermon the next day.[12]

Although Bowling Green's Presbyterians would continue to revere Joseph Lapsley, their founding pastor, it was the earnest, frequently ailing Samuel Calvert who rescued their church. He held a series of revival meetings, which significantly increased membership and offered broader support for his next goal, a new house of worship. Most usefully, by 1833 Samuel and three elders, the merchants Samuel Barclay, John Marshall, and Mathis W. Henry, had recruited other men of means to subscribe funds for a church building. A valuable new member was James Rumsey Skiles, who had returned from law studies in Nashville to farm his family estate and assist in developing the county through several business ventures. In 1822 he had sold to Joseph Lapsley the 110-acre farm where the preacher now lay buried. To Samuel Calvert, Skiles donated a prime lot in town on which to build the new church and one hundred dollars to pay for drawing the plans. Other citizens donated cash or value to the project in the form of labor, real estate, building material, and crops.[13]

The church's future looked promising, but Samuel remained impatient and afflicted with a characteristic worry and gloom. Although

the pace of construction was slow, in summer 1835 he finally admitted
to his journal that the interior work was being completed on a "very
decent" church at the corner of Tenth and State streets, a block from
the public square. He did not allow himself much greater enthusiasm
over the spiritual progress of his flock. At a gathering in the Skiles
parlor where he found some thirty young women among the recent
converts, Samuel's doubt at the depth of their commitment quickly tempered his elation. Perhaps a new church had made Bowling
Green's Presbyterians too proud. "The spirit of piety has seemed to
decline in this place," he charged. "We have as a congregation much
reason for self-condemnation, & deep humiliation before God." Samuel likely did not keep such judgments to himself. His voice would
reappear in Lida's fiction as that of Brother Samuel Wilson, hectoring
his followers to turn away from dancing, horse racing, card playing,
violating the Sabbath, and other worldly snares.[14]

Although Samuel's message was sometimes unwelcome, his
congregation respected his leadership. Late in 1835, after hosting a
meeting of the Synod of Kentucky and expanding their number with
another revival, members voted to raise the salary of their pastor.
Samuel was humbly thankful for the financial reward, since two more
children—Sarah Amanda, born April 14, 1832, and Henry Baxter,
born August 5, 1834—had increased his household to seven. Ever
more frequently coughing and spitting blood, he was now losing hope
in his prospects for a long life.[15]

Samuel Calvert's decline lasted eighteen months, until June 19,
1837, when he died, six months short of his forty-first birthday. A be-
reaved Eliza carefully transcribed his obituary from a Presbyterian
journal, then added her own expression of faith that "through grace,
a joyous meeting where parting is no more" awaited her at the end of
life. Samuel's funeral would long be remembered as the first held in
his new church.[16]

Within the walls of the church itself, Samuel left another important legacy. The initial 1833 subscription list for its construction
had made clear that part of the funds would be applied to the establishment of a female academy. Franklin Jones, a thirty-one-year-old
missionary-teacher from Massachusetts, had promised to contribute
one hundred dollars if Samuel succeeded in reserving room for his
school in the building's basement. By September its future must have

been assured, for Franklin moved to Bowling Green with his new wife, and they formally joined the congregation. On February 7, 1834, the Bowling Green Female Academy was chartered, and Franklin and Mary Kendall Jones opened the school in their home across the street while waiting for the church to be completed.[17]

Like Samuel Calvert, Franklin Jones did not enjoy a long life; like Eliza Hall Calvert, Mrs. Jones, in 1846, found herself widowed with five children. Some in the congregation opposed her succeeding her husband as principal of the female academy, but her supporters would not be moved—nor would they be disappointed. Over the next fifteen years, Mary Kendall Jones made her name legendary among the early educators of Bowling Green. Remembered for her physical beauty as well as her intelligence, faultless character, and strict piety, she and a group of assistants annually transformed scores of girls into scholars and young ladies. Sarah and Emma Calvert became students and later assistant teachers. Their mother, Eliza Hall Calvert, shared a sisterlike bond with Mary Kendall Jones, and their friendship would help Samuel Calvert's descendants through a trial he never could have foreseen.[18]

Samuel's church, unfortunately, did not hold together. In November 1839, two years after his death, half of its eighty-seven members—a group that included Eliza Hall Calvert, Franklin and Mary Kendall Jones, and the donor of the church land, James Rumsey Skiles—formed a separate congregation. Their act of defiance mirrored a new split over denominational doctrine and practice that was more severe than what Samuel Calvert had witnessed as a young preacher. Not only did the New School of Presbyterianism take up the Hopkinsian notion that humans might effect their own salvation, it also showed alarming innovation in its sympathy with abolitionism and in its revival meetings, mixed assemblies in which women might lead the prayer and vocally deplore sin both in themselves and others. Differences in practice, however, did not prevent Bowling Green's two factions from remaining practical; for nineteen years the New School, led by Rev. Archer C. Dickerson, shared the church building with the Old School. Nor did the split imply a less rigorous orthodoxy among followers of the New School; as James Rumsey Skiles would learn, mere rumors of dancing, profanity, intoxication, or other impious behavior required an accounting to Rev. Dickerson and the session.[19]

One of Bowling Green's younger citizens took even more liberty than Skiles in undermining the solemnity of the church. When his oldest son, Thomas, began school in November 1832, Samuel Calvert had been characteristically anxious about the possible corrupting influence of the other boys. "How delicate is the character of a child!" he wrote in his journal. "How easily spoiled!" The parents of his classmates, however, might have had greater cause for concern, for Thomas, like his father, had a youthful "wild streak." A church member described him as one of Bowling Green's "ringleaders of fun & frolic" who played the prankster at all of its religious revivals. More evidence lies in Lida's stories depicting the young Thomas Calvert as a chronic fighter and mischief-maker. In one tale, Brother Wilson's oldest boy "hoodooed" the church bell with a sock tied around the clapper, hoping to suppress its customary summons to the children of town for Saturday-morning religious instruction. In another, he disabled the clock underneath the pulpit on New Year's Eve, then watched with glee as the congregation waited expectantly for midnight chimes that never came. When not playing pranks on adults or fighting neighborhood boys, Thomas would spar with his brother, born Emmons Whitfield but known to all as Joseph Whitfield. It was Joseph Whit, so the tale goes, who exacted a fifty-cent fee from the elders before making the hazardous climb into the belfry to expose his brother's muffling of the church bell.[20]

High-spirited Thomas, nevertheless, could present a serious and dutiful side. From the age of six he had taken charge of the family vegetable garden, and the need to help his mother and siblings no doubt required many other labors of the firstborn son. Not long after his father's death, the twelve-year-old was earnestly filling his copybook with some of Samuel's sermons and essays. A teacher remembered him as a capable scholar and a promising young man, although Thomas would later criticize the long hours of study and threats of corporal punishment that kept him weary and frightened of learning.[21] As he weighed the hopes of his family and community against his resentment of such privations, Eliza and Samuel Calvert's son—the boy who would become Lida's father—entered adulthood both conscientious and ambitious, his capacity for trustworthiness as great as his readiness for risk.

2

"It Did Not Look as We Had Pictured You"

He, who through the vast immensity can pierce,
See worlds on worlds compose the universe,
Observe how system into system runs,
What other planets circle other suns;
What varied beings people every star,
May tell why Heaven has made us what we are.
—Inscription on Thomas Calvert's copybook, 1838

THOMAS CALVERT'S TWENTIETH BIRTHDAY present was a job offer: early in 1846 the owner of a stagecoach company asked him to act as an agent to accommodate passengers disembarking from Cumberland River steamboats. The job, however, was in Nashville, Tennessee, some seventy miles south of Bowling Green. Like his father, Thomas could not look ahead without thinking first of the sorrows attending such a significant change in circumstances. Complicating the prospect of separation from his mother, two sisters, and two brothers was the possibility that nervous creditors would seize the property he was leaving behind for his family's support. After consulting with all parties to whom he was financially or emotionally obliged, Thomas decided to go to Nashville in hopes of improving his net worth.[1]

The young man struggled to acclimate himself to his new surroundings. Nashville was a busy city, its streets crisscrossed with drays and hacks (many, to Thomas's horror, loaded with whiskey), choked with dust when dry, and drowned in mud after a rainfall. Making himself more at home by contacting some former acquaintances, he also received encouragement in letters from his mother and from his friends the Underwoods. Lucy Craig Underwood was a daughter of Mathis W. Henry, one of the Presbyterian elders who had worked alongside Samuel Calvert. Her husband, Warner Lewis Underwood, was a Virginia-born lawyer who would soon be elected to the state senate and later to Congress. Warner's older brother, Joseph Rogers Underwood, was also a lawyer and legislator. A letter from Warner expressed "a strong desire for my success," Thomas recorded in his diary, and he was further pleased when Lucy, whom he respected no less than his mother, included a line of her own.[2]

More often, however, Thomas wandered about Nashville feeling lonesome and worrying about his debts. A month after arriving, he made his first reply to one of his mother's letters to ask if any collection attempts had been made during his absence. He also wrote to his seventeen-year-old brother Joseph Whit for help in a small speculative venture. If he could procure some currency in thalers, German coins popular in trade because of their dependable silver content, Thomas was confident that he could resell them at a profit.[3]

Before long, Thomas decided that a career in the law would better serve his ambition. He may have apprenticed with Warner Underwood's nephew Eugene, who had established a practice in Nashville. In any event, by spring 1849 Thomas had returned to Bowling Green and opened his own office. He was determined to make a success of his new calling and to keep careful control of his finances, but his efforts bore little fruit. He tried to apply himself to his law books in the intervals between clients, but when work did come his way it was less than edifying. After a winter day spent out of town taking a deposition, Thomas confided to his diary that during the ride home he had "thought often of the little hardships & inconveniences a poor d[evi]l must encounter on the road to wealth, and wished I was able to be independent of the small practice of my profession." He continued to pursue other income through speculation in both currency and commodities, but the market was fickle. The year 1851 brought only heavy losses and left him wondering if he should make a new start in a larger city.[4]

If the daily grind of a legal practice and the lure of the speculative market were not enough to draw Thomas away from his office, family, friends, and acquaintances offered ready sources of distraction. He frequented Bowling Green's Aeolian Lodge of Odd Fellows and provided clerical assistance to his brother Joseph Whit, who had opened a store. He left work early to join his friends on riding trips, ideally in the company of young ladies. Although he seemed to be popular, Thomas could not permit himself fully to enjoy these pastimes. Guilt-stricken when he neglected his law practice, he was also disappointed at the lack of intimacy in his friendships. After a sleigh ride one January day, he reflected that he "had a merry time, but I thought often of the office & that I ought to be there and if I had any time to spend sleighing I would prefer making my own selection of company." He did not fail to notice the attachments of the other young men in his circle. Encountering Warner Underwood's niece Jane and her husband, George Rogers, Thomas envied Rogers for having someone to whom he could turn for conversation and advice. He nevertheless disapproved of the short courtship of two local newlyweds, finding "a full knowledge of each other's dispositions" to be indispensable to domestic peace. Still stumbling on the road to financial independence, Thomas comforted himself with a sermon condemning materialism in a husband and wife. Even more than a mistaken faith in another's devotion, he preached to his diary, the "blind hope of happiness in wealth" contributed to marital disappointment, then misery.[5]

Like his father, who had realized that his comfort depended most upon the society he frequented, Thomas continued to search for oases of hospitality. He dropped into Younglove's Drugstore on the public square to sit near its stove and converse with the other men of town. He became something of a fixture at Mount Air, the estate of Warner and Lucy Underwood, where, upon entering the parlor, he was likely to encounter one or another of the family's female relatives and friends. Perhaps it was at these familiar places that Thomas became better acquainted with one of his riding companions, Margaret Younglove.[6]

The ninth of ten children of Isaiah Younglove and his wife, Susannah Yanney, Margaret had been born in 1829 in Johnstown, New York. Both of her grandfathers had served in the Revolutionary War: Dr. David Younglove as a surgeon and Henry Yanney in the New York militia. Situated on a main east-west road forty miles northwest of Albany, Johnstown was well known to travelers for its inns and taverns.

In 1796 Henry Yanney had opened the Black Horse Tavern, one of the largest in the area and located about a mile south of town. Dating from the 1780s, Margaret's childhood home was an even older landmark of early American hospitality. Known itself as the Black Horse Tavern until about 1793, it had been operated for twenty years as Burke's Tavern when Isaiah Younglove purchased it in 1812 to house his shoemaking business and his growing family. Raising their five daughters and four surviving sons, Margaret's parents were mostly spared the sorrows cast over another family, the Cadys, who lived in an upscale home only a few blocks to the north. Three years before Margaret's birth, Daniel Cady, a lawyer, legislator, and wealthy landowner, had endured the sudden death of the last of his five sons. Left without a male heir to carry his name or considerable patrimony, the despondent father had cried out to one of his daughters, "I wish you were a boy!"—inflicting a wound that eleven-year-old Elizabeth Cady Stanton would never forget.[7]

The watershed in Margaret Younglove's life came when she was orphaned at the age of fourteen and subsequently sent to Bowling Green to join two older brothers: Joseph, who had opened Younglove's Drugstore in 1842, and John, who had come to assist Joseph after the death of his partner. Working to establish themselves in their new town, the three siblings nevertheless retained close ties with family back in New York, where Margaret was as well thought of as in Bowling Green. A cousin was warmly appreciative, finding her distinctive among his relatives for her patient and quiet disposition, industriousness, common sense, and want of "those versatile gifts which pour forth a volume of undisciplined ideas." Thomas Calvert's sisters Emma, who was Margaret's age, and Sarah, who was three years younger, were delighted to make the acquaintance of this sensible young woman.[8]

The year 1852, however, brought Thomas reasons to prolong his courtship of Margaret. One development was rather unexpected, given his boyhood history with the local Presbyterians. During the winter Rev. Archer C. Dickerson, who had led the New School for almost thirteen years, had raised such revivalist fervor in town that Thomas complained of being unable to find company outside of church. At the April 25 service, nevertheless, he was so swept up by Dickerson's preaching that he rushed to the pulpit and threw himself into the

arms of the pastor. The next day, a surprised Elizabeth Cox Underwood wrote to her husband Joseph in Washington that Thomas had
declared himself to be "the greatest sinner in the Town. . . . He is more
deeply convicted of sin than any one has been here for a long while. I
saw him this morning weeping in anguish of spirit, and the great solic-
itude of his mother & sister is touching." A week later, Thomas joined
the church at the same time as another convert, Margaret Younglove,
and seven months later was elected a deacon.[9]

A second development gave Thomas financial prospects to accompany his spiritual rebirth. The railroad was coming to Bowling Green.
Thomas had already joined his brother, his friends the Underwoods,
and Margaret's brothers John and Joseph Younglove in subscribing
for stock in the Bowling Green and Tennessee Railroad (BG&T).
Chartered in 1850 on the same day as the Louisville and Nashville
Railroad (L&N), the BG&T demonstrated citizens' firm commitment
to securing service, if necessary from a competing carrier, should the
L&N bypass their town. Deferring his thoughts of starting anew in
another city, Thomas helped survey a route for the BG&T before the
two railroads merged in 1852 and Bowling Green won a place on the
L&N's line.[10]

While waiting for the railroad to be built, Thomas took notice
of other opportunities. Early in 1852 the Green and Barren River
Navigation Company, which operated locks and dams on local water-
ways, lost its superintendent to resignation. The former stagecoach
agent and still-underachieving lawyer affected some deliberation over
"whether it was likely to prove the wisest course in the end for me to
drop my limited practice, & as it were lay aside the law for a salary
of six or eight hundred dollars," but three days later Thomas made a
special trip to Mount Air to pick up a letter from Warner Underwood
recommending him for the position. This time, unfortunately, the passage of his birthday was not accompanied by a job offer.[11]

Thomas rebounded, securing a position in July 1853, as cashier of
the Bowling Green branch of the Bank of Kentucky. Incorporated in
1834, the Bank of Kentucky had anticipated the so-called free bank-
ing era during which hundreds of state-chartered institutions, each
issuing its own currency, had commenced business across the nation
and vastly expanded economic activity. As the day-to-day administrator of his branch, Thomas bore important responsibilities: supervis-

ing the keeping of the books and other records, evaluating the great variety of notes and coin presented to the institution, and reporting to the president and board of directors. He also would have been charged with monitoring the bank's reserves of gold and silver, with which it was obligated to redeem its currency on demand. Despite the tedious and time-consuming aspects of these duties, Thomas must have found the new job well matched to his ambitions. Not only could he enjoy a stable source of income, but he could become more closely acquainted with Bowling Green's growing agricultural, transportation, commercial, and speculative sectors.

A year and a half later, their families celebrated the engagement of Thomas C. Calvert and Margaret Younglove. For Thomas's sisters Emma and Sarah, no woman was a more welcome sister-in-law; in striving to make himself worthy of Margaret, they believed, Thomas would find happiness. For Jane Younglove, her older sister's good judgment was sufficient to invest Thomas with extraordinary qualities. As Margaret's Johnstown relatives gathered around his photograph, Jane excitedly wrote Thomas that "it did not look as we had pictured you in our imagination, although we like your looks very much everyone says he has a fine intellectual forhead [sic], one says it is just the kind of beauty I admire another isn't he handsome!" With the blessings of their families, the couple married at the home of Margaret's brother Joseph Younglove on January 23, 1855.[12]

In the same house, on February 11, 1856, Thomas and Margaret Calvert's first child, Eliza, was born.[13] Known from infancy as "Lida," she joined an extended family of Calverts, Youngloves, and Halls. Her widowed great-grandfather, Thomas J. Hall, and Eliza Hall Calvert, her grandmother and namesake, now lived with Thomas and Margaret. Joseph Whit Calvert was kind and attentive to his new niece, and Lida even visited her northern relatives at the Younglove homestead in Johnstown, New York, where she was bewitched by the gardens of the former Black Horse Tavern. At home, longtime servants also populated her childhood world. Minerva Pollard, the Youngloves' cook, took the Calverts under her wing. Thomas and Margaret regarded Isabella Curd, their own cook and "mammy," as "one of the best women in the world" even though "Aunt Bella" sometimes lost her patience with the young ones. Another servant—perhaps a slave—Uncle George, regularly brought small gifts to the Calvert children.[14]

Lida, indeed, soon found herself the first of a growing family. Born in 1858, Mary was quiet and fragile in health but became a favorite of Aunt Bella and of Thomas, who would remember her in her high chair presiding over happy family dinners. Another daughter, Margaret, was born two years after Mary. In 1864 all the children would spend a summer day with their uncle Joseph Younglove while their mother gave birth to Josephine. Perhaps by this time eight-year-old Lida was weary of the duties that already would have devolved upon the firstborn in such a household. "Lida said when she saw the new baby that she didn't want the thing there," Joseph Younglove reported to his brother John.[15]

As blonde, blue-eyed Josie and her sister Maggie eclipsed the two older Calvert girls, Lida found escape with treasured books—*Alice's Adventures in Wonderland,* Hawthorne's *Twice-Told Tales,* novels, and poetry collections—given her by Uncle Whit and friends. Like any nineteenth-century child in search of amusement, she also became familiar with the topography of her small town—its houses and occupants, commercial establishments, animal and plant life, geographical features, gossip, and folklore—to a degree unknown to modern, urban youth. More than fifty years later, as if recreating a childhood ramble, one of her friends could still tally the landmarks of old Bowling Green—its market, stores, and hotels, "Younglove's Corner" on the public square, the site where farmers sold cider and ginger cake from their wagons on election day, and the stately homes of the well-heeled.[16]

With his young daughters and capable wife by his side, Lida's father seemed destined to occupy one of those large homes. Beyond his bank cashier's job, Thomas threw himself into numerous entrepreneurial activities, trading vigorously in land, debt and commodities, including gold, and in the prosperous cotton market. One of his first investments after marrying Margaret was the acquisition of Vinegar Hill, an undeveloped, fifty-eight-acre tract on the southwest edge of town. He acquired other interests in land through purchase or by taking assignments of notes, liens, and mortgages. He entered into partnerships with a local brickmaker and a lumber mill owner, and appears to have lent money privately, either on his own account or as a factor for others. His wealth grew steadily: by 1860 Thomas had accumulated real estate assets worth $11,000—compared to $550 a decade earlier—and personal property worth $25,000. He also made time for civic duties, becoming a town trustee shortly after Lida's birth, then an elder of the Presbyterian Church when the New School, the breakaway congregation of which his mother was an original member, reunited with the Old School in 1858.[17]

The Civil War, however, brought trials for the Calverts, their families, and neighbors. Although Kentucky had attempted to remain neutral, Bowling Green, located on river, rail, and turnpike routes linking North and South, attracted the attention of strategists on both sides. Its 2,500 citizens, mostly Union sympathizers, greeted Confederate occupation of the town in September 1861 with much trepidation. General Simon Bolivar Buckner commandeered as his headquarters the State Street home of Joseph Younglove, who had removed his family to New York after consigning the house and garden to the care of Aunt Minerva. When General Albert Sidney Johnston took over command, he evicted the residents of Mount Air in order to secure lodging for his officers' families. Warner Underwood, his wife, children, and servants took refuge in a friend's cabin fifteen miles away as Confederate troops helped themselves to his timber, corn, and wheat.[18]

Along with several other elevated locations, or knobs, surrounding the town, Thomas Calvert's Vinegar Hill became the site of one of General Johnston's fortifications. The Confederate authorities also required his formal surrender of the keys to the Bowling Green branch of the Bank of Kentucky, directing the institution to resume business subject to a promise not to fund the enemy. Thomas, however, maintained his entrepreneurial spirit. He dealt in horses and mules, and continued to invest in securities and real estate. He speculated in gold on his own and others' behalf; friends like John L. Row, a local mill owner, maintained an agency account in hopes that the profits would pay down various obligations held by Thomas's bank. Thomas also showed a willingness to do business with military authorities on both sides of the conflict. He and a partner gave the use of a bakery they had recently built first to the Confederates, then, after General Johnston's withdrawal in February 1862, to the Federals. The following autumn, Thomas and another partner secured a contract to furnish Union troops in Bowling Green with beef and other foodstuffs.[19]

The arrival of the Federals did not restore tranquillity to the town.

More than half its population had fled to safety elsewhere, and those who returned found much of it destroyed by Union shelling or Confederate arson. The Underwoods' Mount Air was a burned ruin, and Younglove's Drugstore had been broken into and looted. For Lida, the most regrettable consequence of the war may have been the closing of the Bowling Green Female Academy, where she first attended school. The revered Mary Kendall Jones, now in her early fifties, a teacher since Lida's grandfather built the Presbyterian Church, determined that the time to leave had come. In 1863 she sold her home and departed with her children for St. Louis.[20]

Some citizens found that suspicion over divided loyalties had further damaged their community. Although Thomas Calvert escaped accusations of Confederate sympathy, his partner in the bakery venture did not. Thomas, in fact, grew increasingly alienated from the Presbyterian Church over what he maintained were rebel tendencies in its pastor. As a consequence, in December 1864 the session voted to exclude him, together with several Underwood family members, for lack of attendance and support. These sanctions foretold yet another congregational split when resentment over continuing depredations and Federal martial law after the war sent most of the church into the arms of the Southern General Assembly. The remaining faithful, including the Calverts and Youngloves, established the Second Presbyterian Church.[21]

Other local developments occurred with less rancor. The war had barely ended when the Bank of Kentucky resolved to discontinue its branch operations, and Thomas became one of five commissioners appointed to raise capital for a new financial institution. Chartered in June 1865, the Bank of Bowling Green soon purchased the assets of the Bowling Green branch of the Bank of Kentucky. Most of the directors stayed on, and Thomas retained his position as cashier, making the change largely imperceptible to the public.[22]

Unfortunately, the transfer also carried the seeds of scandal. One of the routine services continued by the Bank of Bowling Green was the acceptance of special deposits from customers. Unlike general deposits, which became the bank's property subject to repayment of the same sum on demand, special deposits were deliveries of specific money or securities for safekeeping. The bank undertook to return the identical property and could neither mingle it with other funds nor apply it to institutional purposes. The customer paid no fee for the service and was generally acknowledged to assume the risk of the arrangement. As cashier, Thomas was well accustomed to issuing receipts for these deposits and recording them in a book kept for the purpose. While still employed at the Bank of Kentucky branch, he had accepted from one depositor more than $20,000 in banknotes and gold coins, property that succeeded to the care of the Bank of Bowling Green. Another customer entrusted bonds valued at $11,500, and the United Society of Shakers, a religious colony of more than two hundred members located a few miles from town, placed more than $72,000 in bonds on special deposit.[23]

Thomas's own fortunes continued to rise. During the 1860s his personal estate increased almost fivefold and his real estate assets more than tenfold, making him the modern-day equivalent of a multimillionaire. He maintained the confidence of friends and business associates who had money to invest, purchasing at one time some $12,000 in gold from a New York broker to fill their orders. He and his family were also held in high personal regard. Lida was not only a guest of the Shaker colony but recalled frequent social visits to the Calvert home by Shaker elders. Margaret Calvert, too, remained a valuable asset to Thomas's career and reputation. Early one morning, a year after the war, he wrote a letter to Johnstown, New York, where she and the children were visiting. After eleven years of marriage, he told her, he remained convinced that she was "of all women in the world the one to make me happy as a wife." Admiring in her an independence and a dignity that was nevertheless free of any attempt "to put on airs," he urged her to "exert an influence on the dear children that will lead them to imitate your example."[24]

Thomas's business interests, however, soon became so demanding that he found less and less time for his bank duties. Margaret's brother Joseph Younglove, by 1869 a director of the Bank of Bowling Green, wrote to Thomas's brother offering him the cashier's position should Thomas not care to keep it, but Joseph Whit, now married and in the furniture business in Louisville, was himself earning too much money to return. Younglove nevertheless wrote again and during one of Joseph Whit's visits to Bowling Green made a personal appeal. More than the need for a full-time cashier may have explained such persistence. Joseph Whit later claimed that Younglove had discovered

Thomas Calvert's misappropriation of bonds belonging to a prominent local physician and customer of the Bank of Bowling Green. He
had confronted Thomas and recovered the bonds within a few days
but then, after failing to find a replacement cashier, had let the matter
drop. He did not—or so Joseph Whit maintained—report the mis-
deed to his fellow directors.[25]

Thomas, meanwhile, continued to outgrow his job in a highly visible manner. On the eastern slope of his Vinegar Hill property he began to build an impressive new home. Local architect D. J. Williams,
whose credits included the county courthouse, the city's waterworks,
and another of its most distinguished residences, designed for his cli-
ent a two-story, asymmetrical brick structure in the Italianate style.
Together with its large stable, the house, valued at $30,000 (more
than $415,000 today), composed a fitting estate for one of Bowling
Green's leading businessmen.[26]

Thomas's triumph, however, was short-lived. Just as his magnificent new home on the hill neared completion, he toppled into
insolvency and disgrace with astonishing speed. The post–Civil War
collapse in prices had steadily undermined the value of two commodities in which he had a particular stake; between 1865 and 1870 the
market price of gold had fallen more than 25 percent and cotton more
than 60 percent. Accounts for materials used to construct the Calvert
house suddenly went unpaid. Joseph Younglove, moreover, could no
longer look the other way as Thomas's performance of his cashier's
duties, including his failure to respond to inquiries about deposits and
his attempts to have checks honored by other banks with which the
Bank of Bowling Green had no credit, grew more and more irregular.
"Come at once," he wrote Joseph Whit in Louisville, and this time
Thomas's brother complied. As word spread of his bank's troubles,
Thomas resigned, then committed a very public act of insolvency. On
October 6, 1870, he transferred his house and all of his other property
to two trustees for the purpose of satisfying his debts.[27]

Learning of this voluntary divestiture of assets, on October 13 two
creditors swiftly petitioned Thomas into bankruptcy. The U.S. district
court in Louisville voided the transfer of his property and called for
creditors to meet on November 14, when they learned that the estate's
liabilities exceeded $310,000 as against assets of some $250,000. By
that time, the extent of Thomas's betrayal had become known as spe-

cial depositors descended on the Bank of Bowling Green and found it unable to produce their notes, bonds, and gold. With more than $60,000 in bonds unaccounted for, the Shakers were among the most seriously compromised. When general depositors attempted to withdraw funds or redeem notes, they too were denied. An early count estimated that some $160,000 in special deposits and $60,000 of the bank's own funds were missing. In modern-day terms, almost $3.1 million was gone.[28]

The predicament of Thomas's friend John Row illustrated how the scandal spread beyond individuals whose property had been stolen to affect, in one newspaper's account, "the pockets of many citizens of this and adjoining counties." At the time of Thomas's bankruptcy, Row was about to be sued by the Bank of Bowling Green for a debt arising out of a bill of exchange. An order to pay drawn by a seller, creditor, or lender, and acknowledged by the debtor, a bill of exchange was a common form of "merchant money," since the creditor might then sell the bill by endorsing it to a third party, who could sell it again or present it for payment. If the debtor proved unable to pay, the first and all subsequent sellers of the bill remained liable for its amount. Not only would merchants use the bill of exchange in place of specie payments, they would commonly draw and endorse bills for each other as favors, lending their good name to the particular transaction and to the negotiability of the document. John Row's bill bore the names of two such "accommodation parties," both of whom faced liability when Thomas Calvert neglected to deposit the profits from Row's gold speculations with the Bank of Bowling Green. Countless other members of the business community, accustomed to endorsing bills and cosigning notes in a collegial sharing of risk, likely were caught in similar webs of obligation.[29]

Deposed at Row's request on November 12, Thomas admitted selling his friend's gold but was otherwise evasive. As the Bank of Bowling Green, which he had rendered insolvent, struggled to make small payments on general depositors' claims, the community's initial shock turned to impatience, then anger. The extent, if any, of the bank's liability to special depositors became the subject of heated debate in legal circles. The Shakers vociferously claimed that their bonds had not just been stolen but converted to the bank's own use and that the directors knew, or should have known, what was happening. Such accusations brought the bank's directors, including its president Joseph Rogers Underwood, now a seventy-nine-year-old retired judge and congressman, under suspicion for possible complicity in the fraud. The bank's charter specifically provided that if convicted they, along with their cashier, faced prison terms of up to twenty years. Fingers began to point in all directions.[30]

Thomas, however, had retained a few friends who were in a position to sense the gathering storm. Within two weeks after giving his deposition in John Row's case, Thomas met with Row outside of town and was warned for his own safety to go home. That night, after the rest of the Calvert family had retired, Row arrived with two associates. The men dug into their pockets and produced $110, which they gave to Thomas. Row then accompanied him to the railroad depot, where the pair stealthily boarded a train out of town.

Thomas's last word to his family had been not a farewell to Margaret but instructions to Aunt Bella to keep the children quiet so they would not wake her. Aunt Bella's duties in this regard had increased only weeks earlier, for on November 10 forty-one-year-old Margaret Calvert had given birth to a son, Edward.[31] Neither he, nor his mother, nor his sisters would see Thomas again for almost thirteen years.

3

Exile

> But while a good writer is able to instruct and please mankind, he has certainly the strangest hold upon them that can possibly be obtained. . . . He can influence individuals, and sway the counsels of nations, whithout [sic] unsheathing a sword or even leaving the tranquility of his own fire side.
>
> —Samuel W. Calvert, as copied by Thomas Calvert

THOMAS'S FLIGHT LEFT HIS VICTIMS beneath a mountain of bookkeeping puzzles and legal proceedings. Indictments filed in the circuit court formally charged him with embezzlement. In mid-December 1870, the bankruptcy court transferred all of Thomas's property to two assignees and instructed them to liquidate his extensive real estate interests. The assignees were also forced to assume the prosecution or defense of numerous lawsuits in which Thomas had become involved in the course of his business or as a result of his collapse. Unable to meet its liabilities, the Bank of Bowling Green soon followed Thomas into bankruptcy. The Shakers recovered some of their money from the bank's assignee but, still unconvinced that Thomas's fraud could have been possible without the guilty knowledge or gross negligence of others, began a decade-long battle to gain full restitution from the directors. As prior custodian of some of the missing special deposits, even the Bank of Kentucky found itself drawn into litigation.[1]

While creditors and lawyers sorted through the financial wreckage, baby Edward and the Calvert women—Margaret, fourteen-year-old

Lida, twelve-year-old Mary, ten-year-old Maggie, and six-year-old Josie—experienced the trauma of sudden poverty and downward social mobility. With little more than their clothing and household furnishings, they crowded into the home of Margaret's brother Joseph Younglove, his wife, Sarah, and their children. Another loss now followed so closely that the children might have been tempted to see their father's removal as its cause. On the evening of February 8, 1871, sixty-six-year-old Eliza Hall Calvert, who now resided with Joseph Whit in Louisville, retired to her room and was found dead there the next morning. She was buried in Bowling Green where, in the displaced Calvert household, a humble piece of furniture evoked her memory. When Eliza first arrived from Tennessee, a member of the church congregation had given her a hickory chair in which she sat to bathe her children and rock them to sleep. "She liked it because it was low and hadn't any arms for the baby's head to get bumped on," one of Lida's stories related. Lida was fond of the chair because, unlike the cherry secretary on which she imagined her grandfather Samuel Calvert composing a "mile-long sermon on election and predestination," it carried no "unpleasant association." Bankruptcy exemptions being less partial, both items survived the dispersal of Thomas's assets.[2]

Thomas himself was now far away. The late-night train from Bowling Green had taken him and John Row to Louisville, where they met with Joseph Whit. After spending another night debating their next move, the men had gathered some clothes and more money and boarded a train for Lafayette, Indiana, where Thomas had his hair and beard dyed. Row and Joseph Whit had then escorted Thomas to Chicago and left him to travel on alone to the frontier town of Greeley, Colorado. A few weeks later, Joseph Whit wrote a letter to his brother promising to send money and advocating even more distant sanctuaries—the "Sandwich Islands or Mexico."[3]

Unwilling to comprehend either the extent of his jeopardy or the finality of his exile—not only had he left home without a word to Margaret, but while in Louisville he had avoided a final opportunity to see his mother—Thomas resisted his brother's advice. Ultimately, however, he was not faithful to his plan to hide in Colorado for the winter, and the vague rumors surrounding his subsequent disappearance attested to its success. Some of his former colleagues believed that he actually fled to Mexico, then to South America. A local history written long afterward claimed that he lived under a rather transparent alias in eastern Kentucky. Thomas may have sojourned in all three locations and elsewhere. He most likely moved at regular intervals from one job and boardinghouse to another and spent at least some time in the United States and its territories.[4]

Back in Bowling Green, Margaret was left dependent upon her own brother's largess and Joseph Whit's, an arrangement made more awkward by Joseph Whit's claim that he, too, was one of Thomas's victims and that Joseph Younglove's silence had compounded his loss. Margaret nevertheless displayed a characteristic determination and practicality by ensuring that the disaster did not interrupt the education of her three oldest children. Although the Presbyterian Church had begun another female academy within a few years after Mary Kendall Jones left Bowling Green, in 1868 Thomas H. Storts, a Baptist minister, had also established a school for girls near Joseph Younglove's home. In January 1871, only two months after their father's flight, Lida, Mary, and Maggie Calvert were enrolled in Storts's school. Lida supplemented her twenty-week course of study with instrumental and vocal music, electives that more than doubled her twenty-five-dollar tuition, but over the next two years, as at least two of the three sisters attended each session, Rev. Storts demonstrated remarkable forbearance in collecting his fees. In spring 1873 he had received against his $308 account only ten dollars in cash and two counterpanes, two blankets, and a set of silver spoons valued collectively at twenty-eight dollars. Lida, however, rewarded his patience with diligent study. She excelled in English literature, won a medal for proficiency in instrumental music, and graduated as salutatorian of her class.[5]

Perhaps Lida's aptitude, combined with the realization that Thomas would not soon return, convinced Margaret to make the further sacrifices necessary to groom her daughter for a paid teaching position. In fall 1873 Lida left for Oxford, Ohio, to continue her education at the Western Female Seminary. Established twenty years earlier, the school was an original daughter of Mount Holyoke Seminary, the pioneering women's institution founded by Mary Lyon. It sought consciously to replicate Mount Holyoke's atmosphere by drawing girls into close familial relationships with their teachers, with whom they lived and studied in the school building, and by incorporating evangelical religious culture into its program of mental training. The seminary also adopted Mary Lyon's strategy for keeping costs, and hence tuition and room fees, at a minimum by assigning students at least one hour of domestic duties each day. Helen Peabody, a Mount Holyoke graduate and teacher, had served as principal of the Western Female Seminary from its beginning, and her students included Martha Smith Calvert, an 1860 graduate and the wife of Lida's uncle Joseph Whit.[6]

Lida entered the first year of a four-year program, studying algebra, English, ancient and modern history, physiology, botany, and the Bible. At first, the reserved seventeen-year-old escaped notice. Lida had been "so modest & retiring that they were just beginning to understand her," Martha Calvert wrote to Margaret after a mid-year conference with Miss Peabody. Her pleasant singing voice and faith-inspired confidence, however, had soon earned the principal's fulsome praise. "She never knew a sweeter or more lovely girl *in every respect* as Lida is," Martha proudly reported. "Miss P. says Lida's *Christian* character is developing *beautifully*—she takes an *active* part in all the prayer meetings—think of Lida's *leading* a prayer meeting with over *one hundred* girls in attendance—Isn't it beautiful?" History teacher Emily Jessup, another Mount Holyoke graduate, concurred with her principal's high opinions in language suggesting that Lida's father's disgrace had been successfully concealed behind the sponsorship of Joseph Whit. Miss Jessup had written to Martha giving "kindest regards to yr. Husband & my congratulations that his name is *so honorably* represented in our house-hold—Lida is a girl any Uncle should be proud of." For good measure, Martha conveyed to Margaret Miss Peabody's understanding that Lida was considered "the prettiest girl in school." Perhaps more encouraging was Martha's own expectation that Lida would be asked to teach at the seminary after graduating, evidence that she was not only excelling academically but absorbing the spirit and discipline of her mentors on the faculty.[7]

Lida, however, spent only a year in Ohio. The school's annual board and tuition of $165, her family's other expenses, and Joseph Whit's deteriorating financial condition undoubtedly contributed to her early withdrawal. Another continuing obligation was for tuition at Rev. Storts's school, where her youngest sister Josie had joined Mary and Maggie. Lida returned to Bowling Green and began to work for Storts as a teacher, rendering $275 worth of service during 1874–75 and ensuring, by her agreement to remain the next year, that the family's account would be retired. Although she contemplated another year at the seminary, ideally with Mary's company and the means for a "comfortably furnished room," Lida's formal education was now behind her.[8]

Soon after Lida's return, her mother, who was never at ease taking charity from her brother and brother-in-law, gave her more reason to continue teaching. In fall 1874 Margaret moved the family some seven blocks northeast of the Youngloves into their own house, a frame cottage on Park Street. Payment of its $1,250 purchase price, probably using funds from Joseph Whit and settlements made with Thomas's assignees of her dower interest in his real estate, suggested how much Margaret valued her independence, but did not signify that her financial condition had stabilized. The former millionaire's wife evidently considered her prospects of earning a living in the national depression of the 1870s—then began taking in washing. Lida's sister Mary also contributed by hiring out her sewing skills, an enterprise that changed the nature of the family's reliance on a former servant. Prior to his bankruptcy, Thomas had agreed to sell Aunt Bella a house he owned, to be paid for with her domestic labor. After his assignees completed the sale in 1873, the longtime cook and nurse, now established in her own home, reversed roles with her former charge. She not only helped Mary learn to sew but either steered work her way or subcontracted her own work.[9]

Although she now needed her older children's help to relieve her financial straits, Margaret continued to seek an education for the younger ones. Her perseverance was admirable, given that only Lida and Mary had felt themselves bound to excel in school; despite possessing a certain native intelligence, Maggie and Josie as well as their brother Edward required much prodding to overcome their indifference to study. Fortunately, one of her mother's old friendships soon provided an opportunity for Maggie to lengthen her education without incurring additional debt. Mary Kendall Jones, having maintained her long association with the Calverts, invited Maggie to St. Louis in August 1876 to attend school and live with her family, an arrangement that would last for the next three years. Not long after Maggie's departure, Josie's schooling came directly under Lida's supervision. When her employer, Rev. Storts, defaulted on his mortgage and lost his school, "Miss Lida," as her pupils called her, established her own private school, first at the Second Presbyterian Church, then in a cottage near Joseph Younglove's home. When Lida was ill, Mary substituted as teacher.[10]

Given her youth and natural sociability, Josie's world was no doubt more carefree than that of her sisters and mother; nevertheless, her diary, kept for some two years beginning when she was fourteen and her father had been gone eight years, shows the family regaining a certain normality. Josie attended Lida's school, sometimes more faithfully than other pupils; one April morning when the circus was in town, she found herself among only three present, and on another spring day was one of two. She spent time with her young friends, attended lectures and concerts, did housework, sewed, and ran errands. Her mother, Margaret, and sister Mary went on rounds of social calls (although on one occasion a visit was cut short by eight-year-old Edward's bad behavior), and received guests at home so regularly that Josie found a Sunday in fall 1878 unusual for its absence of visitors. If her reading was any indication, the family was highly literate: Josie consumed Shakespeare, Dickens, George Eliot, and Charlotte Brontë as well as periodicals like *Scribner's, Atlantic Monthly,* and the children's magazine *St. Nicholas.* When Josie was fifteen, Lida gave her a volume of Tennyson's poems. Other reading matter arrived in the mail that Josie picked up at Younglove's Drugstore: the *New York Tribune* and *Independent,* the *Times* from nearby Glasgow, and no doubt because of Maggie, the *St. Louis Globe-Democrat.* Her diary recorded both the small misfortunes and great sorrows that occasionally darkened her youthful consciousness. When she and Lida cooked dinner one night "every thing went wrong," beginning with the burning of the biscuits. Making one of her few references to their financial circumstances, Josie noted that her mother did not receive a present on her fifty-second birthday. Early in 1879, her uncle Joseph Whit and his wife, Martha, became the parents of a girl who lived only two weeks. A year later, Martha herself was dead.[11]

Josie's diary never mentioned the greatest misfortune of her childhood, and at least one of her sisters also regarded their father's fate as beyond the bounds of conversation. Henry C. Batts, a beau of Maggie's, later admitted to her that he had often wanted to raise the subject "though you have never even remotely referred to it, since I have known you. . . . You never intimated that such a thing would be allowed," he explained, "and I never dared trespass." Almost from the day he left Bowling Green, however, Thomas trod regularly across the consciousness of his children. Enlisting Joseph Whit as trustee, he established a fund, which, though small—generating just twenty-three dollars per month in 1876—contributed to his family's mainte-nance. Remarkably, he also maintained a covert correspondence with Margaret and the children (again, using Joseph Whit as a trusted go-between) that lasted the full term of his banishment.[12]

In contrast to Josie's matter-of-fact diary entries, Thomas's letters spoke in detail to the stresses of his impoverished family, not the least of which was the duty of accommodating his epistolary presence—variously paternal and childish, sympathetic and self-pitying, proud and needy, elusive and intrusive. He responded with ambivalence to the Calvert women's attempts to put the best face on their pre-dicament. Thomas was pleased with Margaret's assurances that her brother Joseph had been generous and that the children, emulating her own lack of interest in showy dress, were satisfied with plain cloth-ing. He grew anxious, however, when Margaret's industriousness took her ever further from the sphere of leisured ladyhood into which he had schemed to place her, and he pleaded with her to retain some of the markers of her former economic and social status. Agreeing with Margaret that "work is a great panacea," he instructed her nev-ertheless not to indulge this philosophy to excess. Instead of ironing clothes, she should send out the work to one of many "poor people" looking for a wage. As Mary came to rival her mother in her unswerv-ing application to household duties, Thomas's letters again counseled moderation, citing the poor health that had so often kept his second daughter at home rather than in school. When she wrote that she and her mother did the ironing by choice, Thomas understood her protest only as a failure to find outside labor that would meet their high do-mestic standards. He never failed to express his regard for Aunt Bel-la, but Thomas also reminded Mary of the embarrassment she must be suffering in working for her "mammy." Like Margaret and Mary, Josie found that even well-meaning references to the family's material condition and morale had an unintended effect. When she reported receiving a purse as a Christmas gift, Thomas doubted that the giver "was making sport of you, but it would seem an almost useless article in your present financial situation." He was unequivocal, by contrast, in his demands of the only person in the household who could now save his mother and sisters from dishonor. Not only did Thomas forbid hiring others to perform chores suitable for his son—Edward should draw water, carry in all wood and coal, and assume responsibility for the garden—he also asked Margaret to report on the seven-and-a-half-year-old's efforts to "earn a living" and help his family.[13]

Besides a kind of compulsory leisure, Thomas promoted two other womanly values, piety and selflessness, as a way of blunting the hardships of his daughters' lives. He urged his children to pray and read scripture, and was delighted when Lida's and Mary's baptism in 1873 signified their "bold stand on the Lord's side." Like other Protestants weary of Calvinist pessimism, however, the anguished sinner who had converted in 1852 did not tender his own fate as an example of divine anger at irredeemable human depravity; he was, he wrote to Mary, only a weak man in need of her prayers. Confessing to Margaret his "coldness and indifference on the subject of salvation," Thomas preached to his family a more liberal ethic based less on reunion in the next world than on self-discipline and autonomy in the present one. He recommended that Mary teach her Sunday school class that "all our unhappiness and misery are the result of our disobedience" and that Margaret impress upon the children "the truth that we are the authors of our own happiness or misery." As he grew increasingly rootless and devoid of friendship, Thomas urged upon his family another, more romantic but scripturally based Protestant creed. "Love one another," he commanded his children. "Urge them to stick close to each other and love one another," he repeated to Margaret. Not only were the children to promote their siblings' happiness and ease the burdens on their mother, but any kindnesses shown within the household should be extended to others, the servants Aunt Bella, Aunt Minerva, and Uncle George receiving special mention. For his youngest daughter, Josephine, Thomas prescribed the traditional remedy for female gloom: "If you would be happy yourself, you must do all you can to make others happy."[14]

Not the least of those seeking the benefits of female altruism was Thomas himself. The arrival of one of his many letters reaffirmed his prior claim on whatever reserves of support and nurturance his wife and children still possessed after a day of domestic labor and desperate economizing. Out of fear that his correspondence would be intercepted and because letters sometimes took months to be delivered, Thomas kept a record of the dates of each, then made a notation when it had been answered. Such score-keeping soon took a manipulative turn when the children were slow to reply. "Think of my loneliness," he protested to Margaret, worried that he was being forgotten. "Maggie must write if only a few lines," he insisted of his fifteen-year-old daughter after recounting the dates of his last four letters. Complaining in 1878 that he had not heard from seven-year-old Edward in more than a year, he was willing to give greater latitude to the boy he had left as a newborn only because his recollection of his father was so slight; but to daughter Mary, bent over her sewing machine, he wrote peevishly to ask why "the one who has no studies on hand cannot drop me a line to say 'all well,' if nothing more." Even Lida, absorbed in her teaching duties, was gently chastised; Thomas asked Margaret to tell her that he had written on her birthday but observed that she had not reciprocated on his. From time to time, Margaret must have dutifully assembled the children and put them to the task of writing their father, but still the results were unsatisfactory: the letters arrived all at once and related the same news. Thomas advocated a rotating schedule in which one child would compose a letter at one- or two-week intervals. Mailing not more than two at a time, assuming that Joseph Whit attended promptly to his forwarding duties, would give him a steady supply and allow him to respond in orderly fashion. The idea gained little cooperation, however, leaving Thomas ever more inclined to criticize. Mary once erred by writing too many lines on thin paper that strained his eyes. He told her that he had destroyed a photograph of her and Edward, apparently preferring none at all to one poorly made. A letter from Josephine passed muster only because, although not as long as those of her sisters, it was "more newsy."[15]

Thomas not only thirsted for news but hung upon every detail of his family's daily activities. In his earlier life as a busy banker and entrepreneur, he might well have taken little interest in his wife's and daughters' domestic work, but now Thomas, like a doting aunt, congratulated Mary when her sewing met Margaret's standards and hoped that her quilts would earn a prize. Seeking to groom them as correspondents, he regularly urged the children to keep diaries (a re-

quest with which only Josie seems to have complied) and expected
them to write of even the most ordinary changes in their lives. After
they moved into their Park Street home, he was anxious to learn about
the house, its furniture, and the barn, and assured Josie that her description of the yard and garden could not be too trifling. "Tell her,"
he instructed Margaret, "to make it minute so that I can see it in my
imagination." He asked for their heights and weights so that he could
visualize his children in people of similar size whom he might meet.
Experiencing his own isolation, the unfamiliar content of the newspapers he procured and his family's delinquency in writing, Thomas
often lapsed into reminiscence. In the centennial year of 1876, he endorsed a proposal to prepare histories of every American county and
offered Margaret a list of local elders who could add Warren County
lore to the record of the nation's past.[16]

Though disappointed that Lida had not remained more than a
year at the Western Female Seminary, Thomas reserved most of his
preaching for her siblings, holding out their oldest sister as a model
and warning Maggie and Josie that they would feel ashamed if lack
of education rendered them less intelligent than their acquaintances.
More often, his references to Lida respected her entitlements as a
substitute provider. After she became a teacher at the Storts school
he vowed to repay, with interest, the wages she assigned to her sisters'
tuition. He made his approval of Josie's music lessons subject to both
Lida's and Margaret's determination that the expense was affordable
and, notwithstanding Margaret's sentiment, deferred to Lida's judgment that funds were insufficient to send Mary on a trip. When Lida
opened her own school he rather vainly offered, through Margaret,
the benefit of his financial expertise to a fellow entrepreneur: "Tell
her to collect closely. It's one of the elements of success and adds
pleasure to the business." Thomas suspected that even his most accomplished daughter was not immune to social embarrassment—
Lida, he supposed, was anxious to have the Calvert house appear
as well appointed as poverty allowed—and no doubt would have
approved when, unlike her plainly attired siblings, she patronized
the town's upscale dressmaker. In personal matters, Thomas was relieved to learn that lack of means had not undermined Lida's powers
of discrimination. He welcomed Margaret's report that, rather than
endure the company of gentlemen "not her equals," the twenty-two-

year-old schoolmistress had determined "to make her books and papers her companions."[17]

Not just her apparent bookishness and reserve but all of her activities over a decade of hardship showed that Lida possessed the self-
discipline and seriousness typical of a girl called upon to stand in for
both an absent father and a brother not yet able to fulfill paternal
expectations. Her father's letters, her sister's diary, and her own later
words, however, suggest that she had suffered many wounds. Thomas's
departure was an obvious blow, but it had also deprived Lida of part of
her mother. As the parent who stayed behind, Margaret remained at
the family's moral center, yet her husband's financial adventures had
exposed the economic and social fragility of her position as a woman
and wife. Her efforts to keep a functioning but frugal household for
five children, moreover, would have left her with little time for their
incorporeal needs. Lida remembered that "use your judgment" was
Margaret's usual response to requests for guidance, and Thomas's frequent admonitions to Mary and Josie to "help and cheer your mother"
made clear the unimportance of any childish troubles they or their
siblings might be longing to share.[18]

If fear and uncertainty became hers to bear alone, Lida nevertheless had reason to remain deeply loyal to her mother. Though
dogged by constant scarcity, Margaret's tireless and unsentimental
orchestration of the family's resources, a habit her status-conscious
husband found almost insubordinate, must have been humbling to
the daughter whose higher education had left her with more of a taste
for gentility than her earning power could accommodate. In an article written years later, Lida recognized both the shortcomings of
such an education and the influence of women like Margaret, arguing
that students who pursued expensive college degrees could learn as
much from mothers whose high standards of housekeeping created
an atmosphere of "cleanliness, order and beauty" as from classroom
lessons. Elsewhere, she defended the woman in need of money who
ignored the wagging tongues of society and made "a brave confession of her poverty by taking up some honest work." For Lida, money
would become only one of many matters begging for honest expression, especially between husbands and wives.[19]

Was Lida less ambivalent toward her fugitive father? Her youngest daughter Cecil—again, many years later—charged that she hated

Thomas for what he had done to the family, yet Lida's relationship with her father was surely as complicated as her and Cecil's would prove to be. Ironically, Thomas's distance from his children seemed to allow him to convey more openly his paternal affection to them, both directly and through their mother. While Margaret was the instrument of his authority, allocating meager funds, sending the children to school, and directing their domestic chores, the lonely father could preserve feminine values of love, mutual support, and connection, not only to humans but to nature; Thomas's most touching mode of expression was the enclosure, in letters to daughter Mary, of pansy seeds or a pressed flower. In hectoring them to keep diaries and write letters filled with detail, Thomas also drew his children's attention to life's ordinary endeavors—tending a garden, teaching Sunday school, piecing a quilt, helping one another—and to the possibility that recording them offered a moment of reflection and creativity at the conclusion of the day.[20]

Lida's bond with her father, however, must have subsisted amid growing frustration and helplessness. If Thomas had been dead her responsibilities would have been no less burdensome, but because he was both alive and in some respects not even absent, her position as his stand-in was far more ambiguous. Even as he acknowledged Lida's contributions to the household, Thomas took for granted his continuing authority in the delivery of fatherly counsel. His letters isolated their recipients behind a veil of secrecy, never using full names and employing a simple substitutionary code in matters of family gossip or debt, yet he routinely asked that he be remembered to selected acquaintances or, more vainly, to anyone who inquired after him. He even kept secrets from his wife, who learned in 1879 that he had sent money to Joseph Whit with instructions to take what he needed before aiding Margaret and the children. As the years passed, Thomas's enforced absence came to resemble more of an orchestrated withdrawal that increasingly mocked his oldest daughter's ability to effect any lasting security for herself or her family.[21]

The true extent of the Calverts' distress, perhaps, lay somewhere between Josie's casual record and Thomas's gloomy one. An unusually positive sign appeared in 1878, when Margaret contemplated building an addition onto her small house, but by spring 1880 her sister-in-law was despondent. "O! Mag," wrote Martha Calvert just before her death, "sometimes when I allow myself to dwell on what has occurred in the past ten years the only wonder is that you Whit or I have lived through them!"[22]

A few weeks later, local perception of the family's need became apparent when seventeen creditors and thirty Bowling Green attorneys petitioned Governor Luke P. Blackburn to pardon Thomas Calvert. The applications made clear that the poverty of his family and the incapacity of its women, rather than any particular forgiveness of Thomas, lay behind the appeal. The attorneys' petition noted that he had left behind a wife and "five small children, four of the children being girls, without any means of support," and the creditors' petition also offered the family's dire circumstances as consideration for the pardon. In a separate submission, creditor William H. Rochester explained that mercy for Thomas was necessary "on account of his family who are almost pennyless [sic]." Rochester understood further that Thomas was not seeking readmission into the community; rather, he contemplated summoning his wife and children to settle with him in a new location. "Mr. Calvert does not propose to return to Kentucky," he wrote, "but wishes to return to the United States and that his family may go to him."[23]

In these attempts to redeem Thomas lay a chance, finally, of relief for the Calvert women, provided that they now joined him in exile. As Lida faced the possibility that her home would be uprooted and, in any event, the likelihood that Thomas's reemergence would again transform her role in the family, the governor only prolonged her uncertainty. Although he had begun implementing a broad program to pardon some of Kentucky's criminals, Blackburn's principal objective was to relieve overcrowding in the state penitentiary, and he declined, at least for the present, to exercise his prerogative on behalf of the fugitive Thomas Calvert.

With Lida's responsibilities continuing to loom before her, certain aggravating questions cannot have spared the intelligent, twenty-four-year-old schoolteacher. If Thomas had come to believe that the God of the Presbyterians no longer saved or condemned men outright, both his recklessness and Margaret's fortitude may well have convinced their daughter that the course of a woman's life remained forever predetermined—by fathers, husbands, children, and her own inner voice calling her to sacrifice. Remembering Thomas's words that "we are the authors of our own happiness," Lida might also have seen as her next duty the discovery of some measure of compensation for her sacrifices—in work, perhaps, or in art, or in love. Little wonder, then, that even as Thomas was praising his daughter's self-sufficiency, she was keeping other company besides books and papers; and even as he complained of receiving no letters, she had begun her writer's life.

4

The Major

And have I wakened thee to life and love,—
Life with its burden, love with thorny crown,
And death that puts an end to all fair things,—
Who might'st have stood in calm and stony grace
And perfect beauty all the ages through?
Forgive me, sweet!

                                    —Eliza C. Hall, "Galatea"

ON SEPTEMBER 15, 1879, Josie Calvert recorded in her diary that her oldest sister had received a fifteen-dollar check from the editors of *Scribner's Monthly* magazine. Expecting that her submission of two poems more than a week earlier "should not come to anything," Josie wrote, Lida "had not told—but when she received 7½ dollars apiece she could not keep it from us a minute." Thanks to the magazine's liberal policy of payment on acceptance, the Calverts suddenly found themselves richer by the modern-day equivalent of some $285.[1]

Though she rightly regarded publication as improbable, Lida made a sensible choice in soliciting the patronage of New York–based *Scribner's*. Begun in 1870, the magazine had built a circulation of 100,000 and ranked with *Harper's Monthly* and the *Atlantic Monthly* as one of the most promising markets for writers. Unlike the *Atlantic*, which relied upon New England contributors, and *Harper's*, which serialized British novels, *Scribner's* advanced the cause of post–Civil War reconciliation by giving special attention to southern authors and topics. Ironically, in view of the direction Lida's writing would later take, its senior editor, Josiah Gilbert Holland, was a firm opponent of woman suffrage and a critic of laws allowing married women control of their own property, but he was otherwise respected for his goodwill and fair dealing. Holland's co-editor, Richard Watson Gilder, was a romantic character who searched for the purest expression of his idealism in poetry. While gradually tempering Holland's use of *Scribner's* as a platform for moral crusades, Gilder maintained the magazine's reputation for courtesy toward its authors. Submitting her work to these gentlemen may have made the difference for a young woman typically possessing little confidence in her ability and, in the style of her grandfather Samuel Calvert, a reflexive pessimism. Fifty years later, Lida remembered that the "brilliant future" Gilder forecast for her "never seemed very brilliant to me," but she could "still recall the leap of my heart at that prophecy." Portions of her first published poem escaped her memory, but she had not forgotten that *Scribner's* had judged her "scrap of blank verse" to be "one of the most exquisite things in the English language."[2]

The poem "Galatea" appeared promptly in the November 1879 issue, and "A Lesson in Mythology" followed in December. Both used Greek myth—Pygmalion and his ideal woman, and Hippomenes' footrace with Atalanta—as the backdrop for a hymn to love. Both also joined the torrent of "magazine poetry"—earnest songs about nature, ardor, beauty, and mortality, most of them composed by women—that ran through the pages of popular periodicals in the late nineteenth century. The December *Scribner's* in particular attested to Richard Watson Gilder's relentless cultivation of such verse. An intrepid reader would have come upon Lida's "A Lesson in Mythology," in the issue's last section of "Bric-À-Brac," only after wading through another section of twenty poems by American women, all of whom, no doubt, had been praised as enthusiastically as she. Although even contemporary critics found their work derivative and sentimental, in rising to the top of what must have been a flood of submissions these contributors could count themselves among the best, and best-paid, of their number. Several of them, including Celia Thaxter, Rose Terry Cooke, Elizabeth Stuart Phelps, Helen Hunt Jackson, Mary Mapes Dodge, and Emma Lazarus, built reputations that transcended their association with magazine poetry. By spring 1880, after Holland and Gilder had published another of her poems, Lida might have seen herself ranking creditably with these working women authors.[3]

In using the pseudonym "Eliza C. Hall" for her *Scribner's* poems, Lida adopted another time-honored practice of the woman writer. Fear of being scandalized by entry into such a public profession had inhibited many of her literary predecessors, and Lida too had most likely had enough of scandal. At the same time, her father's mysterious fate had accustomed her to secrecy, particularly as it gave the holder power not only against the world but over those bound to keep his confidences. By her choice of name, nevertheless, Lida seemed less concerned with creating an impenetrable disguise than with maintaining a nominal distance from the public as she cultivated her voice. At a time when American women were more openly establishing their literary credentials, she could steer a middle course between a masculine pseudonym that would have hidden her aspirations and a "hyperfeminine" one that would have mocked them. In this regard, a name such as "Eliza C. Younglove" may have struck her not as too conspicuous but, given the subject matter of her first poems, too precious, a misrepresentation of both her mother's values and Lida's seriousness about her work. In her grandmother's maiden name, on the other hand, lay a promising combination of sobriety and marketability. Trying to write her way out of a difficult decade, Lida also gave her first clue about the world in which she would attempt to find solace.[4]

She was not, however, the aloof, solitary scribe her father might have imagined. As Josie made clear in her diary, the Calvert women were neither reclusive nor shunned, and only a young schoolteacher's intellectual tastes and a preference for nonexclusive society limited her oldest sister's engagements. Lida made customary visits to the Youngloves and Underwoods—now joined by the 1877 marriage of Joseph Younglove's daughter Emma to Joseph Underwood's son Robert—and attended church socials and gatherings of local literary, music, and even boating clubs. These group activities brought Lida into regular contact with a pool of respectable gentlemen escorts that included three other teachers: Henry M. Woods, a Latin and Greek professor; Malcolm H. Crump, a natural scientist; and William Alexander Obenchain, a teacher of mathematics.[5]

Ironically, these men had come to Bowling Green to practice their professions in the grand house in which Lida's father had intended her to live. After Thomas's bankruptcy and flight, a group of thirteen citizens, under the patronage of the Methodist Episcopal Church South, had purchased his Italianate mansion on Vinegar Hill for the establishment of a school for young men. Warren College opened in 1872 but lasted only four years, its future made untenable by the endowment of a competing school under the will of local farmer and businessman Robert W. Ogden. The trustees of the new school quickly acquired the Calvert house, now enlarged with the addition of a rear wing, from Warren College and adapted the stable for use as a chapel. With sufficient income to pay a small faculty and to educate county boys initially without charge, Ogden College had opened in fall 1877. Its president, the Reverend James Wightman, enrolled his daughter in Lida's school.[6]

Robert Ogden had come to Bowling Green from Virginia, and while professors Crump and Obenchain represented his native state in the school bearing his name, it was Obenchain who best personified the mystique of the Old Dominion. Fifteen years Lida's senior, he had been born on April 27, 1841, in Buchanan, Virginia, the first of eleven children of Thomas Jefferson Obenchain and Elizabeth Ann Sweetland. According to a family story, the failure of Thomas Obenchain's business prompted him to abandon his creditors and move to Wytheville, but unlike Lida's father, he later recovered and paid his debts. Educated in the classics as a boy, William Obenchain had entered the Virginia Military Institute in July 1859. The eighteen-year-old quickly fell under the spell of Maj. Thomas Jonathan (soon to be "Stonewall") Jackson, whose uncompromising attention to duty, both military and civilian, commanded forgiveness of his odd personal habits and uninspired teaching. On April 21, 1861, four days after Virginia's secession from the Union, Obenchain was among the corps of cadets following Jackson to Richmond to instruct recruits in infantry and light artillery. While in Richmond he nervously called on Jefferson Davis, recently elected president of the Confederate states, offered proof of his grades, and secured an army appointment.[7]

By the time he graduated first in his class in December 1861, Obenchain had been transferred from the Corps of Artillery to the Corps of Engineers. In 1864, orders sent the young lieutenant from the malaria-ridden swamps of North Carolina to the Army of Northern Virginia, where he earned the rank of captain and concluded his

Civil War service as one of Robert E. Lee's staff engineers. Two personal encounters with Lee—one in which the general helped him make a fire on a cold, drizzly day in camp, and another after the surrender, when Lee bade him farewell along a country road outside Richmond—would become favorites in Obenchain's repertoire of war stories.[8]

As an epilogue to those stories, Obenchain would explain the general's role in his choice of career. Before the war he had intended to become a lawyer, but afterward, disconsolate over the future of his homeland, he contemplated further military adventures in Mexico. Lee complied with his request for a letter of recommendation but urged Obenchain to remain and serve the South in its time of greatest need. Declining other more prestigious and lucrative positions, Lee himself had settled in Lexington, Virginia, and accepted the presidency of Washington College, a war-ravaged school that had retained only forty students. Destiny now called to Obenchain in the voice of his beloved general. With the sense of duty characteristic of a disciple of both Lee and Stonewall Jackson, he put aside his ambitions and took up the tasks of an educator.[9]

Obenchain began his teaching career in 1866 as a professor of mathematics, civil and military engineering, architecture, and topographical and industrial drawing at North Carolina's Hillsboro Military Academy. In 1868 he became professor of mathematics and commandant of cadets at the newly founded Western Military Academy in New Castle, Kentucky. When the school burned in 1870 Obenchain moved to the University of Nashville, where he occupied the chair of modern languages and was again commandant of cadets. In 1873, suffering from an illness attributable to his wartime exposure to malaria, Obenchain resigned his position and retired to Texas. For the next five years he lived in Dallas, where he traded in real estate and grew stronger through the benefits of homeopathic medicine. In 1878 he returned to Kentucky to resume his teaching career at Ogden College.[10]

While at the Western Military Academy, Obenchain had been awarded the rank of major in conjunction with his duties as commandant of cadets. Like many Southerners whose relatively modest postwar circumstances gave them few other entitlements, he became identified to colleagues and acquaintances by that honorable designation alone. At first glance, the Major seemed an unlikely companion for Lida Calvert, whose family sympathies had rested with the Union, but by the spring of his first year in Bowling Green they had developed a friendship. Lida sent him flowers when he was ill, accompanied him to church, and saw him at club functions. Late in June 1879, he departed for what would become a customary summer visit to his home in Virginia. A few weeks later, Josie noted in her diary that Lida had received a ten-page letter from the Major.[11]

Despite this lengthy outreach, Lida did not appear to pine for the thirty-eight-year-old bachelor professor. In August, Josie recorded her sister's own intention to escape the confines of Bowling Green by saving three hundred dollars to spend the following summer in New York; the publication of "Galatea" three months later suggested that Lida wrote love poetry as much to finance her freedom as to explore her sentiments. The trip to New York never materialized, but in summer 1880, not long after her father's colleagues petitioned for his pardon, Lida contemplated a permanent departure when a former Younglove's Drugstore clerk told her about a vacant teaching post in Colorado. The attraction of the West, with its opportunities for improvisation, independence, and as their father knew, anonymity and the chance to remake oneself, probably became the topic of excited conversation among the Calvert sisters. Only recently had the same prospect been held out to Maggie by a former schoolmate. During her three years in St. Louis, "Marguerite," as her chum called her, had acquired not only a string of admirers that included Mary Kendall Jones's son Charles, but also enough education to stir in her an unfocused ambition. Wondering if Maggie was now spending her time unhappily at home "sewing, reading & idling," her friend asked, "Won't it be fun when you and I go into the wilds of Colorado and teach the heathen what are their names and how old they are? We will only want a cottage with three rooms and a large porch to fix us." Although Lida showed herself more prepared than Maggie to pursue this dream, she soon learned that she had not been elected to the position, prompting a disappointed Josie to exclaim to her diary, "Sad! Sad! Sad!"[12]

Perhaps Josie had wondered whether, barring other such opportunities, the vague outlines of a courtship would soon take shape around her oldest sister and the writer of that previous summer's lengthy letter from Virginia. Her suspicions might have been justified over a few months in 1880, beginning on an August evening when the

Major made his first visit to the Calvert home. She and nine-year-old Edward "had our orders given us," Josie recorded, "and the only way we could see him was by taking off our shoes and peeping through the crack of the door." Allowed out of hiding to attend on his second visit ten days later, sixteen-year-old Josie, by now wryly amused at the ways of her own male acquaintances, regarded this mature and fastidious gentleman with some irreverence. "This evening," she noted, "the Major came down and I had the exquisite pleasure of holding the boll [*sic*] for him to wash his 'lily white hand.'" When the Major left on a trip in November, it was Lida's turn to write—two letters, Josie observed, within a day of his departure.[13]

Lida also continued to compose verse. The October 1880 issue of *Scribner's* had included another of her poetic meditations on love, specifically on the power of its memory alone to atone for "cruel Life," with its past grief, present duty, and immutable future. While not the last of her sentimental verse, "Compensation" marked Lida's final use of "Eliza C. Hall." Her next poem, submitted to the *Atlantic Monthly*, and all of her subsequent poetry, appeared over the name "Eliza Calvert Hall." Confidence born of early success may have encouraged her to imitate writers she admired, such as Sarah Orne Jewett and Elizabeth Stuart Phelps, and the frequency with which three-part names complemented the sing-song quality of so much magazine verse could not have escaped her notice. The unveiling of her pseudonym's initial as signifying "Calvert" rather than her grandmother's middle name "Caroline" suggested further that Lida had determined to reclaim her family name from the taint of her father's misdeeds—and even, perhaps, to show that out of his duplicity might still emerge an authentic, if solemn, voice. Her realism, in fact, received a small rebuke in summer 1881, when the publication of "Felicissima" acquainted her with the tension between artistic freedom and popular magazine editors' guardianship of readers' sensibilities. Like *Scribner's* Richard Watson Gilder, the *Atlantic's* Thomas Bailey Aldrich did not hesitate to edit portions of fiction or verse that he regarded as too unpleasant or controversial. Just as she never forgot the unsparing praise of "Galatea," Lida long remembered Aldrich's rewrite of a stark couplet in "Felicissima."[14]

As the Calverts entered the second decade of Thomas's exile, Miss Lida the teacher, rather than Eliza Calvert Hall, remained their most consistent provider. Her next sister, Mary, continued to labor at home between spells of illness, but restless twenty-one-year-old Maggie had yet to find her calling. "Marguerite's" St. Louis friend urged her to be realistic but not overly self-abnegating. "I won't quote the trite saying 'Do your duty and then you will be happy,'" she wrote, "because I never found it to work." Whether or not she would have agreed, Lida's own sense of duty carried her a small step higher in her profession. Although still disorganized and poorly funded, Kentucky's free school system had benefited from reforms in the 1870s and 1880s that brought greater support through local taxation. By 1883, as a result, Bowling Green had opened its first public elementary schools, and Lida not only was elected to teach but subsequently became a principal. She assumed additional responsibility in 1884 when the county superintendent was empowered to appoint a board of examiners to assist him in certifying the qualifications of new teachers.[15]

In a letter to Josie, Thomas gave his equivocal endorsement of Lida's authority, supposing that male candidates would find it "rather humiliating . . . to be compelled to submit to an examination by a young lady" but hoping that the law allowed her a fee for her services. While this rather patronizing reference to his twenty-eight-year-old daughter contrasted with earlier solicitous remarks made when she filled the vacuum created by his absence, it reflected Thomas's newfound capacity to write fully and freely, for by this time he was no longer a fugitive. On June 8, 1883, Governor Blackburn—having earned the nickname "Lenient Luke" after charges of corruption had further clouded his controversial grants of mercy to thieves, murderers, and vigilantes—had finally issued a pardon to Thomas C. Calvert. Maggie's friend Henry Batts quickly offered warm congratulations and assured her that, in the opinion of the community, her father had been not so much dishonest as unlucky in his "trades and calculations." Thomas himself had hurried home, where he was reunited with his family and with Joseph Whit, now living northeast of Louisville in Pewee Valley.[16]

The ex-fugitive, however, spent only six months in Bowling Green. By spring 1884 he was gone again, looking for business opportunities in Wellington, Kansas, a railroad town south of Wichita, and still resolving to improve the welfare of his family—who did not accompany him, perhaps because they were now more strangers to him than he had cared to realize. His colleagues may also have held Thomas to the terms of their pardon application and insisted that he not remain permanently in the state. As a destination to which other county residents had immigrated before him, Wellington offered some of the community he had longed for while in exile but kept him at a distance from those whose trust he had betrayed. Ironically, after more than twelve years in the wilderness, Thomas returned to boardinghouse life. He found work in a real estate and loan brokerage firm whose principal still maintained an address in Bowling Green, and he again resumed a familiar plea to his family. "I wish some of you would let me have a good long letter," he wrote Josie. Of Margaret, who remained stubbornly but wisely self-reliant, Thomas grumbled to Josie that her mother had "too much ambition," even as he acknowledged his continuing inability to support her or his children.[17]

A further irony presided at Ogden College, where the school year had concluded just as Thomas received his pardon. Major Obenchain left for his regular visit to Virginia; in the fall, upon Rev. Wightman's resignation, Obenchain was appointed Ogden's new president. For matching her constancy in their common profession, Lida's gentleman friend became head of the Calvert home-that-never-was, in the mansion on the hill.[18]

Two years later, on July 8, 1885, the Major became Lida's husband. The pastorship of the Second Presbyterian Church was vacant, so the twenty-nine-year-old bride married her forty-four-year-old groom a block away in the Episcopal Church, his place of worship. Thomas was not present; Lida's uncle, John Younglove, gave her away at the well-attended sunrise ceremony. Wedding gifts of silver, linen, glass, and porcelain streamed in from relatives and friends, including Aunt Minerva and Lida's childhood nurse Aunt Bella. In presentations reminiscent of her grandmother's arrival in Bowling Green more than fifty years earlier, Lida also received two rocking chairs.[19]

"Is your sister to be congratulated? I am sure not so much so as the gentleman if she is anything like her sister," wrote Maggie's friend from St. Louis, wondering, all too humanly, which party had secured the best of the bargain. Although Lida would write enough on the subject of marriage to raise interest about its origins in her own experience, neither she nor the Major dignified any curiosity about the quality of their union. Their six-year-long courtship suggested that at least one of them was cautious, if not reluctant, but the anecdotes collide. Lida's daughter Cecil, whose sudden and bitter reflection on her parents' lives together is difficult both to trust and to ignore, would cite family gossip claiming that her mother was "glad enough" to have her father's proposal. A decade after they married, however, Lida hinted that the Major was glad enough of her acceptance. Objecting to a presumption that personal disappointment had inspired one of her poems about lost love, she replied serenely by way of explanation that "I landed my 'fish' some ten years ago; / More properly speaking he landed me."[20]

The couple, in fact, might have been pressured to take stock of their future because of the continuing possibility, alluded to by Maggie's St. Louis friend, that the Calverts would join Thomas in Kansas. If neither welcomed the thought of Lida's removal to her father's new home, they may have concluded that without the Major's proposal she had no legitimate reason to stay behind. Cecil later maintained that her mother could have struck out in another direction and forged a successful writing career in New York or elsewhere, but Lida—a minor poet by her own admission—could hardly be blamed for lacking the bravado of her daughter's generation; nor could she be faulted if she understood that release from her duty to her family was best secured by taking up another duty. Only the call of matrimony would have justified—indeed, demanded—retirement from her teaching position and from the job of supporting her mother and siblings.[21]

Of course, the possibility that her engagement was a well-considered bargain, rather than a grim compromise, should not be dismissed. For a daughter of Thomas Calvert, the Major may well have personified stability, honor, and respectability. Like Samuel Calvert, he had first exorcised his "fighting blood," then after peace was imposed been shown his duty and taken it up in knightly fashion. While men like Thomas were grasping for wealth and prestige in post–Civil War America, the Major was satisfied to represent a more traditional social order and to espouse honesty and contentment over the calculating pursuit of a dollar. Only once, Lida avowed, did she ever hear him mourn the future that could have been his. "'If circumstances had been different, I might have been something more than a poor school-teacher,' he said," but he never allowed regret or nostalgia to dull his self-discipline. Students could coax him into reminiscing about his Confederate service, but then he would double their assignments for the next day to make up for the time lost.[22]

Lida knew, nevertheless, that the Major's devotion to duty could be oppressive. His "stern sense of responsibility made him sometimes over-zealous and too exacting," she admitted. Students at Ogden College quickly became acquainted with the Major's methods—his dark looks, succinct verbal rebukes, nagging over poor grades, and examinations, which, while fair, "let a boy fall harder than those of any other professor." He required his students to wear their jackets in class at all times, even on the warmest days. He believed, in fact, that the custom should extend to the home, where no gentleman ought to appear before his family in shirtsleeves; similarly, a gentleman did not compromise a lady by speaking with her on the street, nor did he smoke in her company.[23]

Despite his intimidating presence, the young men under his tutelage regarded the Major with great affection, even finding a source of amusement in his overuse of the word "discipline." Much later, Cecil found the same combination of sobriety and charm in her father. "You would enjoy knowing the Major," she assured a friend. "He is so funny & stilted & dignified! Never sees a joke in anything!" Perhaps Lida expressed her infatuation similarly in the early days of their courtship, but ultimately his virtues may have been difficult to comprehend when viewed through the lens of her personal history. The Major had nobly surrendered his ambitions for the sake of an ideal, but could this conscious decision to settle for less pacify a young woman who had been forced to languish in poverty with her mother and siblings? During the years of her father's absence, moreover, Lida's self-command and sacrifice had been neither freewilled nor rewarded—despite her labors, her family had been deemed "penniless" in 1880—while the Major's voluntary declaration of servitude had earned him respect and admiration.[24]

By the time of her marriage, Lida's literary accomplishments had been recognized in her hometown, even if her use of a pseudonym had created some confusion in the local reportage relayed to Louisville. "The little poem contributed by Miss Lida Hall Calvert [sic], of this place, to the Century Magazine, was the recipient of many handsome and merited compliments from the people of the home of the fair authoress," noted the Courier-Journal. Its competitor, the

Louisville Evening Post, even reprinted the poem, "Her Choice"—
fourteen lines that, like the earlier "Compensation," lifted a torch not
to love itself but to "life with memory / of the Old Love." After Lida's
wedding, the *Courier-Journal* noted the union of the Major and "Ida
Calvert [*sic*]," known in literary circles as "Eliza N. Hall [*sic*]."[25] By contrast, the account of the ceremony in Bowling Green's *Times-Gazette*
mentioned her recent tenure as principal of the city's graded school,
but not her writing. The omission was a curious omen, for in her early
years as a wife Lida would confront anonymity, a legal and economic
station that threatened to overwhelm her even as it gave new life to
her pen.

5

Cook, Scullion, Nurse, Laundress

Two happy lovers, leaning cheek to cheek,
Shall read these pages and forget to smile,

. . . . . .

And whisper, as they turn the tear-stained page,
"This book was written in the world's Dark Age."
—Eliza Calvert Hall, "A Forecast"

ON HER WEDDING DAY, Lida's legal status changed from that of *feme sole*, or single woman, to *feme covert*, or married woman. In only a few respects was the event not a watershed. Her civic obligations, for example, remained light; the fact of her sex, rather than her marital status, ensured that she would not be drafted into political office, summoned for jury service, or allowed near the ballot box. Otherwise, marriage reconstituted the former schoolteacher by placing her, as the Anglo-French term suggested, under cover—specifically, under the care and protection of her husband. In practical terms, he was obligated to provide her with food, clothing, shelter, and other necessaries of life, liberally interpreted to mean those comforts associated with their family sustenance, having regard to his economic status and her own background.[1]

Such protection, however, came at a price, for in sheltering women the doctrine of coverture also rendered them unseen and unknown as persons. The eighteenth-century jurist Sir William Blackstone notoriously summarized the English common law from which American jurisprudence had evolved. "By marriage," he held, "the husband and wife are one person in law: that is, the very being or legal existence of the woman is suspended during the marriage, or at least is incorporated and consolidated into that of the husband." Simply put, only the personhood of the groom survived the wedding ceremony.[2]

This principle had long been elaborated in statutes and court decisions confirming a husband's dominion over the life, children, and property of his wife. Many state legislatures had moved to modify or repeal its harsher aspects, but Kentucky, having been excused from both the progressive impulses of northern states and the more liberal property and guardianship rights enacted in reconstructed Confederate states, remained comparatively backward in its treatment of women. At the time of Lida's marriage a wife's legal existence remained submerged in her husband's, causing her personal possessions, contractual rights, and other legal interests, whether acquired before or during the marriage, to become his property. He did not gain ownership of her real estate, but his consent was required for its sale; in the meantime, he had the right to receive the rents. If his wife died and their marriage had produced a child, the husband's right to the income from all of her real estate, known as curtesy, continued for the remainder of his life. A widow, by contrast, obtained a life interest, known as dower, in only one-third of her husband's real estate owned at his death. A husband's property right in his wife's labor allowed him to collect her wages from an employer, and his paternal dominion over their minor children entitled him to include in his will provisions for their guardianship independent of her wishes.[3]

Justifying the perpetuation of such inequalities had never been easy, for none of the standard defenses was entirely logical or consistent. The theory that wives needed protection failed to explain why marriage alone reduced a legally competent single woman to a state of helplessness, or why the man best suited to take advantage of her should become her guardian. The contractual theory—that a wife's property and services were a fair exchange for her husband's support—also faltered when the law persistently refused to allow couples, in the manner of parties to an ordinary civil bargain, the freedom to adjust or waive their entitlements. An enlightened husband's disclaimer, for example, of any right to his wife's earnings did not protect them from attachment by creditors to satisfy his debts.[4]

Perhaps the most common defense of coverture invoked the biblical teachings that a man and his wife became "one flesh" and that husbands were to "rule over" wives, but the law itself had long weakened this "marital unit" theory by allowing a woman, in certain circumstances, to retain at least part of her legal identity. Even though she lost ownership of her personal property, for example, a Kentucky wife's retention of title to her real estate evidenced a separate existence that survived marriage. The legislature also came to the aid, at least temporarily, of a wife whose husband had abandoned her without making any provision for her maintenance; such a woman could apply to the court for power to sell property, enter contracts, and retain her earnings—that is, to live as if she were a feme sole. If the husband repented and resumed his support obligations, however, he could petition the court to have his prior rights restored.[5]

Both English and Kentucky courts departed most significantly from the theory of marital unity in recognizing the equitable doctrine of "separate estates." Prior to marriage, a woman who desired to retain ownership of her property could preempt her husband's rights by transferring it to a trustee; similarly, someone desiring to make a gift to a woman after her marriage could convey it to the trustee for her sole benefit. With her property so insulated from the control and debts of her husband, a wife was then entitled to dispose of it as she pleased during her life or by will, a right otherwise denied her with respect to assets, including land, not held in trust.[6]

In 1868 the Kentucky General Assembly confirmed that the establishment of a married woman's separate estate no longer required resort to trustees; property transferred directly to her with the stipulation that it was for her sole use gave her the same unfettered power of disposition by deed or will. Courts of equity had long been lenient in this regard: in 1852 a circuit judge had agreed with the young lawyer Thomas Calvert that the appointment of a trustee was not required to create a separate estate. Practice, however, continued to vary. In 1858 Joseph Underwood completed transfers of various parcels of land to his son Eugene in trust for his three married daughters and gave each control over the disposition of her share. When Margaret Calvert purchased her Park Street house in 1874, by contrast, the deed conveyed title to her directly "with power to reconvey without the consent of her husband," whose whereabouts were then unknown.[7]

Among the lessons to be learned from this untidy mass of jurisprudence was that the letter of the law, which generally reduced wives to nonpersons, could be tempered by appeals to equity—the spirit of the law—which conceded to women a measure of justice. Both women and men could, of course, twist the law to their advantage, claiming separate estates to shelter assets from a husband's debts or pleading the general rule of coverture to nullify a wife's contracts. Elsewhere, men like Joseph Underwood, acting out of beneficence, and women like Margaret Calvert, acting out of necessity, could employ legitimate strategies to avoid the harsher effects of a male-centered legal system without necessitating its complete overthrow. This circumstance no doubt contributed to the longevity of the regime; three decades after Kentucky had removed most of the inequalities from its statute books, one commentator maintained that the supervision of equity had generously given married women property rights "possibly as complete if not more complete" than the legislated reforms.[8]

Common enough, however, were the trials of women to whom the blessings of coverture had revealed their source, as John Stuart Mill charged in his famous essay *On the Subjection of Women*, in the "law of the strongest." When, for example, a woman possessing substantial personal property married, then died shortly afterward, her wealth constituted a windfall for her husband; if he died first, his next of kin, not his widow, enjoyed the benefit. No more fortunate were women who had contributed to lengthy marriages with unpaid housekeeping, childrearing, and labor in a family business, only to find themselves with little more than their dower rights to wield against a faithless husband.

A few years before Lida's wedding, such a fate had befallen Mary Jane Warfield Clay upon the dissolution of her union with Cassius Marcellus Clay. Clay had spent much of their troubled forty-five-year marriage away from home, earning national recognition through his antislavery crusades as well as his three terms in the Kentucky General Assembly, service in the Mexican War, and eight-year appointment as minister to Russia. Mrs. Clay, for her part, had borne ten children, managed and improved White Hall, the 2,250-acre family estate near Richmond, Kentucky, and judiciously employed her husband's income and business profits to settle his huge debts. She had also fled to her family home in Lexington shortly after his return from his ministership and watched with embarrassment as Clay brought a young Russian boy to White Hall and treated him like the son he probably was. When Clay sued for divorce in 1878 on the grounds of his wife's desertion, Mrs. Clay agreed to relinquish her dower rights in return for possession of any property she had brought into their home or purchased with her own funds. Although unhappy that he had received no rent from her over the long years of his absence, Clay apparently avoided any question of restitution for his wife's supervision of his finances, her enlargement of his estate, or her upbringing of his children who, he confessed, barely knew him.[9]

The divorce, and the fate that could have met them had they not possessed income from a separate family trust, mobilized Mrs. Clay and her daughters against the inequality of men's and women's legal and property rights. One daughter, Mary, brought Susan B. Anthony to speak in Richmond in 1879, an event that led to the formation of the Madison County Equal Rights Association; four years later, Mary became president of the American Woman Suffrage Association. Two other daughters, Sarah (Sallie) and Annie, began supplying articles on suffrage and women's rights to newspapers in Richmond and Lexington. Yet another daughter, Laura, was elected president in 1881 of the newly founded Kentucky Woman Suffrage Association.[10]

Like her sisters, Laura Clay had made her philosophical commitment to the cause after her parents' separation, but more than Mary and Sallie, who were several years older, and Annie, who was ten years younger, Laura had been a close witness to her mother's exhausting domestic burdens during her father's sojourn in Russia. Her early experience had paralleled Lida's in another curious respect as Laura was subject, through her mother, to her father's demands that his children write him regularly. "Let him know all your wants," Mrs. Clay told her, hoping to shame her husband into recognizing his paternal duties.[11] After Clay's return late in 1869, the tension between her parents confirmed their twenty-year-old daughter's fear that the union was irretrievably broken. At the time of Lida's marriage, Laura, at thirty-six, was poised to assume her role as the state's leading suffragist, and the two women's paths would soon cross.

After their wedding, Lida and the Major spent their honeymoon at the resort of Grayson Springs, then joined his family in Wytheville for the rest of the summer of 1885. The Major returned to Bowling Green first, to take up his year's duties at Ogden College, while Lida remained in Virginia until late October. Upon her return, they set up housekeeping in rented premises, perhaps in anticipation of building; nine months before their marriage the Major had paid $350 for a one-third-acre lot at the corner of Chestnut and Fourteenth streets, across from the Ogden College campus. He must have realized, however, that such an undertaking was to be approached cautiously since he now had a wife to support on his annual teacher's salary of $1,400.[12]

The newspaper report of their wedding had called both the bride and groom "prominent in the social circle of Bowling Green," and, in the Major's case, marriage appeared not to reduce any of the activities to which the compliment referred. In 1886, his work as an educator earned him an honorary master's degree from Danville's Centre College. At home, he remained loyal to his church and particularly to his club, of which he was an original member. Formed in 1879 for collegial dining and the discussion of literary, historical, scientific, and political topics, the XV Club brought together fifteen of the town's most respectable lawyers, teachers, and businessmen every two weeks except during the summer, and matrimony did not disrupt the Major's faithful attendance. Neither did it interfere with the cumbersome writing task he assigned himself after each session. In late 1884, he had taken over production of the XV Club minutes, which previous secretaries had kept in rather abbreviated form. With his customary sobriety and attention to duty, the Major took notes of each member's ruminations on the topic at hand—whether European politics, tobacco, China, patents, state education, public improvements, or suffrage—then rewrote them in prose style across page after page of the minute book. Despite his protests that the office was "all work and no play" and his regular plea for a volunteer to replace him, three decades and some 3,300 pages later he would still occupy the secretary's chair.[13]

Lida, on the other hand, had been an original member of the Ladies' Literary Club, a study group for intellectually and socially inclined women founded in 1880 by another Bowling Green teacher, but had dropped out by the time of her marriage. Perhaps she hoped that keeping house for a steadily employed husband would be less grueling than the routines of her family home and that retirement from teaching would make even more time for writing. An eighty-six-line prologue poem, composed for a dramatic program presented by her former public school students in spring 1886, suggested a continued eagerness to exercise her creative talent notwithstanding her domestic responsibilities. The usual incidents of wifehood, however, soon prevailed. Early in 1887 Lida took charge of a new family residence on State Street, considered one of the more desirable addresses in Bowling Green, and on September 19 her first child, Margery, was born.[14]

As one disinclined to remove his jacket even at his own hearth, the Major may have been particular, even fussy, in his standards for their home. After he left for Virginia one summer, Lida expressed relief that having no man in the house made her chores much less urgent, but her own capacity for self-denial allowed few breaks from the treadmill of domestic routine on which she soon found herself. Advice manuals of the day, in fact, recommended the strict scheduling of tasks to enable a woman—and, if she was fortunate, her servant—to keep up with the demands of running a middle-class household: laundry on Monday, ironing on Tuesday, baking on Wednesday, dusting and sweeping on Thursday, scrubbing and scouring on Friday, more baking on Saturday, and every day the usual cooking, dishwashing, and bed making, together with the dressing, feeding, and disciplining of children. Successful completion of the week's routine entitled the homemaker to begin it again on Monday.[15]

A wife, Lida would later complain, was "cook, scullion, nurse, laundress, charwoman, dining room servant, and chambermaid all in one short twelve hours." When available, domestic help neither inspired confidence nor lightened her workload. Not until 1893 did she engage a cook who remained for any length of time; otherwise, the ineptitude of servants added to her housekeeping woes. After her kitchen work was done, there was always "soft Kentucky mud" to wipe up and soft coal dust to clean from furniture, carpets, and draperies. Even if she had found time for writing, Lida saw little in the housewife's lot from which she could draw inspiration. An appreciation of nature, for example, she found wasted on all but the "millionaire or tramp"; the overworked housekeeper marked the seasons of her life only with bouts of spring and fall cleaning and sewing and the "new baby that is laid in the cradle every two or three years." Cooking gave her some satisfaction, at least when it offered an outlet for the creativity she had earlier devoted to poetry. Lida made jelly and preserves, and developed what would be a lifelong talent for bread making, but like the writer of potboilers who yearns to concentrate on literature, she found that a regular trade in stews and soups was required to underwrite the baker's art.[16]

The financial aspects of wifehood were equally burdensome. Reliance upon the Major's modest teaching salary, which did not adequately cover expenses during Ogden College's summer recess, put Lida in a position of dependency that was even more confining than her mother's; as a deserted woman, Margaret had at least been accorded more latitude to earn and keep her own money. Left with an allowance one August while the Major was out of town, Lida complained to Josie at mid-month that she was now "penniless" and awaiting his return to pay some debts. Having exchanged her right to an independent wage for a right to support, Lida may have held her husband to his bargain in a manner that created lasting mutual resentment. Years later, although his wife was again earning an income, the Major remarked broadly that women's "extravagance," and their knowing little about finance except "when they had money to spend & when they didn't," were common causes of marital discord.[17]

Lida was pregnant for the second time, ill, and somewhat distracted when, in Richmond, Laura Clay began to build her state network of women's rights activists. After replacing her sister Annie as a columnist for Lexington's *Kentucky Gazette,* Laura and a colleague, Henrietta B. Chenault, had formed the Fayette County Equal Rights Association in January 1888. Support for the Kentucky Woman Suffrage Association had foundered on the perceived narrowness of its objective, and the two hoped that the county organization's pursuit of educational, professional, and legal advances for women would engage a broader constituency by linking the ballot to causes such as temperance, raising the age of consent from twelve to eighteen, appointing female physicians to mental institutions where women were confined, and reform of married women's property laws. Laura and Mrs. Chenault promoted a speaking tour by Zerelda G. Wallace, a sympathetic lecturer for the Woman's Christian Temperance Union (WCTU), and through her own lectures and correspondence Laura began collecting the names of women across the state who might or-

ganize local societies and circulate petitions in support of a major lobbying effort at the next session of the General Assembly.[18]

Among the many solicited was Mrs. Obenchain of Bowling Green,
but Lida's health largely prevented her from conducting the personal, door-to-door appeals necessary to gain signatures on a petition to
amend property laws. She and a friend on whom she relied for assistance also met with general complacency among her fellow citizens.
"Leading lawyers here declare that in the matter of property holding
&c, woman's rights are better protected than those of man," she wrote
Mrs. Chenault, "and this has kept many persons from signing. I regret
that I have not been able to do more for you." Pressed several times
to help arrange a lecture by Zerelda Wallace, she finally admitted that
poor health had allowed her to mention the matter to only a few sympathizers. Lida suggested to Mrs. Chenault that the clergyman who
had married her to the Major might act as sponsor after he returned
from a summer vacation, but she warned that his progressive views
had already eroded his popularity with his congregation. With this
faint encouragement, Lida concluded her reply. A month later, on
September 21, 1888, she gave birth to her second child, William Alexander Jr.[19]

Lida once hinted that she had been among those "nervous suffragists" whose allegiance to the cause wavered whenever critics in-
sinuated that their homes were unswept and their children uncared
for. Although Alex's birth would have been reason enough to decline
further involvement, another event that same year may have added to
her concerns about negative public opinion. Thomas Calvert was back
home. After making a visit to his wife and children early in 1887, Lida's
father had returned to Wellington in time to witness the drought-
induced end of both the Kansas land boom and his economic prospects. By 1888 he had been permanently reunited with his family in
Bowling Green. His odyssey complete, the former tycoon found work
preparing land surveys and title abstracts, taking depositions, filing
Civil War pension claims, and performing other chores necessary to
the "small practice" of the legal profession from which he had once
schemed to escape.[20]

In Richmond, however, Laura Clay kept Lida on her list of con-
tacts. Laura had become president of the Kentucky Equal Rights Association (KERA), formed in November 1888 to pursue statewide the

goals of the Fayette County organization. She tried again to enlist
Lida's help in the spring after her son's birth but was unsuccessful.
Caring for Margery and Alex, Lida protested, would prevent her not
only from organizing a local KERA chapter but from attending any
of its meetings. No doubt Laura was accustomed to hearing excuses
founded in the demands of home and children, but had she known
of the reappearance of Thomas Calvert during this same period she
might have responded, given her own family history, with even more
than her usual patience.[21]

Laura, in fact, did not have long to wait, for even as Lida was declining specific duties she was pledging herself irrevocably to the cause of
woman suffrage. Her conversion, as she described it, occurred somewhat accidentally, not long after Alex's birth when, perhaps courtesy
of Laura, a few copies of the movement's bible came into her hands.
Published in Boston since 1870 by veteran abolitionists Lucy Stone
and her husband Henry Blackwell, the *Woman's Journal* was a weekly
paper "devoted to the Interests of Woman—to her Educational, Industrial, Legal and Political Equality, and especially to her Right of
Suffrage." After she had finished reading its contents "the deed was
done," Lida proclaimed, and "I knew just where I stood."[22]

That the *Woman's Journal* would galvanize a self-described "ob-
scure woman whose life [was] bounded by the four walls of home" in
a quiet town of less than eight thousand was precisely the intent of its
editors. Suffrage leaders had long recognized the indispensability of
the written word to the success of their mission. As Zerelda Wallace's
proposed lecture in Bowling Green demonstrated, women's isolation,
their inability or unwillingness to assemble in public, and the frequent
lack of a forum in which to do so limited the effectiveness of meetings and oratory. When women did speak, often the mainstream press
either reported the event with disfavor or ignored it altogether. "For
building up a new line of thought in the popular heart," argued another suffragist publisher, "there must be the written word, which shall
be quietly digested and made part of the reader's own thought. Then
the change in belief comes irresistibly, and when the reader avows an
opinion he knows the reason for it." Lida, who with her siblings had
been raised to enjoy literature and popular reading, would have found
this mode of education most accessible, even though she complained
of having to pursue it late at night after her children were asleep.[23]

More than its written format, the *Journal's* content appealed to the sympathies of the educated wife and mother. Begun as the unofficial organ of the American Woman Suffrage Association, the paper had sidelined Susan B. Anthony's *Revolution*, the iconoclastic voice of the National Woman Suffrage Association edited by Elizabeth Cady Stanton. Before it ceased publication in 1870, having contributed to a split of the movement into the two rival associations, the *Revolution* had pronounced suffrage to be a mere "crumb" among the reforms it demanded for woman; more oppressive than the denial of her political rights, one essayist argued, was her "social, and particularly her marital bondage." Elizabeth Cady Stanton had held out constitutionally guaranteed suffrage as the means with which to perform radical surgery on a wide range of social ailments—prostitution and divorce laws, prison conditions, workers' wages, and the institution of marriage itself. The American Woman Suffrage Association, by contrast, focused solely on obtaining the ballot, state by state, as the avenue to middle-class reforms such as equal property rights and access to higher education and the professions.[24]

The *Woman's Journal* accordingly sought to be less abrasive than the *Revolution*, aiming to recruit both socially active supporters and more conservative sympathizers whose interest in suffrage did not necessarily extend to the radical transformation of male-female or worker-employer relations. Readers praised the paper's tone as "neither defiant nor obsequious" and appreciated its avoidance of frivolous "feminine" subjects in favor of serious journalistic and intellectual fare. Its pages offered reports from state associations on suffrage activities and legislative developments, profiles of movement leaders, news about women in clubs, colleges, and the professions, and articles about women's status in other countries. Regular features included editorials, reviews, poetry, fiction, a children's column, and a selection of "news and notes" that both celebrated victories and decried the latest legal, political, or social insults to individual women.[25]

Summarizing her conversion, Lida explained: "I was always a firm believer in justice and what else is woman's suffrage?" If the *Woman's Journal* affirmed her ideals, however, it also must have spoken to more immediate and personal needs—needs of the spirit, rather than those of a woman seeking to recover family wealth or enter a male-monopolized profession. That Lida always dated her new conviction by Alex's birth suggested that she had not been alienated from her maternal role; the dreary, inevitable realities of domesticity, nevertheless, had left her aggrieved and restless. Although she would never have embraced the kinds of risks that had resulted in her father's humiliating expulsion from society, in the "accident" of picking up the *Woman's Journal* Lida seized upon a mission with which to defy the predictable course of her life.[26] She may have dreamed of undertaking such a journey before, as the quiet seminary student leading the prayer meeting, the teacher entering the wilds of Colorado, or the oldest daughter rescuing her family from destitution, but now Lida saw a new opportunity before her. In the wrongs perpetrated against women and in their struggle for justice, the writer had found her stories.

6

Straight to a Woman's Heart

> But suppose we drop metaphor and come down to plain speech.
> —A Kentucky Woman,
> "Why Democratic Women Want the Ballot"

AFTER EMBRACING THE PRINCIPLE of women's equality, Laura Clay had spent several years contemplating what she should do to aid in its realization. She attended college in order to prepare herself intellectually and learned to support herself on farmland leased from her father. For most of her life, she would weave her participation in suffrage campaigns in between cycles of planting and harvesting. She never married.[1]

Upon taking her stand, Lida, by contrast, saw her role in narrower terms. Not only was abandonment of her family out of the question, but the duties of middle-class domesticity, which included year-round housekeeping and management of the perennial servant problem, disqualified her from regular travel or public relief work. Most pre-emptive, of course, were the needs of her children. "My arms were always full of babies," she explained, a recollection not greatly over-dramatized after the birth of Thomas Hall Obenchain on November 2, 1891, gave her the care of three children under the age of five. Between motherhood and the lingering shadow of community disapproval, Lida claimed, it took "a good while" to find the time or courage for what she wanted to do next: take up not the sword but the pen, and "become articulate" about the rightness of her beliefs.[2]

A good while did, in fact, elapse between Lida's conversion and the publication of "Sally Ann's Experience," a short story that both

the author and her readers regarded as her signature protest against
the legal and social injustices heaped upon women. Lida would be
suitably modest about the genesis of "Sally Ann," insisting that the
tale had been conceived out of necessity as she circulated another
petition for the repeal of laws denying married women control of their
own property. Canvassing door-to-door, she was outraged by the testi-
mony, gossip, and recollections she heard: of the wife whose wayward
husband returned long enough to appropriate the money she had
earned to support herself and their children; of the dying mother, unable to make a will, whose small cache of jewelry passed through her
children's hands into those of her husband's new wife; of the drunken
husband who squandered his wife's inheritance; of the couple who
invested their joint savings in a house that, when sold on the husband's
death, yielded only one-third of the proceeds to his widow for her
dower.[3]

Lida recalled that these and other cases of hardship "urged me to
the point where I couldn't keep quiet," but such reticence, manifested
in journalistic profiles and in her autobiographical compositions, must
have amused her intimates. What actually preceded the appearance
of "Sally Ann" was a remarkably unquiet ten years during which Lida
became an accomplished purveyor of pro-suffrage logic and rhetoric
even as she continued to write sentimental verse. In essays and poetry
that crossed and recrossed the terrain of both a wife's grievances and a
woman's essential cares, she intently cultivated the elements of "Sally
Ann's Experience."[4]

Against the background of general male perfidy that she read
about in the *Woman's Journal,* particular men—writers, editors, and
even the Major—facilitated Lida's return to print in the first years of
her marriage. A reminder of her early success appeared in 1890, when
poet and former New York journalist Charles H. Crandall published a
carefully classified anthology of nearly 450 American sonnets. Seeking
to compare his country's output favorably to that of England's, Crandall offered both a host of now-forgotten magazine poets and more
renowned figures such as Oliver Wendell Holmes, Henry Wadsworth
Longfellow, and James Russell Lowell. Among many examples of "irregular sonnets" and sonnets "with Petrarcan octave," he included
two of Eliza Calvert Hall's *Century* poems.[5]

Another selection, "Sunrise," came from the pen of Robert Burns

Wilson, a longtime resident of Frankfort, Kentucky, who had gained
nationwide attention as an artist and poet. In 1885 Henry Mills Alden,
the editor of *Harper's Magazine,* had published one of Wilson's best
nature poems, "When Evening Cometh On." Two years later, while
visiting Bowling Green as a guest of the Major, Wilson may first have
heard of Lida's frustration over the course of her literary development. She long remembered his sympathetic response: "Remember,
it takes a great deal of living to make a very little writing." Given the
routine of her domestic duties and the challenge of writing poetry
with young children underfoot, Lida adapted this observation to her
own circumstances, deciding never to try to compose self-consciously
but instead to wait for "inspiration."[6]

When inspiration did come, Robert Burns Wilson showed some
of the results to his editor at *Harper's.* "All these poems have a distinctive quality. I shall expect greater things from this author," rhapsodized Henry Alden. "Every word she writes is a woman's word, and
goes straight to a woman's heart. It is a great thing to have this power."
He selected a work of six stanzas mourning the loss "to mortal sense,
/ As fragrance shed from Eden's withered rose" of the perfect, archetypal expression of love. "The Unspoken Word" appeared in *Harper's*
just as Lida's third child, Tom, was born.[7]

Like the response from *Scribner's,* Lida kept Alden's praise in her
store of favorite compliments. If she seemed little changed from the
young lady poet who proclaimed "Life, love, and motherhood. What
more could be / But death?" in "Felicissima"—colluding, at first glance,
in the stereotype of her sex as emotional, intuitive, and utterly alien
to the male norm—she was not, in fact, encroaching on her belief in
women's rights. Before the Civil War, this model of female inferiority
had been cleverly turned on its head by the women writers who dominated the market for popular literature. In sentimental novels, poems,
and stories of virtuous girls, devoted mothers, and domestic heroines,
they tacitly asserted that genuine power and strength resided at the
hearth and cradle rather than in the public and commercial spheres
of men. Attributing their work, as Lida did, not to calculation but to
inspiration, these writers also claimed for themselves a measure of the
superiority with which they invested their characters.[8]

Writing as mistress of her woman's heart, rather than its victim,
allowed Lida to transcend some of the most-resented confines of her

domestic life. The aptly titled "My Inspiration" depicts a poet who takes time away from her maternal duties to write but discovers, in her small daughter's gambits for attention, that the woman-as-artist is spiritual kin to the woman-as-mother:

> Sometimes she'll come behind my chair
> And kiss me without speaking,
> Then, all at once, my tired brain finds
> The rhyme it has been seeking.
>
> Or through my study door she peeps
> And throws a smile entrancing;
> Ah, then, the sonnet that I write
> Is brilliant as her glancing.
>
> . . . . . .
> Ah, here she comes and perches on
> My knee—her proper station;
> Take what you will, O, World, but leave
> My brown-eyed Inspiration.[9]

When the manufacturer of Ivory soap conducted a promotion in the guise of a literary contest, Lida smothered her antipathy to housework beneath several poems extolling the capacity of the product to sanctify not only a variety of cleaning tasks but the women who performed them (or who so directed their servants) in an almost mystical purification of their templelike households. Ivory soap was "good for washing the schoolboy's face, / And for cleansing my lady's filmy lace," began the longest of twenty-four lines:

> 'Tis the good little fairy of house-cleaning time;
> At its magical touch all the dirt and the grime
> From carving and frescoes, and bric-a-brac rare,
> From window and door and table and chair,
> From marbles and draperies vanish away,
> And the house is as sweet and as fresh as the May.

Another poem envisioned the beautiful "Clarinda" at her dressing table with "ivory comb and brush in hand":

Her dimpled arms gleam through her lace,
She smiles to see her mirrored face,
And twists and braids the shining rope,
Made clean in suds of Ivory Soap.

Lida offered another, somewhat grittier effort for use only as an advertisement rather than a contest entry. Conjuring up the seasonal ritual in which a woman purged her home's interior of accumulated dust, soot, and residue from oil and gas lamps, and coal- and wood-burning stoves, "The Spring o' the Year" began:

The window panes are dingy;
The curtain's lace is black;
The cobwebs drape the corners,
And the dust fills every crack.

The carpets must be taken up,
The house cleaned through and through;
And housewives say despairingly
"I don't know what to do."[10]

If "Spring o' the Year" better described Lida's own state of mind at winter's retreat, elsewhere she gave similar indications that "My Inspiration," in which the poet writes sonnets with a toddler perched on her knee, was largely a fantasy. Daughter Margery, at least in the Major's estimation, was indeed the "best and sweetest child," but Lida not only had no private study for her children to visit but little on which she actually could write. Noting her ideas on any available scrap of paper, she would collect them in a drawer or under a lamp until, "using an old magazine as a portfolio and writing-desk," she could elaborate upon them. As she picked up and put down these modest tools, conjuring up between household chores a serene, orderly domestic world for the approbation of male critics, Lida might have imagined herself as Louisa May Alcott, from one of whose letters she soon quoted: "I feel very moral to-day, having done a big wash alone, baked, swept the house, picked the hops, got dinner, and written a chapter in 'Moods.'" Her cloak of self-congratulation, however, must have worn thin whenever she found the legitimacy of her aspirations mocked by her own tendency, like Alcott's, to relegate writing to the end of a long list of tasks—or by the sight of the Major, inscribing at his leisure page after page of his club's discussions in its leather-bound minute book while she copied out Ivory soap poems on the backs of page proofs from an Ogden College catalogue. If Lida sometimes resented her family for monopolizing her time and stultifying her literary progress, she also understood, as she no doubt had since she was a girl, that the forces acting on her life were complex. "I came to see," she remembered, "that the children and the servants and home and family and government were all parts of one whole."[11]

When they targeted government as the most likely agent of change, the leaders of the Kentucky Equal Rights Association were similarly frustrated. Armed with ten thousand signatures calling for the reform of married women's property laws, Laura Clay and her talented superintendent for legislative and petition work, Josephine Henry, marched to Frankfort where they addressed the General Assembly on January 10, 1890. Their cause attracted support in the House, where members proposed bills to insulate a married woman's property from her husband's debts, allow her to sue in her own name for unpaid wages, and give a husband and wife equal, one-half interests in the other's estate by way of dower or curtesy. The Senate passed KERA ally William Lindsay's property rights bill by a two-to-one margin but, to the women's disbelief, procedure stood guard over the status quo. None of the House measures was considered, and Lindsay's bill also died there when opponents ensured that lack of a quorum kept it from a vote. Having "knocked at the door of the General Assembly" and been invited inside, the KERA now found itself back on the street. "For very shame's sake," charged Josephine Henry afterward, the legislators made one small concession, enacting a bill giving married women the right to receive their own earnings. If a husband intercepted his wife's wage, wrote Henry, "the employer will have the pleasure of paying it over again to the wife who earned the money."[12]

Laura and KERA secretary Eugenia Farmer endured a similar rebuff early in 1891 when they returned to Frankfort to plead their case before the state constitutional convention. Their hopes rose with the introduction of several unsolicited resolutions in support of both property rights and suffrage, but once more, Josephine Henry reported, "political chicanery and double dealing" prevailed. When the convention adjourned, wives were still without rights to their personal possessions, to household goods bought with their wages, even to guardianship of their children. A husband continued to enjoy a life interest in all of his deceased wife's property, but a widow in only one-third of her husband's. The new constitution, Mrs. Henry concluded bitterly, was "the tomb of justice for Kentucky women."[13]

Clay, Henry, and Farmer, who remained the KERA's chief lobbyists through most of the 1890s, nevertheless seemed energized by these encounters with lawmakers. Greater victories lay within reach, Mrs. Henry triumphantly exclaimed, because "women are standing on the length and breadth of true democracy, and it is like dynamite for men to touch it in their false position." Petition drives soon reinforced the likelihood that school suffrage—the existing right of some women in rural districts to vote for local trustees—could be extended to cities whose charters required revision under the new state constitution. A Louisville group generated one such petition in a matter of hours on the day before the KERA leadership returned to the House in early 1892 to lobby for the latest married women's property bill. As approximately half the legislators and many of their wives listened, Laura Clay introduced Mrs. Farmer, who spoke on married women's fitness for school suffrage, and Mrs. Henry, who catalogued the injustices that attended their lack of property rights. Although the bill failed to emerge from committee, audiences outside Frankfort continued to react favorably both to Clay's and Henry's advocacy and to the suffrage literature they distributed. Eugenia Farmer was particularly convinced that the five thousand pages she had passed out in the course of her work would bear fruit and urged her colleagues to maintain the flow of pamphlets and tracts.[14]

When the KERA held its fifth annual convention at Richmond's Madison County Courthouse in November 1892, the delegates were small in number but confident. After receiving the usual committee reports, they discussed fund-raising, increasing college admissions for women, representation at the World's Columbian Exposition in Chicago, and at Laura Clay's urging, critical study of the Bible in order to enlighten anti-suffrage clergymen regarding "the true position of women as there set forth." Delegates heard papers on industrial education, dress reform, and the merits of the newly founded Populist, or People's, Party. They reserved their greatest enthusiasm, however, for an essay titled "Why Democratic Women Want the Ballot" and submitted under the byline "A Kentucky Woman."[15]

Anxious that it be published, the delegates turned to Clara Bewick Colby, one of the convention speakers, president of the Nebraska Woman Suffrage Association, and since 1883 proprietor of the *Woman's Tribune.* Assembling news of general circulation to accompany her liberal views on suffrage, Colby had published the *Tribune* in Washington, D.C., for part of the last three years while her husband was in government service. Highly regarded by Elizabeth Cady Stanton and Susan B. Anthony, the paper had been identified with the National Woman Suffrage Association until 1890, when the organization reunited with Lucy Stone's more moderate American Woman Suffrage Association to form the National American Woman Suffrage Association (NAWSA). Although the *Woman's Tribune* would lose the contest with the *Woman's Journal* for recognition as the NAWSA's official voice, it retained national prominence and would enjoy the second-longest lifespan, after the *Journal,* of any publication of its kind. Agreeing that "Why Democratic Women Want the Ballot" presented "a most unanswerable argument," Clara Bewick Colby published it three times: in the *Tribune* a month after the convention; in the same month as an issue of the *National Bulletin,* her series of leaflets made available to suffrage organizations for general distribution; and again in the *Tribune* three years later.[16]

The "Kentucky Woman," unidentified until the essay's third printing, was, of course, Lida Calvert Obenchain. If her initial anonymity was a concession to the rules of feminine modesty, it was also a barricade from behind which she launched a rhetorical fusillade that was anything but timid. "I must say at the outset that it seems to me an impertinence for any man to require me to give a reason for wanting the ballot," she began, understanding that a debate framed in such terms took for granted the inequality of the participants. Her reply was in the form of a truth as self-evident to her as were individual liberty and representative government to her Revolutionary War ancestors. "I want this thing because it is my own," she proclaimed. Those who would deny woman the vote because she was "some strange, unclassified creature, some rare exotic, foreign to this world, and utterly unable to exist under its stern laws" had merely reduced her from a human being like themselves to the sum of "the thousand and one frailties" imposed upon her by edict and custom. Even more offensive was the chivalrous argument that likened every woman to a queen or a goddess, and protested her exposure to politics as the equivalent of casting a rose into a cesspool. Suggesting irritably that "we drop metaphor and come down to plain speech," Lida pronounced the flattery hollow and the logic ridiculous. Women were neither queens nor roses but citizens, and politics was not a cesspool but the "science of good government"; further, the chivalry of medieval days was "a disgusting sham, and much of our nineteenth century chivalry is open to the same objection." No real queen ever had to cook, scrub, and sew, sacrifice youth and health to constant childbearing, and seek leave from the legislature to control her own property.[17]

Lida could barely contain her enthusiasm for the budding self-respect of a "lovely Southern woman," a queen by any standard, who had told her, "I don't know that I am very anxious to vote . . . *but I don't exactly like being told that I cannot.*" Striding confidently into the philosophical camp of Elizabeth Cady Stanton and Susan B. Anthony, Lida called upon every woman to stand upon the "solid rock of eternal justice" and claim the vote as a natural right. She understood, nevertheless, that many were far less inclined to advance this "all sufficient, all-embracing reason," preferring instead to wield the vote as a kind of civic housecleaning tool that would speed the enactment of social and moral reforms. Though unimpressed with this "expediency" argument—"If every reform advocated by every party could be carried into effect tomorrow, I would still be a woman suffragist," she wrote—Lida willingly expanded her rhetoric beyond declarations of principle. As a Kentuckian and a writer she was, in fact, well situated to lend her talent on two necessary fronts: refutation of the anti-suffrage arguments that had become more insistent since the Civil War and, of greater importance, the organization of a pro-suffrage constituency that not only was united behind the idea of change but believed itself empowered to make change a reality—what later activists would term "consciousness-raising" among women. Before long, even Eliza Calvert Hall was taken from her poetry and impressed for duty upon this vast and open battlefield.[18]

Perhaps the most troublesome argument for woman suffragists was one that answered their claims to inalienable rights in the style

of "Why Democratic Women Want the Ballot" with an even more
solemn authority: the Bible. In addition to using scriptural references
to uphold laws of coverture, anti-suffragists had long justified their
position with the words of the apostle Paul. Woman was the "glory
of the man," created both from him and for him, and wives were to
be subject "to their own husbands in every thing." Particularly useful
against publicly contentious females were Paul's instructions to his
brethren that women should "keep silence in the churches" and "be
under obedience, as also saith the law. And if they will learn any thing,
let them ask their husbands at home."[19]

The religious argument for denying women a voice nevertheless
prompted fearless responses from Kentucky, where both Laura Clay
and her sister Sallie drew their belief in equality less from the ideals of
the American Revolution than from the spiritual democracy of their
evangelical Protestantism. Like another perceived threat, the theory
of evolution, the achievement of women's rights was not antithetical
to this faith but rather a sign of its approaching triumph. Making the
biblical case in favor of suffrage, itself an exercise in the "higher criticism" of scripture that was part of God's plan for human intellectual
improvement, the Clays contested the universal applicability of Paul's
admonitions. They pointed to the Bible's positive portrayal of numerous female preachers and reemphasized its other, first-mentioned
creation story in which God made male and female simultaneously,
not one from the other. In light of these and other divine prescriptions
for sexual equality, Sallie Clay argued, women who believed their subjection to be God's will rather than men's were as much sinners as the
men who claimed a scriptural license to rule over them.[20]

Perhaps more than her own study of the Bible, both at home and
at school in Ohio, Lida's family history with the Presbyterian church—
Samuel Calvert's struggles with the doctrine of original sin, Eliza Hall
Calvert's defection to the New School, and Thomas Calvert's inability
to take comfort in the promise of joys beyond the grave—would have
acquainted her with the need to reconcile orthodoxy with individual
conscience and experience. Taking up her pen again as "A Kentucky
Woman," she used biblical precedent in another essay received, once
more with great favor, at the seventh annual KERA convention in
Lexington in October 1894. In a lengthy retrospective intended to
show that women had always been fit for the science and art of gov-

ernment, Lida reviewed numerous historical role models, including Isabella of Castile, Catherine of Russia, and Elizabeth I, but began with two figures from the Bible: Esther, who courageously interceded with her king to prevent the destruction of Persian Jews, and Miriam, sister of Moses and a prophetess in her own right, who led the celebrations after the Red Sea engulfed Pharaoh's army. With satisfaction, Lida pronounced Moses "an advocate of woman in politics" and, brushing aside their understanding of history, pointed out to her nostalgic brothers that the "dear old days" of women's exclusion from government did not, in fact, ever exist.[21]

The following January, in honor of Susan B. Anthony's visit to Lexington on her way to the NAWSA convention in Atlanta, a local newspaper granted the KERA's request to publish Lida's essay, "Woman in Politics," and to print extra copies for sale as pamphlets. Laura Clay was undoubtedly pleased at the appearance of another tract that would interest Christian women in suffrage on the grounds that scripture, properly interpreted, stood squarely behind it. This faith in the Bible as a positive force for women's rights, however, soon drove Laura and many other suffragists to distance themselves from the movement's most controversial work of higher criticism and its editor, Elizabeth Cady Stanton. Published in two volumes in 1895 and 1898, *The Woman's Bible* betrayed Stanton's anti-clericalism and her belief that despite its occasional references to sexual equality, the Bible was an instrument of oppression and an obstacle to women's rights.[22]

Standing apart from the hostility to Stanton was Josephine Henry, whose support of *The Woman's Bible* would lead to the end of her ten-year partnership with Laura Clay. Though just beginning her own association with the KERA, Lida also held no strict reverence for clergymen, particularly when they offended an unwritten rule that protected southern suffragists from personal abuse. Two days after "Woman in Politics" was published, a letter in her own name appeared in the *Woman's Journal* castigating a Baptist minister for marginalizing the "woman's rights craze" in Asheville, North Carolina. Lida found his observation that its supporters were, and should stay, unmarried a "specimen of vulgar insolence," a "cowardly insult" that was in shocking contrast to the local newspaper editor's gentlemanly tolerance of the ladies. Two years later, she attacked a less sympathetic Kentucky journalist after Susan B. Anthony appeared at a lecture by

Carrie Chapman Catt in Owensboro. Reminding readers that woman
was merely "an after thought" in the Creator's plan, he had cited the
standard scriptural passages subordinating women to men. Rather
than refute his argument with the merits of the alternative creation
story, Lida eviscerated this example of "boundless egotism" posing as
a "special revelation from the Almighty." Evidently, she marveled sarcastically, the "biology" in the story of Adam's rib was superior to that
of Charles Darwin. She was no more impressed with the claim that
poor physical and mental health in a female was attributable to her
apostasy, haughtily ridiculing "all the Reverends and Right Reverends
and Very Reverends" who urged her to devote her physical energies
to housework and her mental reserves to study of the Ten Command-
ments. While other Kentucky suffragists were more patiently seeking clerical endorsement of their cause, Lida dismissed as irrelevant
the Mississippi bishop who handed down his prescription with vague
quotes from Ecclesiastes and Proverbs. "Women have stopped 'minding' preachers," she snapped, "and not only women, but men, too."[23]

Lida's suffrage writing would have been less useful had she not
understood that such irreligious, anti-male rhetoric was easy sport.
Wisely, she also provided more positive copy that downplayed movement setbacks with evidence of progress: praise for Louisville's South-
western College of Homeopathy for admitting women students, for
example, and supportive quotes from men, particularly prominent
southerners whenever they proved as open-minded as northerners.
The KERA's petition drives, however, had shown Lida that the most
challenging subjects for a woman suffragist were women themselves.
In the lucky event that they had, as she wished, stopped minding
preachers, they remained isolated across gulfs of education, age, and
geographical distance. Marriage, with its complex rules of social con-
straint and legal dispossession, further separated wives not only from
single women but from married women of other economic classes. In
the South, the symbolic position of women was particularly incom-
patible with the ballot. Compassionate, innately virtuous, exercising
indirect influence on the coarser male sex and perceived to be under
constant threat from predatory blacks, the southern lady of the 1890s
inspired efforts not to expand but to restrict the franchise, thereby
restoring the orderly, patriarchal, white-dominated society that had
predated the Lost Cause. Tradition-bound and oriented more to their

roles as members of a family than citizens of the state, such women could be indifferent to suffrage at best and, at worst, openly opposed. Their resistance gave more weight to men's anti-suffrage arguments and shook the confidence of women who harbored sympathy for the cause, undermining their ability to perceive themselves as members of a working constituency with the power to effect change.[24]

Perhaps with Henry Mills Alden's praise in mind, Lida—or, rather, Eliza Calvert Hall—soon was confronting this stumbling block for the movement. Forgoing recitations of abstract principle or pro-suffrage literary and historical precedent, Eliza sought to influence both the faithful and fainthearted in a candid, more intimate style. Appropriately, she began her task in the pages of an independent weekly whose publisher was known for her influential friendships. St. Louis–born Mary Katherine "Kate" Field had parlayed her foreign travels, cosmopolitan wit, and intimacy with notables such as Dickens, Anthony Trollope, and the Brownings into a career as an actress, lecturer, and journalist. In 1890 she began *Kate Field's Washington,* a newspaper that Lida, always appreciative of publications that improved upon the fare of the typical woman's page, enjoyed for its commentary, short stories, and verse. While Eliza Calvert Hall contributed at least six poems throughout the paper's five-year existence, she also wrote several outspoken essays concerned not with political liberation through suffrage but with psychological liberation through altered self-perception— leading, she hoped, to changes that would extend far beyond the ballot.[25]

Beginning with a simple anecdote, Eliza recast a revered feminine trait into a social ill no less odious than the masculine fault with which it was so often contrasted. In "The Sin of Unselfishness," a group of women gathered around a casket remember the meekness and self-abnegation of the deceased but find it strange that her children have failed to follow her example. "Strange! Not at all," Eliza retorted. "The inevitable outcome of the woman who never thinks of herself is the husband, the son, the daughter who never thinks of anything but self." Such a woman—an "enabler" or simply a "doormat" in modern parlance—was a sinner, guilty of ignoring Christ's admonition to "Love thy neighbor *as thyself.*" Eliza contrasted the conspicuous display of martyrdom, which turned wives into slaves, and husbands and children into tyrants, with a "noble self-esteem," which attracted respect and thereby fostered true unselfishness in one's family and oneself. Mourning the effect on her offspring of a woman's pernicious self-effacement, the essay raised a compelling vision of women's collective power to better society simply by standing up for themselves at home. Those who paled at the thought of following Laura Clay into the chambers of the General Assembly could take heart in this alternative course of action.[26]

Behind Eliza Calvert Hall's sermon on sinfulness lay a more subtle intellectual exercise, one that induced her readers to reevaluate the traditional connotation of words like "selfish" and "unselfish." In this pursuit, Lida was soon pleased to invoke both the religious and scholarly authority of Richard Chevenix Trench, the Anglican archbishop of Dublin, theologian, poet, and philologist who had died only a few years earlier. His famous 1851 work, *The Study of Words,* may first have been brought to her attention by the Major, a devoted book collector who enjoyed sharing tidbits of etymology with the members of his club. Rereading its pages, Lida had found an answer to women who resisted attempts to "thrust" the vote upon them, yet objected to legal incapacities that classified them with "idiots." They had no complaint, she wrote, in light of the ancient Greek definition of "idiot" as not a mentally deficient person but a private individual who neglected the proper development of his intellect by declining to involve himself in public life.[27]

Archbishop Trench's chapter on the "morality" of words also allowed Eliza Calvert Hall to demonstrate how conventionally unselfish women further cloaked their degradation in the lexicon of polite middle-class femininity. "We are not accustomed to think of plain speaking as a Christian duty," she observed, writing "On the Duty of Calling a Spade a Spade." As a consequence, she charged, the well-bred woman curried the favor of others by renaming their stupidity "conservatism," excusing their cruelty as "peculiar," and lauding her own tolerance as "Christian charity." A "very *un*-Christian moral cowardice," in fact, motivated the woman who denied both the ignorance of those around her and her own judgment of it, making her—to follow Trench's prescription of "an ugly word for an ugly thing"—a liar twice over. Cowardly acts also abounded, Eliza complained, in the day-to-day habits of status-seeking, fashion-conscious, overconsuming wives, absorbed in the "servile imitation of others no better than we are." Such women were derivative souls, "second-hand" in their ideas, opinions, and morality—in everything except their new clothes and parlor furnishings.[28]

Reading these essays, subscribers to *Kate Field's Washington* must have been struck by this new edge to Eliza Calvert Hall. Except for "A Forecast," which predicted that future lovers would recoil at the misbegotten chivalry of the nineteenth century, her poems had none of the urgency of her prose, nor did she defend them with as much vigor. She and her husband shared a "hearty laugh," she reported to *Kate Field's*, when her most recently published verse elicited a playful comment from New York's *Commercial Advertiser* about the romantic prospects of its author, mistakenly thought to be Miss Field herself. Eliza's response was less forgiving, however, when a Chicago reader known only by his initials "J. E. W." accepted her advice to "call a spade a spade" and characterized as a "job lot of misfits" the suffragist clubwomen of his acquaintance. Barely affecting patience with someone who had so openly admitted his incomprehension of ordinary English, she suggested that the gentleman purchase a "textbook of logic and study for a few months" in order to understand the difference between a truth told for truth's sake and the reactionary gibes of "conservatives" like him, whose malice masqueraded as candor. "I knew that Eliza Calvert Hall would rend J. E. W. the moment she got hold of him," wrote Kate Field gleefully.[29]

While men could be handily dismissed as victims of their own intellectual shortcomings, Eliza tried to be more philosophical in her judgments of the self-effacing mothers, complacent matrons, and "second-hand" women of her experience. Publications such as the *Woman's Journal* had avoided demonizing females who stood outside the movement, preferring instead to excuse their conduct as merely the internalization of generations of oppression. Eliza concurred, if somewhat grudgingly. Pity, she confided, was the only appropriate response to the "wretched little" woman who wasted her money on the latest fashion despite knowing it would make her look "like a fright," or who cobbled together silver and cut glass from her neighbors to hold an elaborate dinner party at which her pretensions fooled no one. Pity, too, the "dear little creature" who began every conversation by chirping "John says . . . ," in mimicry of the uninformed opinions of her husband. Sadder still was the wife of another "John" who

meekly surrendered the memory of her undiminished self: suggesting
to her husband that they make an excursion to the springtime woods
she found so rejuvenating in her youth, she returns her love of nature to an inventory of unsatisfied yearnings as he retreats behind
his newspaper. Such "mental poverty" differed only in degree from
that of Eliza's most pathetic example, drawn from the report of a missionary traveling through eastern Kentucky. Stopping at an isolated
mountain cabin, he had accepted a drink of water from its occupant
and, in the course of their conversation, was stunned to learn that she
had never heard of Jesus. "I live so fur from the big road," was her
humble explanation, "and John never tells me nothin'." Just as she
had found the words "unselfish" and "conservative" to be swaddled
in false meaning, Eliza likened these unfortunate nineteenth-century
women to mummies, trapped in the "moldy winding-sheets of Preju-
dice and Custom." She believed, nonetheless, that patient unraveling
of each would reveal a soul that was not simply a receptacle for the
"rotten opinions of dead ancestors" but "something that was once a
living thing made in the image of God."[30]
     Seeping too often into the modest faith of Eliza Calvert Hall,
however, was the frustration and pessimism of Lida Calvert Obenchain. The two seemed to wrestle for the same pen, one attempting
to show compassion for her all-too-human sisters, the other yearning
to throttle them for their thickheadedness. In her treatment of men,
Lida had imagined that a righteous verbal ambush was sufficient to
expose their foolishness and hypocrisy. Turning her gaze on women
such as the "little, laboring, trusting wife" beholden to the opinions
of her husband, Eliza tried to save her own "small reputation . . . for
sweetness" and not waste words, only to surrender to the same fantasy
of angry confrontation. "Some of these days when I am suffering from
an unusual dearth of Christian charity," she warned, "I am going to
forget my inborn and my acquired politeness and be for once just as
mean as I possibly can be. I am going to turn on that innocent Mrs.
'John.'" After Eliza rehearsed a tongue-lashing of the hapless woman,
her anger turned to resignation as she abandoned both John and his
wife to "find out what I, in my impatience, would have them learn
long before the appointed time for learning it."[31]
     Lida's frustration recalled that of her grandfather Samuel Calvert,
who berated his parishioners for failing in the work of their own salva-

tion even as he despaired of knowing whether such salvation was pos-sible. Although prepared to make allowance for the poor creature "fur from the big road," Lida remained convinced that the woman who declined at least to struggle against her moldy winding-sheets would face judgment for denying her God-given self. Unselfishness "is the source of half the woes of this life—*and the next,*" was the malediction that intruded upon Eliza Calvert Hall's parable of the meek, selfless creature in the casket. Unless God had readied for them a "second-hand heaven," women who lived in slavish imitation of the habits of their wealthy neighbors courted a similar purgatory.[32]

Perhaps Lida was concerned about her own salvation; after all, every time she exercised "Christian charity" and failed to turn on the wives of "Johns," she must have sensed her own moral cowardice. On the other hand, she understood that women who defied convention risked personal, social, and intellectual capital, sometimes earning nothing but gossip and ostracism as "cranks." She deplored oppo-nents who, claiming that the vote would render them less feminine, denied justice to women on aesthetic grounds, but she conceded that such rhetoric effectively associated suffrage with unlovely outcasts—"gaunt, spectacled women" aggressively lobbying congressmen—and commonplace, even vulgar behavior. Even where southern activists strove to appear respectable and conventionally ladylike, critics hint-ed at the undue influence of their grotesque northern sisters. Eliza Calvert Hall had tried to soften this imagery with an anecdote about a woman in a small southern town whose nonconformism sprang from an inward-looking, spiritual need. Wishing to enjoy a certain view from a certain window, she had built her cottage with its front facade a quarter-turn from the entrance gate. Eliza professed nothing but goodwill for such a woman, who acted "out of the fullness of her own heart, and not out of the emptiness of somebody else's heart," but admitted that since no one had dared to emulate her commonsense challenge to custom, both cottage and occupant stood "solitary and alone."[33]

By the late 1890s, Lida's sharp, informed argument and commen-tary had assured her of space in the pages of leading women's journals. Each anti-suffrage parry that she deflected, however, each historical role model that she invoked, and each slumbering conscience that she tried to awaken was a goad to the literary imagination of "Eliza Calvert

Hall." In a social world bound by stale, unoriginal opinions, she recognized firsthand the attraction of "the theatre, the novel, anything that will give us a chance to study human nature" and envied the insight that poets, dramatists, and novelists of the reform-minded nineteenth century had brought to issues such as anti-imperialism, agrarianism, socialism, and the single tax. Given the manner in which critics tended to portray advocates of women's rights, Lida was particularly convinced that the movement could achieve its goals more quickly by securing not just the intellectual high ground but the aesthetic high ground. Reviewing the poetry of Charlotte Perkins Stetson, she applauded Stetson's ability to present her case for equality of the sexes with "the lofty altruism, the delicate humor, the delightful wit, and the keen reasoning from analogy" that rendered it unanswerable on any level of discourse. Stetson had supplied a necessary element of "picturesqueness" that not only would appeal to the mind of the most progressive and ambitious woman but would "touch the heart of the most conservative and domestic wife that ever cooked her husband's breakfast." Lida cautioned that she was not referring to the sweet, romantic brand of picturesqueness that writer William Dean Howells had complained was so lacking in the agitation for women's rights; she contrasted the picturesqueness that valued aesthetic sense over moral perception with a clear, well-drawn "picture-ness," the truth of which rendered even a homely subject beautiful.[34]

In her worshipful review (which Stetson herself remembered as "a most flowery article") Lida might also have been praying for the literary future of Eliza Calvert Hall. Not only did she endorse the application of rhyme, lyric, and story to the cause of social reform, she claimed that consecration to a cause was "the crowning glory and blessedness of genius." She yearned to inform minds and hearts about the denial of justice to women, yet she also apprehended the cost. Literature written with a purpose did not gain immortality, either in the estimation of critics, who disqualified it as genuine art, or in the popular imagination, where it ceased to resonate once the particular reform had been achieved. Like the selfless woman dedicated to family and domesticity, such writing could fill its sphere but not overflow the limits, and even Stetson's verse on behalf of "the woman movement" would live only so long as it was useful. No matter, insisted Lida, for longevity measured by usefulness was "immortality enough."[35]

In Stetson's other poems, however, Lida hailed that familiar subject in which she knew artists and art could aspire to perpetual life: "the thoughts and emotions of the universal woman-heart."[36] She had already flirted with such mysteries in her youthful poetry, but as "A Kentucky Woman"—a propertyless wife, weary mother, overworked housekeeper, temperamental Christian, and passionate suffragist, as well as a writer—she had come to view them intimately only through the lens of grievance. Would Eliza Calvert Hall ever transcend her own circumstances and dwell in the realm of the true artist, or would she find that the devotion of her art to the reform of women's lot was, in fact, "immortality enough"?

7

Money and Marriage

> And when the honeymoon is over, the woman who has been
> endowed with all her husband's goods, finds that she has to ask for
> every cent she spends, and if she doesn't ask she will never have a
> cent to spend.
>
> —Lida Calvert Obenchain, "The Evolution of Justice"

"I AM GETTING FAMOUS RAPIDLY," wrote Lida in August 1894
to her sister Josie, who was visiting Mary Kendall Jones in Missouri.
Over the past six months, Eliza Calvert Hall had published three essays in *Kate Field's Washington* and two poems, one in *Kate Field's*
and another in the *Arena,* a review devoted to issues of interest to reformers. Two submissions under Lida's own name had also appeared
in the *Woman's Journal* and the *Woman's Tribune.* Her home life was
somewhat unsettled: money was scarce, the Major and young Alex
were in Virginia, her sister Mary had been seriously ill, her cook was
also sick, and Lida, aged thirty-eight, was pregnant with her fourth
child. She was, nevertheless, in reasonably good humor, asking Josie
to tell one of Mrs. Jones's sons that "I am going to send him some of
my woman suffrage documents. No doubt it will shock them all," she
added mischievously, "to know that I am an 'unsexed creature' who
wants to vote."[1]

None of Lida's sisters had married, and none would. Mary uncom-
plainingly assisted their mother Margaret at home and skillfully plied
her needle for family and friends. Although Mary Kendall Jones's son
Charles still pined for her, and Henry Batts, her admirer at the time

of Thomas Calvert's pardon, had begged her to reciprocate his declarations of love, Maggie had kept her own counsel. She had begun teaching third grade at the public school, where even the superintendent found himself complimenting her personal charm as well as her dedication to her work. Josie had become an assistant to Mrs. Carrie Taylor, whose large dressmaking firm Lida had patronized when she was a schoolteacher. Two weeks before Lida's letter, Mrs. Taylor's husband had asked Josie to return promptly from Missouri to help with orders for the fall season's wedding fashions. Avoiding any stigma that might have followed the children of Thomas Calvert, Josie became the Taylors' trusted employee. When they departed on buying trips to New York and Europe, they left her in charge to answer mail, collect accounts, and sign company checks.[2]

Had they chosen to marry in 1894, the other Calvert sisters would have escaped many of the legal disabilities that had been forced upon Lida. On May 16, 1893, the General Assembly had finally approved a married women's property bill. Signed by Governor John Young Brown on May 18, the new law included provisions giving a wife the power to dispose of her estate by will and reserving the right to use and rent her own real estate free of her husband's control or debts. "We Kentucky suffragists are all smiles," Josephine Henry reported to the *Woman's Journal*, even though the final measure was more conservative than the KERA had hoped. Amendments to raise the age of consent for females from twelve to sixteen and to equalize dower and curtesy rights had failed, and a wife remained unable to sell or mortgage her real estate without her husband's consent or permission of a court in lieu thereof.[3]

The next year Laura Clay, Josephine Henry, and Eugenia Farmer made five more lobbying trips to Frankfort as the General Assembly considered bills to liberalize the law still further. Proposed measures from both houses were referred to a joint committee for reconciliation, and while Laura Clay credited its successful passage to Mrs. Henry's eloquence and parliamentary maneuvering in the House, the final bill remained associated with one of the Senate committee members, Louisville lawyer Rozel Weissinger. Signed by the governor on March 15, 1894, the Weissinger Act expanded the 1893 law to give wives control over both their real and personal property. It recognized a married woman's separate legal existence, allowing her to sue and be sued as if she were unmarried and to make any contract subject only to the continuing right of her husband to consent to a sale or mortgage of her real estate. The act also equalized dower and curtesy, giving surviving spouses a life interest in one-third of their deceased spouse's real estate as well as the right to one-half of his or her personal property.[4]

Although the KERA's paid membership numbered only four hundred, the persistent lobbying of its leaders, together with their use of petitions to demonstrate widespread support for property rights, had contributed significantly to the legislative gains for married women in 1894. Another breakthrough that same year demonstrated how progress on voting rights could be achieved through well-organized activism. After the 1891 state constitutional convention, Eugenia Farmer had urged local KERA chapters to petition the committee revising city charters to include a provision allowing women to vote in school board elections. Women in Covington, Newport, and Lexington, the state's second-class cities (having populations between 20,000 and 100,000), heeded Farmer's advice; in Covington and Newport they also petitioned their city councils, and in Covington obtained the endorsement of their state representatives. Despite the failure of a general school suffrage bill, Governor Brown signed legislation updating second-class city charters on March 19, 1894, giving women in those cities voting rights withheld from their less influential sisters in Louisville, the state's largest and only first-class city.[5]

In the style of a loyal movement foot soldier, Lida expressed only momentary satisfaction with the decade's gains. While she credited the KERA with having "swept from the statute books of Kentucky every vestige of the barbarous common law of England as it related to the property rights of married women," still standing were laws respecting guardianship of children and the age of consent that "would disgrace the pagans." Subsequent judicial interpretation of the Weissinger Act also would have prolonged her sense of injustice. In 1898, the Kentucky court of appeals held that the act could not operate retrospectively to deprive a husband of his common-law rights in his wife's property if their marriage had occurred prior to the date of its passage. A woman such as Lida, therefore, was only entitled to full control of property she had acquired after March 15, 1894.[6]

On March 25, 1895, Cecilia "Cecil" Obenchain, probably named after a sister of her great-grandmother, Eliza Hall Calvert, became the youngest sibling of seven-year-old Margery, six-year-old Alex, and three-year-old Tom. Perhaps more clearly than any legal watershed, the arrival of Lida's fourth child highlighted a growing divide between the opportunities that had been available to her and those now imaginable for younger wives and single women. By the time of Cecil's birth, women in Kentucky had breached many barriers to their independence and participation in public life. They had gained admission to most colleges and professions, and were serving as postmasters and county school superintendents. The formation in 1894 of the Kentucky Federation of Women's Clubs reflected their commitment to organized civic activism on behalf of education, the protection of children, urban beautification, and, occasionally, suffrage. That same year, the Senate elected its first woman enrolling clerk, and in 1896 a woman would become state librarian. A woman had first passed the state bar examination in 1892.[7]

The fact that these gains had been realized without resort to the vote, however, gave nonsympathizers an excuse to remain indifferent to the suffrage movement even as they benefited from revised property laws and greater access to education and the professions. Lida was deeply offended by the "moral idiocy" of such women who, in her view, now enjoyed the spoils of a battle from which they had remained aloof. Comparing them to guests who repudiated the acquaintance of a hostess after partaking of her food, drink, and hospitality, Lida issued a challenge intended to sting any woman, particularly a southerner who considered herself to be "of enlightened conscience and high breeding." Given that no such woman would accept a privilege obtained through the indelicate, "strong-minded" conduct of others, she must either refuse to avail herself of it or openly admit her debt to those "despised and rejected" suffragists who had endured condemnation and scorn on her behalf. This, Lida declared, was simply "*a point of honor.*"[8]

Appropriately, Lida revived the theme of honor in a lengthy paper written for a grand celebration of southern progress. When the Tennessee Centennial Exposition opened at Nashville in May 1897, the Tennessee Suffrage Association sponsored an Equal Suffrage Convocation in the Woman's Building on the exposition grounds. Although Lida later credited this event with her realization that "nature never

intended me to be a public speaker," she participated with Laura
Clay and suffragists from Tennessee and Alabama in a three-day program of addresses and songs. Taken together, their speeches linked
a woman's identity to both past and future, and her cause to both
tradition and revolution. Laura reiterated the Christian argument for
suffrage, speaking on "The Bible, and Woman as Found in It," while
Lida, in the midst of a centennial showcasing southern womanhood,
hailed "this army of short-haired, plain-faced, stern-voiced reformers with their uncompromising logic, their strident voices and their
disagreeable habit of calling things by their right names." Returning
to her best and most fiercely held argument, that the vote belonged
to women as a matter of justice, she scolded the Daughters of the
American Revolution for their preoccupation with the bloodlines of
their ancestors rather than the principle that "taxation without representation is tyranny." She called again upon her conservative sisters,
who sat "wrapped in silks and laces" protesting that they now had
all the rights they wanted, to acknowledge the "'unwomanly' women
who had sense enough to know what rights women ought to have and
courage enough to demand those rights."[9]

Lida also raised a point of honor with men who resisted such demands even as they wrapped themselves in the attributes of chivalry,
mercy, kindness, and charity. Understanding that a show of these derivative sentiments allowed them to deflect charges of injustice, she turned
to a far more potent accusation, that of dishonesty. At the source of a
thief's criminal behavior, she argued, was a deficient sense of justice,
one that failed to recognize his victim's right to possess the property he
had stolen. Similarly, the man who interposed himself, chivalrously or
otherwise, between a woman and her civil and political rights was not
only lacking a sense of justice, he was behaving as dishonestly as if he
had robbed her of the money in her purse. Any reason he gave for his
opposition—that women had enough rights, that they did not know
how to use them, or that they would use them to bad effect—would
be transparently dishonest if the word "money" were substituted for
"rights."[10]

In a speech ringing with calls for a republic "whose every law is an
embodiment of pure justice," the question of a woman's purse lurked
as a bitter aside. Lida realized that laws protecting property did nothing to alleviate the ongoing state of poverty most women suffered

within marriage. She was fond of observing that after being endowed at the altar with her husband's worldly goods, a wife commonly had nothing to spend but what she asked for or (in another instance of dishonesty born of injustice) stealthily removed from his pocket. Confined to a monthly allowance, begrudged a few extra dollars at Christmas, and prevented from earning her own wages by domestic duties and childrearing, she suffered either the personal indignity that came with begging or the marital discord that came with demanding.[11]

While Laura Clay agreed that control over her own means of subsistence was essential for a woman's genuine liberty, Lida's grievances about money tempted her to use rhetoric that many southern suffragists avoided, at least publicly, as too radical. Late in 1897 she wrote a series of articles for the *New York Times* that succeeded in raising the eyebrows of even a few northerners. Relaying to the *Times* an excerpt from the Greenup County, Kentucky, *Gazette,* she deplored the report of a wife who had committed suicide after being chastised by her husband for extending credit to a customer of his store. Lida wrote a simple epitaph for the woman: "Died for lack of a separate purse." Without money, kept ignorant of family finances, and denied the status of a business partner, she had the means neither to perform an act of charity on her own account nor to avoid humiliation by her "anthropoidal ape" of a husband. Lida hoped that every wife would some day receive an income, either through her own business or through recognition of the monetary worth of housekeeping, in order to confound men's demand for domestic labor in exchange for minimal support. In the meantime, revisiting a comparison that had scandalized antebellum southerners, she pronounced marriages like those of the suicidal woman's to be "a form of slavery." Responding to Lida's letter, a New York reader was sympathetic but counseled a more moderate approach. "You can't pay a woman for nursing her own children or baking her own bread," she wrote, asking whether husbands demanded their wives' housework any more than wives demanded their husbands' office work. She agreed, nevertheless, that openness about finances was critical to the emotional health of a marriage, especially for women who had left their fathers' comfortable homes or their own wage-earning positions out of love for poor men.[12]

Lida also provoked a response when she advocated conduct that valued gender solidarity over economic self-interest. A wealthy wom-

an, she argued, ought to practice a kind of virtuous extravagance by
targeting her spending to benefit those further down the income scale.
More than a large gift to her church or the purchase of luxury goods,
for example, payment of a higher fee to her seamstress would better
solve the problems of unemployment and depressed wages. Another
Times reader took issue, fearing that such overpayment would inflate
the price of labor beyond the means of less wealthy women. Rhe-
torically clenching her teeth, Lida was quick to assure her: "As I am
a woman of moderate means myself—very, very moderate means—I
am not likely to overlook the claims of this class to consideration." Unlike New York's wealthy, she explained, no one in her small town possessed enough money to distort the market; in any event, all women
should purchase as much higher-priced work as possible and econ-
omize in other ways. Providers of services ought to display similar
altruism, charging less if they worked for "pin money" than if they
constituted the sole support of their families. Lida thanked the reader
for her "bright and courteous criticism" but, rather than retreating
from her position, warned that further elaboration of her views might
render her letter too radical even for the *New York Times*.[13]

Although they could have undermined acceptance of her suffrage arguments, Lida did not confine her more controversial ideas
to a northern forum. Speaking at the Tennessee Centennial Exposition, she expressed sympathy for the labor movement even as she
acknowledged its association with communism and anarchism. She
reprimanded Charlotte Perkins Gilman (formerly Stetson) for her
failure to credit suffragists with intermediate reforms such as property rights; not surprisingly, given their shared antipathy to housework,
she endorsed Gilman's call for cooperatives to provide families with
precooked food and other domestic services. When Ellen Glasgow
published her first novel, *The Descendant,* in 1897, Lida praised the
choice of a woman suffragist and her socialist husband as its main
characters. She was particularly gratified to see this "little Virginia
girl" puncture the stereotype of the traditional southern woman, but
Glasgow was only among the more visible. "This revolt of women from
the bondage of the accepted ideal is a more serious affair than the
careless observer might think it to be," warned Lida. Though pres-
ently experiencing "no clamor for the ballot," her region was home
to masses of unnamed women who were earning wages, meeting in

clubs, participating in school elections, and speaking out publicly on national politics. Within each of these "conservative" southerners, she insisted, lurked a potential subversive.[14]

In her series for the *New York Times*, Lida had included other progressive pieces defending women's college education, older woman–younger man marriages, and the right of the "literary woman" to exemption from household chores. This last topic drew her back to her theory of literature, which she had first explored in her review of Charlotte Perkins Stetson's poetry. Instead of analyzing the nature of immortal art—whether it sprang from the application of genius to a purpose, or from the expression of an archetypal "woman-heart"—she considered writers such as George Eliot, Elizabeth Barrett Browning, and George Sand, linking their greatness to their freedom from domestic burdens. Lida qualified her own argument, however, when she challenged the stereotype of the literary woman as an unfit wife and mother. No doubt she took special pride in dismissing the notion that a woman who wrote a story for the *Century*, a poem for *Harper's*, or an essay for the *Atlantic* had an intellect "developed beyond the point of safety." The biographies of famous women writers, on the contrary, had left her "dumb with admiration" for their ability to produce timeless literature while fulfilling the duties of nurse, laundress, cook, and housemaid. Anxious to claim in principle the same relief from domestic constraints granted to literary men, Lida, nevertheless, was unwilling to admit defeat before those same constraints or even to divorce them from the sources of literature itself.[15]

This theme became particularly relevant when the breadth of Lida's *New York Times* pieces, combined with her iconoclastic views on money, caught the attention of John Brisben Walker, editor of *Cosmopolitan* magazine. In early 1898 Walker had purchased the Bacheller Syndicate, founded by journalist Irving Bacheller to supply newspapers with feature stories, sketches, and serialized fiction. The contract he offered Lida with the now-renamed International Literary and News Service would have given her a unique opportunity to claim the privileges of a literary woman; still, she declined. Syndicate work promised to draw much of her attention away from Cecil, who was still very young. For Lida, that settled the matter.[16]

For someone so aggrieved by the burdens of domesticity, Lida's decision seemed remarkably free of regret. Although she would never abandon the dream of becoming a newspaperwoman, at the time she had no reason to feel completely thwarted. Recent support for her efforts to juggle wifehood and writing had arrived in the form of a flattering letter from James Lane Allen, the Lexington native whose short story collections such as *Flute and Violin* and best-selling novels such as *The Choir Invisible* had made him one of Kentucky's most popular literary voices.[17]

When Lida told her brother of Allen's letter, he too responded positively. Now in his late twenties, Edward was still finding his way. At seventeen he had left Ogden College and entered the U.S. Military Academy at West Point. Despite his high standing at Ogden, which included distinction in arithmetic, he was discharged from West Point two years later for deficiency in mathematics. After several years assisting his father in real estate work and briefly attending school in Indiana, Edward took a low-paying, temporary job at the Tennessee Centennial Exposition, where Lida had lectured. There, he mocked a festival patron's claim to high status as rather "codfishy" and, when he caught a cold, likened his runny nose to "a W. C. T. U. drinking fountain," but had no flippant reply to James Lane Allen's praise of his sister. "I have believed allways [*sic*]," he told Josie, "that she could make herself a living and a name with her pen if she should choose to devote her time to literature. However I think raising up one kid as good as Margery—to say nothing of the rest of her rising family—is even a better way than that of serving the Lord."[18]

Whatever frustration she may have experienced over his stodginess and his modest earning capacity, Lida also benefited from her husband's interest in writing. In addition to a personal account of his beloved Stonewall Jackson, the Major's own publications included articles on bass fishing and state revenue legislation, an essay on character for an anthology of inspirational thinking, and, later, contributions to *Confederate Veteran* magazine. When he met with fellow members of the XV Club, literary figures and the state of literature were among the many subjects discussed in detail. Along with Robert Burns Wilson, to whom he may have introduced Lida when she was seeking a venue for her poetry, the Major was acquainted with James Lane Allen, who had lectured in Bowling Green around the time *Flute and Violin* was published. Lida's own work attracted his interest and comment. Just as he had shared her amusement over the misreading of

her poem in *Kate Field's Washington*, the Major teased her by warning that her *New York Times* essay advocating "virtuous extravagance"
would have all husbands protesting the incitement to their spendthrift
wives.[19]

More important than his tolerance of Lida's style was the Major's
sympathy for her message. Though Cecil would claim that her mother resented his attachment to his men's club, its minutes recorded
his strong support of her right to vote, sometimes in stark disagree-
ment with colleagues his wife would have unhesitatingly termed "anthropoidal apes." The Major echoed Lida's outrage at "the tendency
of the man, the self-constituted lord of creation," to classify women
"with minors, idiots, & lunatics" and blamed English common law
for their fall from positions of rank and influence to near-slave status.
He agreed that the recent gains of Kentucky women, especially their
property rights, were attributable to "patient & persistent agitation of
the question, in the face of misrepresentation and ridicule."[20]

By the time Lida received the syndicate offer, the Major had also
become familiar with her persistence in another matter. For almost
two years, both later recalled, a typewritten sketch had traveled back
and forth "like a weaver's shuttle" between Bowling Green and the
publishers of major periodicals in the East. Unlike her poetry, Eliza
Calvert Hall's first attempt at fiction had been less than enthusiastically received. The editor of the *Ladies' Home Journal* praised its
literary qualities but was typically squeamish in declining to publish
the story, pronouncing it "irreverent" and not likely to be received in
the "right spirit."[21]

Fortunately, on one of its trips east the manuscript reached the
offices of the *Cosmopolitan*. Under the editorship of John Brisben
Walker, who had read Lida's essays in the *New York Times*, the magazine had achieved a circulation of more than 300,000. For one dollar
a year, subscribers received a well-illustrated monthly that combined
the quality magazine's literature, travel accounts, and discussion of
social and political issues with the more timely and sensational reporting common to newspapers. A man of wide business as well as
journalistic interests, Walker focused less on aestheticism and moral
uplift than the genteel purveyors of magazines like *Scribner's*, but he
maintained strict control over content. He reserved about one-quarter
of each issue for fiction, serializing novels but more frequently turn-

ing to short stories in order to accommodate a broader, less leisured audience. Work by H. G. Wells, Bret Harte, Sarah Orne Jewett, Arthur Conan Doyle, and Frederic Remington had recently appeared in the magazine alongside that of lesser-known writers, whose manuscripts crossed Walker's desk at the rate of more than fifteen thousand a year.[22]

With the Spanish-American War in its third month, the nonfiction sections of the July 1898 *Cosmopolitan* were distinctly martial in tone. Two articles, one by Walker himself, discussed technical aspects of weaponry. Theodore Dreiser contributed a portrait of a Connecticut cartridge factory, and Irving Bacheller reported on a cavalry encampment near Chickamauga. Other articles profiled the wartime American government, Napoleon Bonaparte, and German emperor William II. The issue also included an essay examining the merits of various oratorical styles; its author most favored extemporaneous addresses that were free of digression, warning that a speaker, "having chosen the impression he wishes to produce, must limit his energy on that occasion to the production of that single impression."[23] The five short stories that month promised lighter fare, but in hindsight a reader might have concluded that one of them was better classified with the magazine's nonfiction offerings. Amid the *Cosmopolitan*'s meditations on conquest, both military and verbal, appeared the tale of "Sally Ann's Experience."

8

Sally Ann's Experience

> It is only a plain tale of plain people told in the plain dialect of a plain old woman.
> —Eliza Calvert Hall, "Why I Wrote 'Sally Ann's Experience'"

"COME RIGHT IN AN' SET DOWN. I was jest wishin' I had somebody to talk to. Take that chair right by the door so's you can get the breeze." With the opening sentences of "Sally Ann's Experience," Eliza Calvert Hall introduces one of that species of plain southern folk whose isolation has cultivated both her sense of hospitality and her talent for storytelling. The invitation is extended to the story's unnamed female narrator—an outsider, but one who enters this scene of rural homeliness without condescension or unease. It is June in Kentucky, and even though clover and bluegrass renew the face of the landscape, her hostess is preoccupied with the past.[1]

"Yes, I'm a-piecin' quilts again," Aunt Jane tells her guest. Rummaging in the garret, she has come across a long-forgotten bundle of calico scraps. As she cuts and arranges them, each evokes a vivid memory of the garment from which it came and the woman who sewed, purchased, or wore it. Among the flowered and colored bits of cloth is a black and white piece, a humble token of reuse and making-do that hints of a certain severity, especially when matched to the name of its donor, Sally Ann Flint.

"Did I ever tell you about Sally Ann's Experience?" Aunt Jane asks, before returning to a time forty years ago when both her church and her congregation were "out o' fix." The men of Goshen Church

have managed to repair its roof and windows, and the ladies' auxil-
iary, tellingly named the Mite Society, is ready to spend twelve dollars
it has saved for the improvements.[2] The women meet and agree to
purchase a "cyarpet" to cover the bare floor, but are dumbfounded
when their treasurer, Elizabeth Taylor, abruptly informs them that the
cash is missing. Warnings from the minister's wife—"Judge not"—and
from Sally Ann, who fears that the male parishioners will be justified
in their claim of women's unfitness to handle money, convince the
society to close ranks until the matter can be resolved. By the next
morning only one of its members, Milly Amos, has confessed the secret to her husband, Sam; she was, Aunt Jane recalls, a woman with
"mighty little sense to begin with, an' havin' been married only about
two months, she'd about lost that little." Sam Amos questions Aunt
Jane, who tells him sharply to mind his own business.

A month passes before "'Lizabeth," looking pale and anxious, reappears one night for the prayer meeting. The service proceeds as
usual until the minister, Parson Page, issues his regular call to the
brethren to give their past week's experiences of the Lord's grace. Before the most tiresomely faithful among them can speak, Elizabeth, a
slip of paper in hand, appears in front of the pulpit. "I've somethin' to
say," she announces. She admits to taking the carpet money—"I only
meant to borry it," she explains—to pay for a trip to Louisville, where
her daughter from a previous marriage lay dying. Three times she had
asked her husband, Jacob, to finance her travel and he had refused.
Distraught and praying for guidance, she had spied the Mite Society's
cash in her bureau drawer and, on the mantel, her mother's brass candlesticks, for which a Louisville woman had once offered her fifteen
dollars. Presented with a way both to make the trip and to replace the
money, Elizabeth concluded that "the Lord was leadin' me."

In hindsight, she confesses, "it must 'a' been Satan." She had managed to spend a few hours with her daughter before she died, but the
purchaser for the candlesticks was out of town, forcing her to leave
them with a relative and accept a promise that the money would follow in a few days. Unfortunately, the woman had delayed her return
home, and Elizabeth had not received her check until after the Mite
Society meeting. "I reckon it's a judgment on me for meddling with
the Lord's money," she says, resigned to the likelihood of her expulsion from the congregation. Offering up the check, she nevertheless

admits that she does not regret the actions that have so tormented her conscience.

The congregation sits in awkward silence as Elizabeth waits, trembling, for the first stone to be cast. Suddenly, a woman is by her side. It is Sally Ann. Aunt Jane recalls praying that "the Lord Jesus would jest come in" and help Elizabeth before realizing that this small figure in an "old black poke-bonnet and some black yarn mitts" would "do jest as well."

"I reckon if anybody's turned out o' this church on account o' that miserable little money, it'll be Jacob and not 'Lizabeth," Sally Ann observes calmly. "A man that won't give his wife money to go to her dyin' child is too mean to stay in a Christian church anyhow." Not pausing for a reaction, she continues:

> "And things is come to a pretty pass in this state when a woman that had eight hundred dollars when she married has to go to her husband and git down on her knees and beg for what's her own. Where's that money 'Lizabeth had when she married you?" says she, turnin' round and lookin' Jacob in the face. "Down in that ten-acre medder lot, ain't it?—and in that new barn you built last spring."

Sally Ann's confrontational manner rouses Silas Petty, one of the old deacons. He reminds his brethren that a woman's religious experience is welcome in the house of the Lord, but her abuse of an elder must be subject to the apostle Paul's command: "Let your women keep silence in the church." These words, however, hold no authority for Sally Ann, who once confided to Aunt Jane that she had as little use for the "'Postle Paul" as for Judas Iscariot. Perhaps, she retorts, the long-dead apostle might rise from his grave and address the matter of Deacon Petty's own wife, "workin' like a slave for twenty-five years" only to sit up every Saturday night washing her one good petticoat for church the next morning. "I can give my experience, can I? Well, that's jest what I'm a-doin'," says Sally Ann, catching fire, announcing her intention to speak not only for Elizabeth Taylor and Maria Petty but for "the rest of the women who betwixt their husbands an' the 'Postle Paul have about lost all the gumption and grit that the Lord started them out with."

The men nervously realize what lies in store for them. Feigning illness, Job Taylor rises and starts quietly for the door, only to become Sally Ann's first target. "I've knelt an' stood through enough o' your long-winded prayers, an' now it's my time to talk an' yours to listen," she says. After Job meekly returns to his seat, Sally Ann recounts the heartbreaking decline of his now-dead wife after he took the money she had carefully saved for new furniture. "You told her that she and everything she had belonged to you," she reminds him, but his legal justification is, like the apostle Paul's edict, merely a convenient shelter for his "natural meanness." She warns that a higher authority, a judge heedless of both Kentucky law and selective Bible-quoting, will hold all the husbands accountable for stealing from their wives. Like an accusing angel, Sally Ann points her finger. "Job Taylor, you killed Marthy," she charges, "the same as if you'd taken her by the throat and choked the life out of her."

Clearing his throat and shuffling his feet, Dave Crawford makes the next ill-advised attempt to break Sally Ann's hold on the assembly. In an earlier territorial dispute, Aunt Jane recalls, Sally Ann had successfully sued him over the placement of a fence, prompting him to disparage her as a "he-woman"; now, he stumbles into the crosshairs. "You're one o' the men that makes me think that it's better to be a Kentucky horse than a Kentucky woman," Sally Ann declares. Like Job Taylor's wife, "pore July" Crawford has found rest in the graveyard, but Sally Ann is delighted that Dave must now pay someone to cook for his farm hands while he lavishes attention on his prize mares.

Aunt Jane laughs as she remembers how Sally Ann, in the manner of one possessed, similarly "had her say" about almost every man in the church. Singling them out by name, she tells how these petty, tightfisted husbands exploit their wives' sense of duty and countermand their generosity until the marriage of the typical Goshen woman becomes a treadmill of self-denial and demeaning improvisation. Not even the good Parson Page escapes indictment; Sally Ann admits her refusal to contribute toward a suit of clothes for his trip to the Presbytery. She is tired of seeing finery on the backs of clergymen, she explains, while their wives carefully recycle their own meager wardrobes, appearing at church in "an old black silk that's been turned upside down, wrong side out an' hind part before, an' sponged an' pressed an' made over till you can't tell whether it's silk or caliker or what."

Moreover, complains Sally Ann, some of Parson Page's sermons "ain't fit for nothin' but kindlin' fires." In particular, his preaching on the fifth chapter of Ephesians inexplicably stops short at the twenty-fourth verse, which pronounces wives to be subject in everything to their husbands as the church is subject to Christ. Noting that she has never heard a sermon on the twenty-fifth verse, Sally Ann proceeds to the pulpit, "same as if she'd been ordained," and reads "what Paul said about men lovin' their wives as Christ loved the church, an' as they loved their own bodies." Reconciling the two passages is, for Sally Ann, an unnecessary intellectual exercise: "I'd jest say that when Paul told women to be subject to their husbands in everything, he wasn't inspired; an' when he told men to love their wives as they loved their own bodies, he was inspired." Closing the Bible, she again demands to know "who's to do the turnin' out" of Elizabeth, given that the rolls of Goshen Church bear the name of no man "good enough to set in judgment on a woman."

With Sally Ann showing no sign of desisting, a desperate Parson Page seizes a hymnbook and urges the congregation to sing "Blest Be the Tie That Binds." His diversionary tactic fails halfway through the first verse as the women, led by his own wife, gather around Elizabeth to offer their friendship with handshakes, hugs, and tears. Although they have witnessed the entire incident solemnly, as if enduring one of Parson Page's sermons on "'lection and predestination," they now depart for home flushed with the effects of "a reg'lar love-feast."

That spring, every wife in the community appears wearing new clothes—"an' such a change as it made in some of 'em," Aunt Jane adds, hinting of a more lasting internal transformation. For her part, Aunt Jane wonders if Sally Ann's message did not come directly from the Lord, as she had claimed; in any event, she concludes, this "turrible free-spoken" woman did more good for the marriages in Goshen "than all the sermons us women had had preached to us about bein' 'shamefaced' and 'submittin'' ourselves to our husbands."

Hoping to prolong the story, her guest asks whether Sally Ann had included Aunt Jane's own husband in her experience. "La! no, child," is her testy reply. "Abram never was that kind of a man, an' I never was that kind of a woman." On the return home that night he had suggested "sort o' humble-like" that she buy some fabric she had recently admired but had laughed knowingly when she assured him that it was already safe in her bureau drawer awaiting the dressmaker's needle. "You see," Aunt Jane explains,

> "I never was no hand at 'submittin'' myself to my husband like some women. I've often wondered if Abram wouldn't 'a' been jest like Silas Petty if I'd been like Maria. I've noticed that whenever a woman's willin' to be imposed upon, there's always a man standin' 'round ready to do the imposin'. I never went to no lawbook to find out what my rights was. I did my duty faithful to Abram, and when I wanted anything I went and got it, and Abram paid for it, and I can't see but what we got on jest as well as we'd 'a' done if I'd a-'submitted' myself."

Abram and all the others, of course, are now gone. As the story concludes and the narrator departs, she looks back to see Aunt Jane lingering in her doorway, gazing across the fields at the church graveyard.

With the gentle humor that was his trademark, Peter Newell, a well-known children's book author and artist, illustrated the story's four most dramatic moments. Above the title, the reader sees the Goshen women comforting Elizabeth while Parson Page stands to one side, gaping fishlike as he sings "Blest Be the Tie That Binds." One full page shows the women's subdued reaction as a downcast Elizabeth reveals the disappearance of the Mite Society's money. On another page a shifty, crouching Job Taylor attempts to withdraw "easy-like" from the prospect of Sally Ann's wrath. The final illustration captures Sally Ann beside a shaken Elizabeth, commanding Job Taylor to "set right down an' hear what I've got to say." Her accusing stare and open mouth, her black dress and prim white collar make sport of both Elizabeth's mild demeanor and Parson Page's self-serving religiosity. In magisterial pose, chin raised, arm outstretched, and finger pointed, she is the picture of righteous outrage.

For a story that was both comedy and tragedy, gentle reminiscence and angry manifesto, Lida could not have chosen better than the literary form that had been a staple of American magazines since the 1870s. Appealing to Americans' post–Civil War interest in the diverse regional traditions of their expanding republic, writers of "local color" stories had delivered countless tales constructed around the dialect, settings, and customs of New England, the West, the Southwest, and especially the South. Reading of Bret Harte's California miners, Mary Noailles Murfree's Tennessee mountaineers, Hamlin Garland's prairie farmers, Sarah Orne Jewett's Maine villagers, Kate Chopin's Cajuns, and Joel Chandler Harris's plantation folk, middle-class readers indulged their curiosity about fellow countrymen and took pride in the mythology of their own region. Twenty years before "Sally Ann's Experience," Lida's first published poem had appeared in the same issue of *Scribner's* as the opening installment of *The Grandissimes*, the novel that established George Washington Cable as a skilled conjurer of the personalities and atmosphere of Creole Louisiana.[3] The early 1880s had seen the first of James Lane Allen's stories set in Kentucky, and a decade later he inspired John Fox Jr. to begin writing of the feudists and moonshiners of eastern Kentucky as well as the more sophisticated culture of the Bluegrass.[4]

Like the sentimentalist writers who were so popular before the Civil War, many local color writers were women. Although the term "local color" was first used in reference to George Eliot's *Romola*, some practitioners acknowledged the influence of even earlier works, both at home, for example, in the stories of Harriet Beecher Stowe and Rose Terry Cooke, and abroad in the "village sketches" of Englishwomen Mary Russell Mitford and Elizabeth Gaskell. Sometimes these stories were melodramatic and openly propagandistic. As a girl, Lida had read Dinah Mulock Craik's *A Brave Lady*, serialized from 1869 to 1870 during the debate in Britain over married women's property legislation. The novel's heroine resolves to leave her weak, financially irresponsible husband after he appropriates money from the local school fund, but realizes that she will be denied the right to her earnings or to custody of her children. Only when her husband becomes incapacitated is she free to think and act for herself. Reviewers objected to the story's graphic descriptions of domesticity gone horribly wrong, but the struggles of the heroine and her six children (all of whom eventually die) must have struck fourteen-year-old Lida, in her own straitened circumstances, as alarmingly plausible.[5]

Besides the day-to-day realities of marriage, American writers used the medium of local color to take up with readers some of life's other more intractable aspects. Chief among their concerns were two with which Lida also struggled: the oppressiveness of the Calvinist belief in salvation solely by grace, and the dilemmas of an urban culture dominated by money and a rural one dominated by scarcity. In order to explore these questions without offending either readers or editors, writers often located their stories in the past, adding dollops of sentimentalism and assigning characters unusual dialect, habitat, or customs. As a further mediating device, writers might employ a well-educated onlooker (as Craik had done in *A Brave Lady*) to act as narrator; in some cases, he or she would pass along a story related by yet another, further insulating the reader's sensibilities by means of a "double narrative."[6]

Reading the same magazines in which she dreamed of publishing, Lida would have become well acquainted with these techniques. The title of her own first story was a curious echo of "Mrs. Flint's Married Experience," a grim tale by Rose Terry Cooke set in early New England. Fearing a lonely old age, a well-off widow remarries, then literally starves at the hands of her cruel, dogmatic husband. When she tries to leave him, the church where he is a deacon expels her. She is forced to seek forgiveness of her sin, but, mercifully, death saves her from the obligation to reconcile with her husband. "You've killed her as good as if you took an axe to her," hisses a woman friend to the deacon. "You can take that hum to sleep on."[7]

Women and the church clashed to more comical effect in Harry Stillwell Edwards's "Sister Todhunter's Heart." Set in the village of Sweetwater, Georgia, the story recounts an ill-advised attempt to discipline "a disagreeable old thing" made violent by the provocations of her slippery, alcoholic husband. Before the parson can begin the condemnation proceedings, Sister Todhunter enters the church, seats her three-hundred-pound bulk in a chair, and instructs him to "go on with yer lies. I'm ready." Before long, she has turned the service into a circus, telling all she knows about the drunkenness, snobbery, laziness, and usury of the parishioners. A battle ensues as the men finally carry her outside, chair and all, and deposit her in a wagon. Though some of the onlookers secretly regard her as the victor, she is expelled from the church for talking "too plainly." Only when this "awful presence" reappears and brusquely nurses the parson's dying baby back to health does he learn not to judge a woman's character by the whisperings of others. "Trouble and worry sometimes sorter crusts over er woman's heart, so that ev'ybody can't see hit, Parson," she explains, "but hit's there all the same."[8]

Anyone familiar with her suffrage rhetoric would have recognized in "Sally Ann's Experience" the crust of Lida's decade-old frustrations with clergymen, conservatives, and "second-hand people." Luckily, in her fictional world Eliza Calvert Hall is free to tailor the opposition in a manner that best serves her utter disdain for it. Nowhere among the plain farmers of Goshen is an articulate southern patriarch who might have confounded her realism with the logic peculiar to male codes of honor, chivalry, and protection. Deacon Petty invokes the apostle Paul against Sally Ann, and Parson Page interrupts her with a hymn, but both, despite their relatively high status, are made ridiculous and irrelevant. Job Taylor and Dave Crawford also attempt to censure Sally Ann, but their underhandedness and the verbal explosion they ignite recall KERA officer Josephine Henry's vision of men in their "false position," which is "like dynamite" to touch. Most cleverly, Eliza not only preempts her opponents but appropriates a church, the very center of their patriarchal authority, as the setting for her story. Seizing upon the allowance for a woman to relate her "experience," she gives Sally Ann the highest courtroom in which to make her charges.

Sally Ann's experience is a formidable blend of the spiritual and the temporal. Her spiritual experience recalls the Calvert family's New School Presbyterianism, which urged fearless condemnation of sinners while straying from traditional rules of gender and hierarchy in the conduct of its services. Challenging the men's harsh Calvinism, Sally Ann practically curses them, warning that their miserly habits will trump their claim in law and scripture to rank among the elect. With regard to women's behavior, she deconstructs the Bible's call for subservience by identifying it with a long-dead, fallible man, the apostle Paul, and her homespun higher criticism applies a simple test, the presence or absence of male self-interest, to determine whether the will of God inspired his admonitions. Not only does she claim the right to interpret scripture for herself, but her likening of Paul to Judas even hints that she regards the apostle, with his careless juxtaposition of human and divine commands, as a traitor to God's will. Enduring "about a hundred an' fifty sermons" on the twenty-fourth verse of the fifth chapter of Ephesians has left Sally Ann cynical about the motives of clergymen, but in spite of her frustration she does not repudiate the sacredness of the Gospel; on the contrary, her own study of the twenty-fifth verse—"Husbands, love your wives"—impels her to speak from the pulpit, "same as if she'd been ordained."

Even though her talk reminds Aunt Jane of "the day of Pentecost an' the gift of tongues," Sally Ann's experience draws its greatest power from mundane, observable reality. Much as Lida would have gathered from her door-to-door petitioning, Sally Ann has seen and heard of the unending toil and almost comical scarcity endured by Goshen women. From these scraps of eyewitness and hearsay—Maria Petty's late-night washing, July Crawford "with her head tied up" cooking for farm hands, ministers' wives turning their silks inside out—she pieces together a pattern of mistreatment long institutionalized in law and custom. The other women secretly share her understanding— "There ain't a woman in this church," she informs Job Taylor, "that don't know how Marthy scrimped and worked and saved" for new furniture—but this common perception does not embolden them to collective consciousness until Sally Ann "calls a spade a spade." Flinging aside the veil of feminine reticence that, together with masculine delusions of marital privacy, has abetted the men's "natural meanness," she breaks the dual yoke of husbands' oppression and wives' acquiescence.

Aunt Jane's cheerful recollections do not deny that individuals like Sally Ann are unusual and not a little unnerving. Sally Ann claims no personal impoverishment at the hands of a man, and with her lawsuit over Dave Crawford's fence she has successfully repulsed the only known attempt to confine her. With his illustration of her dress and posture, Peter Newell confirms that she is something of an oddity—"turrible," a "he-woman" who becomes "possessed" by the compulsion to relate her experience. Through Aunt Jane's mediation, however, the reader must conclude that the depth of Sally Ann's conviction springs not from any pathological militancy but from the clarity of her understanding of justice. Taking on the other women's burdens as her own and diverting scorn away from them, Sally Ann is Lida's strong-minded, stern-voiced reformer who has "sense enough to know what rights women ought to have and courage enough to demand those rights." When the Mite Society was considering how to spend its twelve dollars, Sally Ann vetoed a proposal to send it to "furrin' missions"; paying for the heathen to hear the Gospel, she argued, would only give them a "chance to damn theirselves" if they refused to repent. By the end of the story, Sally Ann has likewise denied Goshen's morally nearsighted husbands and their sinfully unselfish wives the chance to damn themselves—proof indeed that she will "do jest as well" as Jesus in the role of savior.

Anticipating the reaction of middlebrow magazine editors to this bold characterization, Eliza Calvert Hall has Aunt Jane admit that comparing Sally Ann to Jesus is "sort o' like sacrilege." Through Aunt Jane's matter-of-factness, she also assures the reader that what Sally Ann incited forty years ago was less a revolution than a course correction—a periodic "reprovin'" of the men—beneath which the foundations of the community remained intact. The Goshen women's new clothes, modest symbols of their recovered "gumption," underscore their femininity; so, too, does their compassionate nursing of Elizabeth when she falls ill only a week after the prayer meeting. The relationship of Aunt Jane and Abram further demonstrates that a wife's unwillingness to submit need not jeopardize her love of her husband or the institution of marriage; the exercise of mutual respect, in fact, is a better guarantee of marital stability than confinement within the roles of imposer and imposed-upon.

Reactions to "Sally Ann's Experience" indicated that Lida's combination of humor, sentiment, and realism had successfully matched that of the most admired local colorists. Her sister Maggie proudly sent the *Cosmopolitan* to an old friend, who responded with alacrity. "It is hard on men & Ky farmers in particular, but there is too much truth in it all," he admitted, before forwarding the issue to his bride-to-be in Scotland. Lida soon began to fill a scrapbook with similar messages of praise from across the country. The first letter she received came not from a beleaguered wife but from an elderly Illinois man. "The truth of all you say and the eloquence with which you say it have caused my tears to flow even while convulsed with laughter at the living picture you place before my eyes," he cheered. A second aging correspondent also alternated between laughter and tears as he marked numerous places in the text for future reference. Like the first writer, he had been inspired by the story to reflect upon the utter nobility of his now-dead wife, but rather than brooding on his sins or lapsing into regret over his failure to appreciate her, he was buoyant—as if, in speaking for ill-used women everywhere and forever, Sally Ann had expiated

his guilt. In a real-life version of the story's ending, he made a promise
to Lida: "Whatever the past, no Sally Ann shall ever have cause in the
future to rise up and relate her experience to me!"[9]

Three months after its publication in the *Cosmopolitan*, "Sally
Ann's Experience" was reproduced in the *Woman's Journal*, then serialized in the *White Ribbon*, the official paper of the WCTU in far-
away New Zealand. As readers clamored for reprints of the story, its
irreverent speeches and use of dialect endeared it to dramatic readers
and elocutionists. Over the next year, Isabel Garghill Beecher, a popular performer on the Lyceum and Chautauqua circuits, gave some
thirty readings, including one before a Wisconsin audience of five
thousand. The reaction, she wrote Lida, was always the same: "tears
for poor Lizbeth [*sic*] and peals of laughter and rounds of applause as
Sallie [*sic*] Ann piles up her points."[10]

As payment for "Sally Ann's Experience," Lida would have received no more than the magazine standard of one cent per word, or
approximately fifty-six dollars. The fact that her entitlement to this
money, at the age of forty-two, was finally on sound legal footing would
have given her no small satisfaction, but readers' understanding of her
"irreverent" story was her true reward. Notwithstanding the enactment of married women's property law reform, won only recently in
Kentucky but better established in other states, most wives remained
"fur from the big road"—unenfranchised, unappreciated, unpaid for
their household labor and child care, and unless they were among
the minority who possessed separate estates, beholden to husbands
for their material well-being. Like the continued denial of suffrage,
the dynamic surrounding their access to money had perpetuated an
atmosphere of dishonesty. As a consequence, readers reacted not with
outrage but with sympathy when Elizabeth rationalized her taking of
the carpet money as "borrowing" and when the Mite Society determined that withholding the news of its missing cash was strategically
more important than the cash itself. Everyone knew a bride like Milly
Amos, who had so quickly internalized her own unworthiness that she
could not help but betray another woman, and a wife like Elizabeth,
whose confession at the prayer meeting arose from the same sense of
unworthiness. Even Aunt Jane, who possessed Lida's ideal of "noble
self-esteem," resorted to a minor but common subterfuge when she hid
her newly bought fabric from her husband Abram. By Lida's own ad-

mission, the small intrigues of these plain people carried "no glamour of romance" or "startling plot," but their reenactment in the modern-day marriages of rich and poor, urban and rural alike, ensured the story's popularity. It might have been rendered a dead letter on the statute books, but "as long as the spirit of the old English common law survives in man," Lida explained, "the financial relations between husband and wife will continue to be a theme certain of touching the universal heart."[11]

Writing of the Goshen women's tortuous relationship with money—whether their own, their husbands', or someone else's—did Lida reconsider the audacious conversion of funds that had so tragically altered her own family history? At the time of Thomas Calvert's pardon, Maggie's friend Henry Batts was already disposed to regard his behavior as regrettable but not criminal. Years later, Lida's daughter Cecil defended her grandfather's "unfortunate speculation," asking if he was not merely trying, "in the only way he knew, to make more money for his family."[12] Even if Lida's father deserved to have a "Sally Ann" speak for him, he never beheld her in his lifetime. Only weeks before the story was published, on May 19, 1898, Thomas Calvert died.

9

A Jumble of Quilt Pieces

I ought to give up press work & everything else & devote myself to
writing novels poems & stories, but I love justice too well for that.
                                                    —Lida Calvert Obenchain to Laura Clay

A WEEK AFTER HIS FATHER'S DEATH, former West Point cadet Edward Calvert began the military career that would steer him
through the rest of his life. Enlisting as a private in the army, he was
assigned to the First U.S. Cavalry and sent to train in South Carolina.
Seeing him pass through Columbia, a friend of Maggie's remarked on
the plainspokenness he had already displayed in his letters from the
Tennessee Centennial; Maggie should tell her brother, she wrote, not
to refer to a Confederate veteran as a "rebel," since "he fought for the
cause he thought was right." At the outbreak of the Spanish-American
War, Eliza Calvert Hall, too, had remembered the men in gray, but in
her poetic imagination the call to intervene in Cuba and the Philippines had overcome sectional bitterness. "It's strange," said her old
soldier, "but I reckon it's true: / For it's jest one country, and jest one
flag, / And we're all a-wearin' the blue!"[1]
    Her patriotic instinct aside, Lida soon found that for a woman suf-
fragist in the age of American empire the blue was as threadbare as a
Goshen wife's made-over silks. By 1898 four states had granted women
full suffrage, and twenty-three states and two territories had enacted
forms of school suffrage, but a twelve-year-long fallow period was beginning. Some leaders, most notably Susan B. Anthony and Elizabeth
Cady Stanton, supported American imperial policies in the hope that

their loyalty would be rewarded with the ballot. Lida herself observed that Red Cross work and other good behavior during the war had left women deserving of suffrage as never before; she even held out reports of Cuban "Amazons" battling the Spanish as an answer to the argument that women should not vote because they could not fight. She fumed, however, when young American women and schoolgirls flocked to appearances by the hero of Santiago Harbor, Captain Richmond Pearson Hobson, and regaled him with requests for kisses. That so many approved of such "osculatory patriotism" in substitution for "the dignified, well-bred, and effective way of a legal voter" prompted her to quote one of her favorite aphorisms, from Mrs. Poyser of George Eliot's *Adam Bede:* "I'm not denyin' the women are foolish: God Almighty made 'em to match the men."[2]

Before long, Lida's commitment to suffrage "on the ground of simple, plain, old-fashioned justice, without any mixture of expediency" placed her firmly in the anti-imperialist camp. "I cannot understand," she wrote, "how any suffragist can uphold this Administration in the matter of the Philippine war." President William McKinley's denial of self-government to Filipinos, on the ground that they required protection from both external aggression and their own unfitness, mirrored men's attempt to placate women with chivalry and mercy instead of justice. "This government of ours is not a republic," Lida charged, since it governed women with the aid of their taxes but without their consent. Once exported as a tenet of empire, such a narrow conception of citizenship would become even more difficult to unseat at home. With suffragists largely unsuccessful in grafting their cause onto the anti-imperialist movement, she could only warn that the next presidential election would determine whether America was to fulfill its republican ideals or whether it would, through its own injustice, implode like the empires of old.[3]

Even if they supported imperialism, suffragists at the turn of the twentieth century faced the difficult task of broadening democratic rights at a time when racism and xenophobia, expressed through voting restrictions such as poll taxes, residency requirements, and literacy tests, were methodically shrinking the electorate. With a black population that was small in comparison to other former slave states', Kentucky was largely free of such restrictions, but Lida's colleague Laura Clay recognized that legal disfranchisement eroded one of the

most compelling expediency arguments available to southern suffragists, namely that giving the vote to women would strengthen the political hegemony of an educated, affluent class of whites. Laura had
been further disappointed when, in 1895, restructuring within the
National American Woman Suffrage Association effectively scaled
back the work of a special committee she had organized three years
earlier to develop suffrage campaigns throughout the South. As the
national and many state associations slipped into the doldrums, Laura
tried to combat the loss of momentum. From her position on the board
of the NAWSA, she encouraged state officers to open membership to
all persons paying a modest annual fee regardless of their ability to attend meetings or perform specific tasks. Designed to capitalize on pro-
suffrage sentiment and refute the contention that most women were
uninterested in voting, what came to be known as the Kentucky Plan
generated more financial support for the national organization and
broadened the pool of sympathizers to whom literature might be circulated. More than ever, promotion of suffrage through the written
word became necessary to sustain the movement.[4]

  Though Lida would soon prove to be one of Laura's most valuable allies in this effort, Eliza Calvert Hall continued to write of
Aunt Jane and old times. Within nineteen months after "Sally Ann's
Experience" the *Cosmopolitan* had published two more of her stories,
"The New Organ" and "Aunt Jane's Album." These returns to Goshen,
however, did not betray the urgent need, like that which had possessed Sally Ann, to "pile up points" against men. Sally Ann, in fact,
withdrew to the background, becoming an ensemble player in an expanding network of human interactions. In the tradition of the best
local color writing, Lida also sank deeper into her settings, bringing
more of western Kentucky's visual, auditory, and olfactory elements
to her stories. Aunt Jane's world emerged more vividly as a sanctuary,
a charmed place of escape for the reader, even if its pastness gave it
limitations with which Lida herself was growing impatient.

  The characters and incidents of "The New Organ" promised a
light-hearted and meandering sequel to "Sally Ann's Experience."
While she prepares dinner, Aunt Jane tells her visitor the story of
the Mite Society's purchase, three years after the carpet, of an organ for the church. Even though it is a modest specimen not "much
bigger'n a wash-stand," most of the men object simply because the

idea has originated with the women. Among those witnessing Deacon Petty's condemnation of "Satan's music-box" is Sally Ann, but rather than looking to her for a speech, the women deflect the criticism with amused tolerance. Their confidence prompts Aunt Jane's husband, the sensible but usually taciturn Abram, to warn his brethren that "there ain't no use tryin' to stop 'em when they git their heads set on a thing."⁵

On the Sunday of the organ's debut, the congregation has invited a group of "Babtists" to attend and a soloist from Louisville to play and sing a voluntary "the way they do in the city churches." Recalling the scene, with the parishioners dressed in their best, the open windows of the tidy little church admitting the sounds of birds and rustling trees, the humble instrument decorated with fragrant honeysuckle and "Miss Penelope" ready at the keyboard, Aunt Jane loses herself in one of her "flashes of silence." Needing no explanation, her listener understands this pause as a moment of transcendence in which the breeze outside the door and the scent of flowers in the yard have become those of long ago, Aunt Jane is again seated beside Abram in their battered old pew, and life is "like a watered garden in the peaceful stillness of the time 'jest before church begins.'"

A pot boils over on the stove, disturbing Aunt Jane's reverie. Led gently back to her story, she tells how the service is spoiled by Uncle Jim Matthews; an opponent of the organ, he also constitutes a longtime "rock of offense to the whole church" because of his insistently loud, atonal, clumsy singing. As the men look on gleefully, Uncle Jim overwhelms the soloist's beautiful voice with his "squawkin'" and "hollerin'." Miss Penelope sings on, unflustered, but the women seethe in anger, and Milly Amos, the choir's lead soprano, has to restrain herself from "reachin' over and chokin' the old man off." Lying seriously ill that summer, Milly is still resentful, warning her husband that if he allows Uncle Jim to sing at her funeral "I'll rise up out of my coffin." She rallies, however, after he replies affectionately, "Well, Milly, ef it'll have that effect, Uncle Jim shall sing at the funeral, shore."⁶

Behind its humor and sentiment, "The New Organ" considered the dilemma of the woman artist, a theme that appeared regularly in the work of female writers at the turn of the twentieth century. Having gained a measure of financial power, the members of the Mite Society yearn to realize both a musical and spiritual vision, but a man's

"hollerin'" literally drowns them out. The story offers three responses
to such a dehumanizing fate. Miss Penelope, the soloist, remains serenely focused on her art, her personal and professional detachment
keeping her oblivious to Uncle Jim and to the cruel delight of his
brethren that so infuriates the local women. Milly Amos's response is
more complex. She suffers an illness that recalls Elizabeth's in "Sally
Ann's Experience," yet her husband's tenderness ensures her recovery. Her singing will be heard again, but at Uncle Jim's funeral, where
she finds herself weeping with regret for her mean-spirited remarks
about his voice. Unlike Miss Penelope, she must measure her quest
for creative autonomy against the ties of marriage, church, and community.[7]

Aunt Jane herself is the model for the third response. Throughout
her reminiscence, she has held court in her kitchen, peeling apples
for dumplings, steaming potatoes, boiling vegetables, and browning
butter. Together with her storytelling talent, these culinary skills mark
her as a successful artist within her own sphere—natural, rural, and
matriarchal, one that synthesizes creativity and social harmony. Like
Sarah Orne Jewett's woman writer who returns every summer to Mrs.
Todd, the "supernaturally attuned and yet ultra-earthbound mother"
in *The Country of the Pointed Firs* and other stories, Aunt Jane's visitor is drawn into this nurturing world.[8]

"Aunt Jane's Album" presented an even more compelling vision of
a female utopia. Approaching her elderly friend's home, the narrator
is captivated by the scene, a blend of nature, art, and maternal love—
lilacs in the foreground, an orchard in the middle distance, low green
hills on the horizon, and in the midst of these visual layers, a clothes-
line strung with a collection of colorful patchwork quilts. Greeting her
visitor from the "cavernous depth" of her sunbonnet, Aunt Jane explains that she is giving them their "spring airin'." After the two carefully fold the quilts and return them to the house, Aunt Jane begins
to review them as she would albums and diaries, a capacity she first
demonstrated at the beginning of "Sally Ann's Experience." Brought
back from the past are the milestones of her own life, interspersed
with the faces of the children, neighbors, and friends whose dresses
and aprons are represented in each block and pattern.[9]

On this occasion, however, no scrap of "caliker" reminds her of
Sally Ann's scrap with the men of Goshen Church; the males in this

reminiscence are reduced to marginal presences, overwhelmed by the creative imperatives of the women. Aunt Jane evokes a dominant female aesthetic in which the emotional impetus behind a quilt's creation is as important as the beauty of its design and the fact of its use; so, too, is the quality of the hand-stitching employed to piece the design and, in what was commonly the contribution of a group of women, to attach the completed design to its padded backing. Describing her friends bent over her quilting frame, Aunt Jane recalls an easy blend of individuality and community. She shows her visitor the distinctive stitching of each woman that ultimately benefited her as designer. She displays a collection of sterling silver cups, premiums that her many quilts have earned at a succession of county fairs, but with equal pride recalls the year in which she and Sally Ann secretly arranged for an unlucky, untalented neighbor to capture the prize.[10]

While Lida was no stranger to a needle, she would have known that a story about quilts was something of a literary gamble. Her own mother "went to piecin'," as Aunt Jane would say, at an early age, her fine stitches earning her the deference of her sisters, but by the time of Lida's marriage quilting was increasingly identified with old-fashioned female decorum and, in the words of suffragist Abigail Scott Duniway, "woman's unpaid subjection." Writing for the Kentucky Equal Rights Association in 1895, Lida herself had decried attempts to label such a pursuit, in contrast to political participation, as innately feminine. "Can you imagine Lucy Stone," she asked, "devoting her life to the piercing [sic] of patchwork quilts, or Susan B. Anthony with no higher ambition than the acquisition of bric-a-brac or the giving of 'pink teas'?" The narrator of "Aunt Jane's Album" experiences a similar sense of distance from this world. She is taken aback at the sheer number of quilts, no doubt reflecting on the time consumed in their creation, and is helpless to discern any variation in their stitching. She observes that the collection lacks a crazy quilt, a style considered more up-to-date than patchwork, and when Aunt Jane expresses bemusement at a granddaughter's wish to hang one of her quilts in a doorway, supplies her with the "new-fangled" word, *portière*, for this modern use.[11]

Like many other writers, nevertheless, Lida found quilting irresistible as a metaphor for the bittersweet realities of women's lives. Echoing "The New Organ," the story addressed women's struggle for

creativity within strict gender roles and rejected the assumption that
their artistic expressions, particularly those associated with domesticity, were inauthentic or trivial. One of Aunt Jane's quilts is patterned
after an ancient mosaic that her granddaughter sketched during a trip
to Florence, and her emotional investment in all of her quilts is such
that, unlike other household possessions, she declines to donate them
early to expectant heirs.[12]

Gently but insistently, Aunt Jane also uses this antiquated craft
to raise the eternal question of mortality with her younger listener.
"Here's a piece o' Miss Penelope's dress," she says, caressing one of
the quilts, "but *where's Miss Penelope?* Ain't it strange that a piece o'
caliker'll outlast you and me?" What else, indeed, remained of most
ordinary women, "lying in sad, neglected graves on farm and lonely
roadside"? A hard worker all her life, Aunt Jane realizes, nevertheless, that "'most all my work has been the kind that 'perishes with the
usin','' as the Bible says." No one will remember the floors she swept,
the tables she scrubbed, or the clothes she mended, but when her
descendants look at her quilts they will think of her and, "wherever I
am then, I'll know I ain't forgotten."[13]

More important, if works, and not merely grace, also opened the
door to heaven—if freely determined acts could confound the spiritual poverty of Calvinist preordination as well as the material scarcity
of existence—then a quilt was both a woman's tangible legacy and a
blueprint for salvation. Aunt Jane proves as adept at plain sermoniz-
ing as Sally Ann when she explains:

> "You see, you start out with jest so much caliker; you don't go to
> the store and pick it out and buy it, but the neighbors will give
> you a piece here and a piece there, and you'll have a piece left
> every time you cut out a dress, and you take jest what happens
> to come. And that's like predestination. But when it comes to
> the cuttin' out, why, you're free to choose your own pattern.
> . . . And that is jest the way with livin'. The Lord sends us the
> pieces, but we can cut 'em out and put 'em together pretty
> much to suit ourselves, and there's a heap more in the cuttin'
> out and the sewin' than there is in the caliker."

Faith, however, is indispensable to the work. She cautions that "while you're livin' your life, it looks pretty much like a jumble o' quilt pieces before they're put together; but when you git through with it, or pretty nigh through, as I am now, you'll see the use and the purpose of everything in it. Everything'll be in its right place jest like the squares in this 'four-patch,' and one piece may be pretty and another one ugly, but it all looks right when you see it finished and joined together."

Curiously, after observing that a quilter does not go to the store and deliberately choose her calico, Aunt Jane reverses herself a paragraph later and declares: "You don't trust to luck for the caliker to put your quilt together with; you go to the store and pick it out yourself, any color you like." Was this, in fact, the interjection of the story's author, mindful that, for her generation, taking "jest what happens to come" left women restitching the old black silks of the American "sexocracy"[14] rather than sporting the new garments of justice?

As a contented Aunt Jane laid her folded quilts in piles and pronounced her work completed and good, Lida remained uncertain which style of cutting out and sewing, that of the artist or the polemicist, would suit for her own salvation. Early in 1900 Lida accepted a demanding assignment from the KERA. She became its press superintendent, a position that required her to keep newspaper editors across Kentucky generously supplied with ready-to-print suffrage material forwarded to her by Laura Clay and the NAWSA. Not satisfied merely to distribute syndicated literature, Lida added letters and commentary of her own in response to local and out-of-state developments, editorials, magazine articles, and political speeches that came to her attention. So quickly did she begin her work and so diligently carry it on that in little more than a year Laura could report to the NAWSA's annual convention the placement of over five hundred suffrage articles in Kentucky newspapers.[15]

Unfortunately, just as Laura was crediting Lida's efforts with a significant increase in pro-suffrage opinion, racial and class divisions engineered a severe setback. In Lexington, Democrats had supervised and won the 1901 school board election, but grew doubtful of their ability to prevail in future contests because of their poor performance in registering voters. The next year, playing on fears that higher Republican registration would deliver control of the schools to black women and illiterates, the city's representatives in Frankfort introduced a bill to repeal the 1894 law granting school suffrage to women in second-class cities. Laura, who had continued to promote school suffrage statewide, assembled a committee to lobby against the bill, but, through a partisan process that reportedly raised tears in her eyes, it passed.[16]

For the next several years, Lida continued her work in the face of more disappointment. Despite a 154 percent increase in 1901, membership in the KERA still numbered fewer than one thousand, and she was among a mere handful of women systematically courting the southern press on behalf of the cause. For a time, Laura Clay became less available for consultation, diverting more of her energy to committee work with the NAWSA after the repeal of school suffrage in Kentucky. Lida also endured personal uncertainty and loss. Three years after entering the army, her brother Edward had risen to the rank of lieutenant and been sent to that "shameful war" in the Philippines. On November 9, 1902, her sister Mary, as quietly resigned to her domestic burdens as Lida was vocally resentful, succumbed to the chronic ill health that had followed her through her forty-four years.[17]

Hailed as a "gentle, unobtrusive, Christian woman," Mary was the subject of several affectionate tributes in the local newspapers, publicity that the KERA's press superintendent might have envied in her search for editors willing to give suffrage a hearing. Lida continued to mail syndicated and original articles to both new and established publications, and if rebuffed, tried again when they changed ownership. After her list of newspapers reached 100—out of a total of 226 in Kentucky, according to her directory—she would mail submissions to half of them one week and half the next. Her statewide reach—north to the *Carrollton Democrat,* south to the *Tompkinsville News,* east to the *Hazard Enterprise,* west to the *Mayfield Messenger*—sometimes prevented her from determining whether the articles were being printed, but over time she was able to classify about one-third of the newspapers on her list as "likely to publish" and the rest as "doubtful" or "unfriendly."[18]

Among those in the last category was the *Louisville Courier-Journal,* which dutifully reported news of the women's rights movement but editorially deplored it. Lida had once complained of a leading Ken-

tucky paper whose editor dipped his pen in "nitric acid" when writing of reform-minded women; without doubt she was referring to the
unrelenting opposition of the *Courier-Journal's* Henry Watterson,
scourge of the "Sillysallies and Crazyjanes," for whom only prohibition
deserved equivalent doses of ridicule. The state's largest city was generally hostile territory. "There is not a paper in Louisville friendly to
Equal Rights," Lida grumbled to Laura Clay, recently returned from
a campaign in Oregon, before asking her for the names of prominent
local women who might intercede at both the *Courier-Journal* and
the *Post*. As more writing under Lida's byline appeared, perhaps all
too exclusively, in editors' mailboxes, she resorted to the use of several
pseudonyms. In 1906 she sent Laura a copy of the observations of "Elsie Haller" on a recent feminine popularity contest conducted by the
Courier-Journal. Pronouncing it the "only honest election ever held
in Kentucky," Miss Haller noted that all the candidates and a large
number of the voters were women and that no defeated candidate
had disputed the results—"a pretty good argument," she concluded,
"for woman suffrage." Pleased with the point she had made, Lida then
regretted not having signed her real name to the piece.[19]

   The indifference of her sex to voting in genuine elections was
a continuing complaint in Lida's work for national suffrage publications. With politics a frequent topic of conversation, not only in Kentucky but nationwide, in the progressive call for reform of industry,
agriculture, and commerce, she was mystified by women's apparent
failure to connect the desire for change with the casting of a ballot.
How, she asked, could they plead club work as a reason to avoid agi-
tating for the vote when the club movement itself, with its turn from
genteel literary pursuits to civic activism, grew out of women's early
associations on behalf of suffrage? How could they nod agreeably as
men invoked the purifying effect of female morality upon civilization
while telling them that politics was not their sphere? Why did they indulge their most "rabid political partisanship" during a gubernatorial
or presidential campaign, listening to speeches, devouring newspapers, and declaring for a particular party, when lack of a vote rendered such expressions utterly superfluous? Possession of "an atom of
common sense," Lida charged, should at least make such women suffragists from expediency, but once more she could not suppress her
disdain for an argument based upon less than justice. After Louisville

endured another round of corrupt municipal elections in 1905, she proposed that as a compromise measure women be given the right to count the votes cast by men. With mothers supervising, ballots would neither appear nor disappear under mysterious circumstances. The woman "who has spent fifteen or twenty years picking up things and putting them in their right places," she pointed out sarcastically, "has had a magnificent training for taking charge of a ballot-box."[20]

At the time of her observation, Lida herself had been in charge of a household for twenty years, and her children were benefiting from their upbringing by intellectual if not especially carefree parents. In spring 1905, seventeen-year-old Margery received a diploma in reading and dramatic art from the Pleasant J. Potter College, a school for young ladies located near Ogden College on Thomas Calvert's former Vinegar Hill estate. Sweet-tempered, perhaps rendered somewhat fragile by a childhood bout with whooping cough, Margery had demonstrated her own interest in literary pursuits as an assistant editor of Potter College's student magazine. Alex, almost seventeen, enjoyed the family library as much as long walks in the woods or along the Barren River. In fall 1905, he entered his senior year at Ogden College, where he was working to overcome both a stammer and what he later claimed were his parents' unduly high expectations of him. Tom, almost fourteen, was a freshman at Ogden College, and ten-year-old Cecil was learning to play the violin at Potter College.[21]

By the time her sons returned to school, Lida had completed nine "Aunt Jane" stories. Hoping to publish them in book form, she circulated the work to eight New York publishing houses. Although the collection opened with the popular "Sally Ann's Experience" and included three other stories previously printed in the Cosmopolitan, it earned praise but no acceptances. "They all say it will not be a financial success," Lida wrote Laura. "A volume of short stories rarely sells well." Conditions at home, moreover, were hardly favorable to other projects. She had taken in two students as boarders, but after the family's longtime cook married, leaving behind only a thoroughly unsatisfactory servant girl, she and Margery were forced to assume most of the housework. Lida claimed to have made the best of the situation, downgrading the midday meal from dinner to lunch, cutting back on meat and other "superfluous and unwholesome food," and prodding all of her children to cook for themselves, but domestic chores relentlessly sapped her energy and concentration. As she tried to maintain her press work and find a book publisher, her stress became more evident. "No cook, two boarders, a bad attack of bronchitis, such is my present estate," she complained to Alice Stone Blackwell, who had succeeded her mother, Lucy Stone, as editor and publisher of the *Woman's Journal.* Anxious, nevertheless, to help a local student compose a graduating essay, she asked Alice to send her some back numbers of the *Journal* containing biographies of notable American women. Lida suggested a few names before offering, as an afterthought, to reimburse Alice for a mailing in excess of five issues. "My wits are so scattered," she confessed. "I cannot remember many distinguished women just now."[22]

At the root of Lida's worries was, predictably, money. For her work as press superintendent, the KERA promised her five dollars per month—which paid for the washing, she confided to Laura— together with fifteen to twenty-five dollars for stationery and postage. Unfortunately, Isabella Shepard, the KERA's treasurer, was a poor correspondent who neglected to advance funds regularly. Lida obtained credit at local bookstores for envelopes but, when unable to borrow from the Major, had to pursue Mrs. Shepard for the money to buy stamps and postcards. Conscious of both the value of Lida's press work and her prompt handling of correspondence, Laura responded with expedited checks and sympathy.[23]

Although she expressed every intent to carry on her work, faithfully reporting to Laura on the circulation of her latest articles and asking how the newspaper in Lexington, where Laura now spent part of each year, was "behaving itself," Lida had additional, more pressing financial concerns. In recent years, Ogden College had struggled. With a steady decline in enrollment already under way, its "Dark Ages," as insiders called the period, had commenced about 1900 when a revered but aging faculty member retired. By 1902 the Major's annual salary as president had dropped to $1,250, and Ogden had scaled back its curriculum to high school–level instruction as a further cost-cutting measure. Enrollment continued to stagnate until, in 1905, despite a special appropriation to the Major for advertising, a mere fifty-six students were in attendance.[24]

As Alex Obenchain graduated in June 1906, Ogden's trustees yielded to pressure to reinstate college–level work but also carried out a long-standing threat to reorganize the faculty. The Major, now sixty-five, was permitted to announce his resignation as president on the advice of his doctor, but Lida revealed the humbling truth in a letter to Laura. The five members of that "unspeakable board of trustees," she declared, had "kicked the entire faculty of Ogden College out of the back door, so to speak, just three weeks before school closed." They had then rehired the Major, but as a regular professor of mathematics at an annual salary of only $1,000.[25]

Lida was grim and resentful, perhaps remembering her relative helplessness after her father's flight and during the campaign to secure his pardon. "We may have to leave the state," she confided to Laura. "Major will remain in Ogden only until he can get a better place. The situation is intolerable to any one with an atom of pride & self-respect and he wouldn't be in it if he had taken my advice." Although his friends from his years in Dallas, Texas, where Alex had secured a railroad job immediately after graduation, were urging the Major to relocate there and open a school, the future remained uncertain. More "chaos" descended in October, when the Obenchains' house on Park Street, about seven blocks southwest of Lida's mother and sisters, was sold, and the new owners tried to raise the annual rent from $200 to $300. After a fruitless search for other accommodation, they bargained the landlords down to $250, and Lida began restoring the household that she had already packed up in anticipation of a move.[26]

The approach of the KERA's annual convention, where her press work was bound to receive the usual high praise, only added a further note of gloom to Lida's correspondence. She warned Laura that she was capable of no more than a written report; travel to meetings was impossible, given her current financial straits. In early November, a few weeks before the convention opened in Ashland, she sought desperately to forestall Laura's summons. *"Please don't ask me,"* she begged. With only a young black boy helping in the house, she was "nervous and worn out with domestic work and worry." She was enduring some "tedious dentistry" in order to save her teeth, "for of course a woman who wants to vote mustn't be ugly." Concluding that the KERA should have a press superintendent with the time and money to accomplish what ought to be done, she cried: *"I am not that woman."* The convention delegates, however, believed otherwise. In addition to passing a resolution commending the General Assembly for raising the age of consent from twelve to sixteen, they reelected Lida to her position.[27]

Although the stress of the past year had left Lida, as she later remembered, a "thin, small tired worn-out creature," she continued to believe that both she and Aunt Jane had a future in the literary world. The stories she had circulated "*will* find a publisher and they *will* be a financial success," she vowed to Laura. "Of that I am sure." Convinced that she must now write enough to make up the shortfall in family income, she could not resist adding that her task would be easy were it not for cooking, sewing, housework, and the usual "domestic drudgery."[28]

When Lida's faith in her book was finally rewarded, she efficiently inserted the news in a report to Laura detailing her suffrage activity. The KERA's treasurer had sent enough money to cover at least two press mailings in January 1907, particularly if Lida reduced submissions to newspapers on her "doubtful" list; friendly papers, she calculated, might also do with less because even they could not print everything she sent. The Louisville papers were still ignoring her, but an editor in Frankfort, after several months of consideration, had endorsed woman suffrage. She recommended that a friend living in Oklahoma, where Laura had recently campaigned, be sent some literature—and, Lida reported, the Boston firm of Little, Brown, and Company would soon publish her book. "The critics say it is a literary success and I confidently expect it to be a financial success," she declared. "I want all my friends to hope for me and pray for me to this end."[29] Laura most certainly obliged, no doubt grateful that the imminent release of *Aunt Jane of Kentucky* had not distracted one of her most talented foot soldiers from the cause.

10

Aunt Jane of Kentucky

Her method is simplicity itself.
—*New York Times*

EVEN AFTER BECOMING PRESIDENT, Theodore Roosevelt read at least one book every day. His tastes were as far-ranging as his youthful adventures in the West: novels, poetry, ancient and modern history, essays, speeches, memoirs, and biography, in both English and French. His light reading showed the influence of his mother and aunt, refined daughters of Georgia who had shared with him their anecdotes and nostalgic tales of the Old South. As a consequence, Roosevelt's volumes of Mark Twain, Charles Dickens, and Edgar Allan Poe were likely to occupy the shelf alongside Bret Harte, Octave Thanet, Owen Wister, and "the quaint, pathetic character-sketches of the Southern writers—[George Washington] Cable, [Charles Egbert] Craddock, [John Alfred] Macon, Joel Chandler Harris, and sweet Sherwood Bonner."[1]

At a White House reception in mid-May 1907, the president was exercising his considerable skill at finding common ground with every citizen whose hand he shook. When he learned that the lady passing before him was from Kentucky, he momentarily held up the receiving line to praise that "fine old State" where his daughter had recently enjoyed a visit. "Oh, by the way," he asked,

have you read that charming little book written by one of your clever Kentucky women—"Aunt Jane of Kentucky"—

by Eliza Calvert Hall? It is very wholesome and attractive. Be sure that you read it.[2]

The end of the month found the president in Lansing, Michigan, for an address to the graduating class of State Agricultural College and some twenty-five thousand onlookers. In a speech that considered both the problems and opportunities of modern agriculture, Roosevelt maintained that the quality of rural life depended upon the availability to laborers of "social and intellectual advantages as well as a fair standard of physical comfort." Not to be forgotten was "the one who is too often the very hardest worked laborer on the farm—the farmer's wife." To help a husband lighten her burden, much useful guidance was available in the popular literature of the day. "You will learn the root principles of self help and helpfulness toward others from 'Mrs. Wiggs of the Cabbage Patch,' just as much as from any formal treatise on charity," declared the president—and, he continued,

I cordially recommend the first chapter of "Aunt Jane of Kentucky" for use as a tract in all families where the men folks tend to selfish or thoughtless or overbearing disregard of the rights of their womenkind.[3]

Sally Ann was back in the bully pulpit.

When Eliza Calvert Hall promptly thanked him with an autographed copy of her book, Roosevelt just as quickly clarified his position in a letter of acknowledgment. In Michigan he had emphasized that while no wife should be an "overworked drudge," the first duty of the "normal woman" was to be the keeper of home and family, that nucleus of civilization where she reigned superior to any public servant.[4] Returning to this doctrine, he cautioned Lida that Aunt Jane, who was "so good and so wise," must not become the pawn of "self-indulgent, selfish, short-sighted women, cold in heart and in temper," who sought to disguise their cowardly avoidance of the duties of motherhood by pretending to "wise or lofty motives"; further, he added in a handwritten postscript, "she must not give aid and comfort to unsexed or sexless creatures by a jest which they may take for earnest!" Lida, no doubt, regarded this concern as utterly misplaced; a decade earlier, she had addressed a critic who similarly feared that access to higher education created "he-women" who would neglect the ideals of wifehood and motherhood. No men's college, she observed, was ever deemed suspect for its failure to inculcate the ideals of husbandhood and fatherhood; meanwhile, she scoffed, "one would think that woman's ideals had been created by the Almighty and then left lying around loose, and that man was made for the purpose of gathering up these fragile things and shielding them from the rough clutches of Vassar, Wellesley, and Bryn Mawr students; and all the time he is making a spectacle of himself the ideals are as safe as a pearl in an oyster fourteen fathoms down in the sea."[5]

If Roosevelt's eminence preempted a similar rejoinder, so too did the public's eager embrace of *Aunt Jane of Kentucky.* The book, in fact, was selling well even before the *New York Times* printed excerpts from its first chapter under the headline "'Husbands, Love Your Wives,' Roosevelt's Message to Americans," and its advertising touted "The Book Pres. Roosevelt Recommends." Published by Little, Brown, and Company on March 30, 1907, *Aunt Jane of Kentucky* had quickly secured a place on *Bookman's* April list of most popular new releases, ranking fifth in Cincinnati, fourth in Boston, second in Rochester, New York, and first in Louisville. In May it was the sixth-most-requested title in downtown New York City. In June, after the presidential endorsement, it ranked first in Baltimore, second in Louisville, third in Cleveland, and fourth in Buffalo, Cincinnati, and Detroit. Laura Clay wrote Lida that the two Lexington booksellers she patronized "could not keep it on the shelves." By July it was in its third edition, and two London firms were negotiating for a British edition. Within a year Lida's permission was sought for a French translation, and Helen Keller became one of *Aunt Jane's* readers after the book was set in type for the blind.[6]

Little, Brown, in addition, did not neglect the sales advantage presented by its celebrated first chapter. Customers ordering the book at $1.50 could obtain, at no extra cost, an additional, separately bound copy of "Sally Ann's Experience." Magazines also rushed to capitalize on the reappearance of the story. The *Woman's Journal* printed it for the fourth time, and in October 1907, with *Aunt Jane of Kentucky* in its sixth edition, Lida took great satisfaction when the *Ladies' Home Journal,* which had originally rejected "Sally Ann" as too irreverent, paid two hundred dollars for the right to deliver the story to its one million readers. The *Cosmopolitan* printed it again the following summer, on the tenth anniversary of its original publication. Noting that demands for copies of the 1898 issue in which the story first appeared had "come into this office with remarkable regularity," the editors added Eliza Calvert Hall's explanatory essay recalling the legal disabilities imposed upon women that had fired her indignation and imagination.[7]

President Roosevelt might have rested easier, nevertheless, when reviews of *Aunt Jane of Kentucky* largely ignored its political subtext and concentrated instead on the artistic merits of the collection as a whole. "Grant that the title suggests antique rural sentiment, and you have said all that may be said in dispraise," declared the *New York Times*—mindful, notwithstanding the president's enthusiasm, of the shortcomings that had contributed to the waning popularity of "quaint, pathetic character-sketches" and stories in dialect. "For Aunt Jane is not false, nor cheap, nor shallow, and the stories that are put in her mouth exhale the very breath of old gardens and country roads and fields." Even the name of the author conveyed sincerity, although the reviewer made the traditional assumption that women's writing derived wholly from experience and not imagination. "Without doubt, Eliza Calvert Hall (what a good name it is!) knows very well the original (or originals) of her aunt Jane, and has sat often and receptively at her feet."[8]

Several critics compared the stories favorably to those of the best-known local colorists. "What Mrs. [Elizabeth] Gaskell did in 'Cranford,' . . . and what Sarah Orne Jewett and Mrs. [Mary E.] Wilkins [Freeman] have done for similar plain, homely life in New England, this author does for Kentucky," reported the *Syracuse Herald*. The book possessed "the unfailing good taste which distinguishes the country stories of Miss Jewett, and which makes simple things in Miss Hall's hands worth the telling," noted the *Brooklyn Eagle*. While more distant reviewers carelessly generalized the stories' settings as the Bluegrass, those closer to Lida's home knew better. "It is not only Kentucky rural life we see, but life right here in Warren county with the 'knobs' we love all around us, and our scenery everywhere; . . . that Aunt Jane lives right here, about Bowling Green, we feel and know," enthused a local paper.[9]

Of all the book's characters, Aunt Jane naturally drew the most affectionate regard. The *Outlook* found her "perfectly delightful," with her "merry, wise comments upon folks and their doings, her absolutely sane religion, her enjoyment of the present and her happy hope of the future." From her homespun environment, she evoked a simpler life long overtaken by "the age of haste, restlessness," and "expense of nerve force." At the same time, the human strengths and foibles lying at the heart of her tales gave them a universal appeal, which, agreed Lida's fellow Kentuckian and author Nancy Huston Banks, marked "the value of all creative writing."[10]

Although Lida's essay accompanying the *Cosmopolitan* reprint made clear that the attitudes once enshrined in English common law continued to oppress women, Henry Blackwell of the *Woman's Journal* was among the few reviewers to dwell on this theme. As Lida had praised the work of Charlotte Perkins Stetson, he applauded *Aunt Jane of Kentucky* not for a picturesqueness that drew sighs of nostalgia but for a "picture-ness" designed to unsettle minds and change hearts. He reminded readers of Sally Ann's "sharp wit and free-spoken criticism" which was "true to the life," and focused on similar elements of discord in some of the book's other stories: a wife's domestic rebellion in "Sweet Day of Rest"; a young woman's seduction and abandonment in "Milly Baker's Boy"; and another wife's observation in "The Baptizing at Kittle Creek" that "principles ain't the only thing a woman has to give up when she gits married." Divulging the real name of a contributor already familiar to *Woman's Journal* readers but not yet widely known as *Aunt Jane's* author, Blackwell valued the book for its genial but transforming effect on consciousness.

> Surely Mrs. Obenchain has a Shakespearean touch, which shows that a woman may give her readers the good gospel of women's rights in object lessons that "point a moral and adorn a tale." Let every suffragist buy this book and lend it to the "antis" of her acquaintance. They will become full-fledged suffragists before they know that they have been subjects of conversion.[11]

Such an interpretation, however, remained rare amid reviews sprinkled with adjectives like "quaint," "wholesome," "charming," and "entertaining." Lida's local newspaper even blamed the "age of haste"

from which the book was a respite on "the clang of woman's multitu-
dinous calls to the 'higher life,'" and *Catholic World* frowned when
the musings of Aunt Jane's more sophisticated visitor disturbed the
"rusticity and simplicity of the anecdotes."[12]

Ironically, the version of "Sally Ann's Experience" that appeared
in *Aunt Jane of Kentucky* and subsequent magazine reprints facilitated this swell of sentiment. Since its publication in 1898, Lida had
made revisions to the story, one of which, perhaps, was merely a matter of delicacy: gone was Sally Ann's claim that she had "as little use
for the 'Postle Paul as she had for Judas Iscariot." Without comment-
ing on Elizabeth Taylor's fate under the laws of dower, Lida also ami-
ably dispatched her husband, whose meanness had precipitated her
mishandling of the carpet fund. "Jacob died the follerin' fall," Aunt
Jane now recalls, "and 'Lizabeth got shed of her troubles. The triflin'
scamp never married her for anything but her money."

More significantly, Lida reframed "Sally Ann's Experience" with
new paragraphs at its beginning and end. Before turning over the nar-
ration to Aunt Jane, her visitor provides a brief but vivid introduction of her elderly friend. Dressed in purple calico and a gingham
apron, with a white handkerchief pinned at her throat and a "substantial structure" of a cap tied under her chin, Aunt Jane is "in perfect
correspondence with her environment"—rag carpet, shuck-bottomed
rockers, high bed, bureau, and mahogany table. The "sweet old tre-
ble" in her voice bears a slight lisp from lack of teeth, but her soprano
laugh is that of a young girl's. The handiwork in her apron pocket has
been temporarily neglected while she applies her "slender, nervous
old fingers" to her quilting project. Setting both Aunt Jane and her
memories far into the past, the narrator confesses that the woman
and her surroundings "always carried me back to a dead and gone
generation."

After Aunt Jane has related Sally Ann's experience, she gathers up
her pieces of calico, as if closing her book of stories, and returns her
listener to the present. "Things is different from what they used to
be," she now observes. The previous summer, her son-in-law had told
her "how a passel o' women kept goin' up to Frankfort and so pester-
in' the legislature that they had to change the laws to git rid of 'em. So
married women now has all the property rights they want, and more'n
some of 'em has sense to use, I reckon"—certainly more than she

herself needed, with a husband as fair-minded as Abram. Where Lida was quick to pay tribute to Laura Clay and her "little band of women who for ten years struggled to free the married women of their state from the captivity of unjust laws," for Aunt Jane such developments are merely a footnote to her own ongoing story of contentment.[13]

Aunt Jane of Kentucky's illustrations also cast its subjects in the gentle light of long ago. By late January 1907, the task of executing the book's frontispiece had fallen to Beulah Strong, a Paris-trained artist who had taught at Potter College, where Margery and Cecil attended school, and who would shortly assume a professorship at Smith College in Massachusetts. Anxious not to detract from Lida's work, Beulah applied herself conscientiously to the assignment, drawing upon the expanded description at the beginning of "Sally Ann's Experience" to portray the book's central character. Swathed in cap and calico, Aunt Jane sits in her rocking chair, a patchwork quilt from the stack behind her laid across her lap. With her hand resting gently on the fabric and a far-away expression on her wrinkled but full face, she has been caught in one of her "flashes of silence."[14]

Beulah also executed fourteen illustrations in pen and ink—a head-piece to open each of the nine stories and, due to lack of space, tail-pieces at the end of only five. The editors at Little, Brown compounded her struggle with this delicate work. "They scrutinize every button & kittle handle in the little drawings," she wrote Lida, adding that the "august publishers" had finally accepted her fourth rendering of a skittish horse for the story "How Sam Amos Rode in the Tournament." In their mid-nineteenth-century dress, Beulah's human characters struck the appropriate note of quaintness, but she worried when the lips or noses of her ringleted females "did not quite come out" and wished that she had drawn the young rake in "Milly Baker's Boy," with his frock coat, high collar, and cravat, leaning closer to his diminutive conquest. For "Sally Ann's Experience," she illustrated two quiet moments—the narrator seated before Aunt Jane, absorbed in her tale, and Aunt Jane's gaze across the field at the cemetery—instead of the more dramatic turns chosen by Peter Newell for the *Cosmopolitan*. The limitations of pen and ink forced her to abandon her sketch of the climax of "Mary Andrews' Dinner-Party," in which a widow enters a dark, locked cabin to discover that her husband has compulsively hoarded the family's discarded clothing and household goods. Beulah

Strong, nevertheless, completed her work on time and well enough, according to the reviewer for the *Hartford Courant,* to place her "in the front rank of illustrative artists."[15]

Praise of *Aunt Jane*'s literary and artistic qualities, especially after the sudden fame conferred by President Roosevelt, increased public curiosity over the true identity of Eliza Calvert Hall. Although the *Woman's Journal* quickly named the author and summarized Lida's writing credits on society and politics as well as in fiction, other presses diligently searched for a woman who more resembled Aunt Jane than Sally Ann. She was, confided her publishers, the wife of a Kentucky professor and the mother of "many children" who had modestly hoped that her March book would be as successful as her youngest daughter, a March baby. When *Aunt Jane of Kentucky* reached an eighth edition of ten thousand in November 1907, the *New York Times* revealed Lida's name and noted her early verse in "the old violet covered Scribner" as well as her critical essays in the *Times* and other papers. Mrs. Obenchain "has lived a very quiet life," insisted the *Saturday Evening Post.* She had published some poems and considered becoming a journalist, but then had "succumbed to a happy state of domesticity."[16]

One of the most cloying profiles of Lida appeared in August 1908, just as *Aunt Jane* reached its eleventh edition. Journalist and photographer Ewing Galloway visited the Obenchain home to interview "one of Kentucky's noblest women" and her husband, a "Southern gentleman of the old school." He found not only the "mistress of a household that bespoke family devotion and true Southern hospitality" but a "great soul in tune with God and Nature" who possessed the "power to bring before our vision the divinity of commonplace things." While their discussion fixed on three topics—family, literature, and woman suffrage, with Lida claiming greater interest in the third than the second—Galloway assured his readers that his subject was "far from being narrow"; in particular, she had channeled her advocacy of suffrage into dignified persuasion rather than "shrieking in public places and being arrested" in the style of her British sisters. While Lida must have known that President Roosevelt's support of suffrage was, as he himself admitted, "tepid," she graciously expressed her admiration for the man who had brought so much notice to *Aunt Jane of Kentucky.* She also hastened to praise her four children, of whom she was prouder than anything she had ever written, and sent Margery in search of Cecil so that her youngest, with Lida's accompaniment on piano, could give an impromptu violin recital.[17]

Behind these expansive portraits of a contented wife and mother lay a genuine improvement in Lida's domestic circumstances. Since fall 1906, when they had endured the Major's demotion and the untimely increase in their rent, the Obenchains had moved to their own home across from Ogden College at the corner of Chestnut and Fourteenth streets. The location was familiar, although the path to it had been somewhat circuitous. The Major had first acquired the Chestnut Street lot shortly before marrying Lida but had sold it in 1904. In prior years, he had also purchased vacant land in the next block south, near the family's rented house on Park Street; Lida's sisters Maggie and Josie had even invested in an adjoining lot. No residences had materialized on these tracts, but in September 1907 the assured success of *Aunt Jane of Kentucky* coincided with a decision by the current owner of the Chestnut Street lot to sell it. The Obenchains accordingly reacquired the property, on which the seller had recently built a house—but this time, the name on the deed was Lida's, not the Major's.[18]

Lida was pleased with both her new home and its purchase price of $2,950. The Dutch Colonial Revival–style cottage was "a marvel of comfort and convenience," she reported to Maggie, then visiting in Johnstown, New York. Expecting never again to have another reliable servant, she hoped that its amenities would allow her to devote less time to housework and more to writing. Until then, the usual stresses of moving had to be overcome. "I shall be glad to get settled for I realize that I am too old to be dragged about from house to house any longer," she wrote. Having her furniture currently split between the new house and the old created the "awfulest mess," but with the *Cosmopolitan* asking for more stories, her ambition was to secure a room and desk for herself and return to work. While the debt incurred to purchase the house also left Lida wishing that royalties from *Aunt Jane* were payable earlier than the following February, she believed the burden worthwhile in order to secure a home for her children.[19]

To another correspondent, Lida reported more cheerfully that she was "very busy preparing to move into the house that 'Aunt Jane of Kentucky Bought.'" After the book achieved the highest sales by a new author in 1907 and remained on *Bookman*'s most-popular lists through June 1908, Aunt Jane generously drew the necessary royalties from her apron pocket. On September 3, not long after Ewing Galloway's visit, the third and final note for the house was retired. Lida was now, in fact as well as in law, a married woman with property.[20]

She was also growing more ambitious. "I am going to quit writing Aunt Jane stories next spring," she told Galloway. "I am tired of writing dialect and I find it difficult to keep from permitting it to corrupt my English." Plans to publish her second book of stories were under way, but "after that," she said, "I will try to write something else."[21]

As fluent as Lida was in the language of local color, in *Aunt Jane of Kentucky*'s closing story she had already ventured away from dialect to give a hint of her restlessness as she anticipated her next literary endeavor. "The Gardens of Memory" lavishly celebrated a place as necessary to Aunt Jane's home, and Lida's own, as a kitchen. As if obeying Thomas Calvert's long-ago instructions for Josie's description of the flowers in their yard—"make it minute so that I can see it in my imagination"—Lida did not immediately invoke the charm of her elderly friend's lilies and "daffydils"; rather, in the inward-looking style that *Catholic World* judged as distracting from the simplicity of Aunt Jane's anecdotes, her narrator begins with an examination of the gardens of her own past.

One such garden had flowered impressively in the brief summer of the north, on the grounds of a house once known as the Black Horse Tavern. Wandering its paths in the footsteps of Revolution-era patriots, her child's imagination in flight, she had absorbed the colors and fragrances of its "well-kept beds where not a leaf or flower was allowed to grow awry." Though happy within its borders, she had not been entirely at liberty; amid the exotic fruits and rare berries of its trees, she admitted, "we children ate by stealth, and solemnly declared that we had not eaten."

The second, a southern garden, survived faintly as part of her earliest memory. Out riding on a pleasant day in the country, she had encountered it near a "heap of blackened, half-burned rubbish" that had once been a house. Abandoned and weed-infested, it nevertheless offered a host of snapdragons free for the taking, with no need to seek permission. "And as long as I live," she continued, remembering her companion in that small adventure, "the sight of a yellow snapdragon on a sunny day will bring back my father from his grave and make me a little child again gathering flowers in that deserted garden."

Such were the two plots—Margaret Younglove's ordered sanctuary and Thomas Calvert's boundless ruin—that had framed Lida's own childhood. She brought them forth with equal tenderness, even dedicating *Aunt Jane of Kentucky* to both her mother and father, but Lida remained the querulous daughter in search of her own garden. "Brick walls and pavements hemmed me in," her narrator complains in "The Gardens of Memory," and "robbed me of one of my birthrights." As she grew older, she and her playmates had tried to possess wild patches in the woods, but their impetuously gathered bouquets "withered and were thrown away before we reached home," victims of a wastefulness not confined, in retrospect, to youth. She had also kept geraniums in pots and courted public patches of blossoms she found in town. Within the boundaries of the latter another child might have been content, but her encounters were unsatisfying—the Indian peach tree inspired only "melancholy thoughts," the honeysuckles had no perfume, and the roses, so alluring in color and form, lacked robust thorns and proved "sickening-sweet" in odor, bringing only "disappointment and disgust."

Eventually, however, the narrator rewards both herself and the patient reader by drifting into Aunt Jane's "gyarden." Like the calico in her quilts, it is "a record of the years in leaf and blossom," an egalitarian Eden where humble sage grows alongside aristocratic roses, and the seedlings transplanted by her Virginia-born grandmother provide a living link to the past. The little snake passing beneath her hoe evokes a humorous story, the faces of long-dead friends reappear in the flowers, and finally, a "flash of silence" descends in which Aunt Jane accepts the prospect, some day, of leaving this paradise behind for the next.

All of these recollected gardens, the narrator insists, brought "rich aftermaths" to her senses; nevertheless, she confesses, "when Memory goes a-gleaning, she dwells longest on the evenings and mornings once spent in Aunt Jane's garden"—the only one in the story, Lida confirmed later, that was imaginary.[22]

Eliza Caroline Hall Calvert, Lida's paternal grandmother, from whom she took her pen name. (Courtesy Kentucky Library, Western Kentucky University)

Thomas C. Calvert, Lida's father. Outwardly prospering as a lawyer and banker, he fled Bowling Green after being forced into bankruptcy and exposed as an embezzler. (Courtesy Kentucky Library, Western Kentucky University)

Margaret Younglove Calvert, Lida's mother. Practical and independent, she ensured her family's survival after Thomas Calvert's financial ruin. (Courtesy Kentucky Library, Western Kentucky University)

Eliza "Lida" Calvert. As a child, Lida read novels and poetry, frequented the county fair, and visited the gardens of her Younglove relatives in Johnstown, New York. (Courtesy Kentucky Library, Western Kentucky University)

(Below left) Mary Calvert, Lida's sister. Though fragile in health, she became, in her father's words, the "quiet industrious housekeeper who thinks that every moment must be improved at some handy work." (Courtesy Kentucky Library, Western Kentucky University) *(Below right)* Margaret Calvert, Lida's sister. Her father expected Maggie to excel in school because she had the "best mind" of any of his children. (Courtesy Kentucky Library, Western Kentucky University)

Josephine Calvert, Lida's sister. During her father's long absence, Josie obeyed his instructions to keep a diary in order to preserve more detail for her letters. (Courtesy Kentucky Library, Western Kentucky University)

Edward Calvert, Lida's brother. His fugitive father expected the young boy to "earn a living" and help his family. (Courtesy Kentucky Library, Western Kentucky University)

Lida Calvert Obenchain. Before marrying at twenty-nine, Lida helped support her family by teaching school and writing poetry for popular magazines. (Courtesy Kentucky Library, Western Kentucky University)

William Alexander Obenchain, Lida's husband. Commonly addressed as "the Major," the dignified Virginian supported women's rights and suffrage. This photograph accompanied an essay he wrote for *Signal Lights: A Library of Guiding Thoughts by Leading Thinkers of To-Day* (Marion, Iowa: Waffle and Maddock, 1892).

After Thomas Calvert's bankruptcy, his newly built mansion became the home of Warren College and later Ogden College. Lida's husband became Ogden's president in 1883. (Courtesy Kentucky Library, Western Kentucky University)

Laura Clay (1849–1941), founder of the Kentucky Equal Rights Association. Laura praised Lida's decade of press work for the KERA, while Lida credited her with keeping "my coward soul" on the "path of duty." (Courtesy Special Collections and Digital Programs, University of Kentucky Libraries)

For the *Cosmopolitan*'s first publication of "Sally Ann's Experience," in July 1898, Peter Newell drew an outraged Sally Ann commanding an errant husband to "set right down an' hear what I've got to say." The story became the opening chapter of *Aunt Jane of Kentucky*.

Illustrating the 1910 book version of Lida's most famous story, G. Patrick Nelson depicted a more gentle, refined-looking Sally Ann.

For the frontispiece to *Aunt Jane of Kentucky*, Beulah Strong imagined Aunt Jane among her patchwork quilts—"my albums and my
di'ries."

The success of her first book prompted Lida to refer to her Chestnut Street cottage in Bowling Green as "the house that 'Aunt Jane of Kentucky Bought.'" (Courtesy Kentucky Library, Western Kentucky University)

Lida in Aunt Jane-like repose, probably with part of her husband's vast book collection in the background. (Courtesy Kentucky Library, Western Kentucky University)

Margery Obenchain Winston and son Val. Her sweet-tempered older daughter's early death made Lida "a pessimist forever." (Courtesy Kentucky Library, Western Kentucky University)

William Alexander Obenchain Jr., Lida's older son. His World War I military service marked what was probably the happiest time in Alex's troubled life. (Courtesy Kentucky Library, Western Kentucky University)

Thomas Hall Obenchain with his aunt Josie Calvert. Lida's second son built a successful business career in Dallas, Texas. (Courtesy Kentucky Library, Western Kentucky University)

Major William A. Obenchain and grandson Val Winston. (Courtesy Kentucky Library, Western Kentucky University)

Lida with her grandchildren, Margery and Val Winston, for whom she cared during their mother's illness. They are "pretty and wonderfully bright," she wrote her own mother, "but more trouble than any children I ever saw." (Courtesy Kentucky Library, Western Kentucky University)

Lida with her third grandchild, Thomas Obenchain Jr. (Courtesy Kentucky Library, Western Kentucky University)

Lida in her Dallas garden with her daughter Cecilia. As arthritis and rheumatism overtook her mother, Cecil struggled with the duties of companion and caregiver. (Courtesy Kentucky Library, Western Kentucky University)

Lida's sisters Maggie (*left*) and Josie Calvert. (Courtesy Kentucky Library, Western Kentucky University)

11

Seeing Double

Ah! Eliza Hall, God bless you,
Since you've made our tired hearts young,
And may never griefs distress you
Half so real as those you've sung.

                    —*Chicago Record-Herald*

WHILE THE *WOMAN'S JOURNAL* found a suffrage argument en-
coded in *Aunt Jane of Kentucky,* another periodical noted an element
missing from Eliza Calvert Hall's stories. Her tales of rural life, the
Arena assured its more discriminating readers, were honest represen-
tations of the genre, but a "striking omission," namely the "absolute
absence of the negro from the canvas on which Aunt Jane's pictures of
the old days are painted," detracted materially from their "wonderful
living reality." The *New York Times,* on the other hand, remarked un-
critically upon the same absence, praising the stories for evoking the
"sentiment of two generations ago among the plain and solid folk of
that part of Kentucky where the darky was not sufficiently present to
complicate seriously the social structure." Such different impressions
of Kentucky's past reflected the contradictions of a state in which the
cultures of North and South had intersected, where citizens had been
both slaveholders and Unionists, and were as likely to trace their roots
to Pennsylvania as to Virginia.[1]

    In her next series of stories, the first of which appeared in the
Cosmopolitan only six months after *Aunt Jane* was published, Eliza
Calvert Hall did not alter her formula to suit the *Arena*'s critic. Hav-

ing mourned the tendency of dialect to corrupt her English, Lida was doubtlessly unwilling to descend further into the nonstandard spelling and grammar used by local colorists to give voice to the "darky," even though she would not have denied that the black folk of her experience had stories to tell. In an 1894 monograph on Bowling Green's Civil War history, she preserved a favorite anecdote about Aunt Minerva, that "famous cook of the old Kentucky type" who had served General Buckner during his occupation of the Younglove home. After the war, when Buckner visited the city as governor, Aunt Minerva presented him with her long-overdue account for wages, which he promptly paid. Nor did Lida fail to see that in the racial politics of Civil War Kentucky lay the themes of timeless literature. She appreciated that a mere compilation of historical events and reminiscences of the men who witnessed them could not fully capture the "light and shades" of opinion that had animated the conflict in her home state. Between the planter convinced of the divinity of slavery and the equally stubborn emancipationist, she knew of less easily drawn characters—the Unionist whose loyalty faltered when denied compensation for his slaves, for example, or the legislator "ready to eat his own words" in support of Lincoln when his constituents objected. "What a wealth of material is here!" she declared. Not only should a suitably nuanced, "Rembrandt-like picture" of the political cauldron of 1861 be undertaken by a talented southern novelist, but for such a work to be truly great "its scenes must be laid in Kentucky and in the little town of which I write."[2]

Lida, however, was not an artist who easily blended the complication of race on her own canvas; she was a suffragist from a state that, as one historian famously observed, had waited until after the Civil War to stand with the Confederacy. While she could be contemptuous of the mythical Old South, with its idealization of male chivalry and its women "wrapped in silks and laces" insisting that they neither wanted nor needed the vote, she continued to subscribe to its notions of caste, freely complaining, in common with other southern suffragists, of the enfranchisement of black men ahead of white women while avoiding any kinship with similarly oppressed black women. During the election year of 1896, she had cast a cynical eye on the ladies who campaigned enthusiastically for free silver and offered flowers to favored local candidates. "Why did they not know," she asked, "that a ragged, coal-black negro with a greasy ballot in his hand is a more interesting object to a politician than half a million beautiful women with their roses and chrysanthemums and ribbons?"[3]

After solving the "negro problem" by restricting black men's access to the ballot rather than offering it to women, southern Democrats had opposed universal woman suffrage as a threat to this resurgent white supremacy. Insisting that white women's votes would counteract those of both black women and men, Laura Clay nevertheless recognized the difficulty in overcoming fears that such women would not visit the polls in sufficiently large numbers to give the desired result. Placed on the defensive, she and other southern suffragists waded more deeply into legal and intellectual quagmires as they attempted to reconcile principle and opportunism, individual freedom and racial hierarchy, women's rights and states' rights. As early as 1890, the old abolitionist Henry Blackwell had joined in a proposal to Mississippi's constitutional convention to restrict suffrage to literate women. Rationalizing this approach on the ground that the votes of better-educated (and usually white) women would redound to the benefit of black women, in 1906 Laura and the KERA called for an amendment to Kentucky's constitution on the same terms. Among those closest to Lida, the Major, who supported woman suffrage as "a matter of right and justice," favored a literacy qualification for both women and men.[4]

In her suffrage writing, which had slowed but not stopped in the months surrounding the publication of *Aunt Jane of Kentucky,* Lida did not as clearly endorse limitations on the right to vote; in the case of white men and women, she certainly rejected the notion that the former, no matter how well educated, could adequately represent the latter at the polls. She agreed, however, at least in regard to certain pressing social questions, that the judgment of an enlightened class of both sexes ought to be substituted for that of the general population. Answering a claim that the average woman's indifference to the ballot was an "unanswerable argument" against suffrage, Lida observed that many average citizens had slowed the advance of the public good through indifference to progressive measures such as sanitation, child labor laws, and women's education and property rights. The achievement of human progress, she declared, "means the setting aside of the opinions and wishes of average people, and in the long run the world is governed by the small first class, the men and women who love justice."[5]

Perhaps because Lida did not exclude the possibility of educated
blacks' joining this class, the NAWSA issued The "Unanswerable Argument" Answered in pamphlet form even as its relations with southern
suffragists were increasingly complicated by the latter's whites-only
preference. Lida, nevertheless, was capable of no more empathy for
blacks than for the "silks and laces" set. Eliza Calvert Hall, too, found
that neither captured her imagination. Composing Aunt Jane's single extended reminiscence of the Civil War, she relied instead upon
her most authentic voice, that of the ordinary, unenfranchised wife
who glared at the world through the lens of her own marginality. "In
War Time" returns Aunt Jane to memories of her mother, Deborah,
a strong and capable woman to whom even her father defers, but who
quickly realizes the limits of her influence at the outbreak of hostili-
ties. "You men have got this thing in your own hands," she tells her
husband, "and us women'll have to put up with whatever comes." She
then watches in anguish as two sons enlist, one to fight for the North
and the other for the South. As the rest of the community fractures
along the same lines, a neighbor congratulates her for serving her
country by giving a child to each side of the "great question" to be
settled. "Country!" she snaps. "You men never told me I had a country
till you got up this war and took my sons away from me." When both
fall at Shiloh, the only great question that haunts her is whether a
hasty battlefield burial had kept their bodies safe from the vultures.[6]

"In War Time" included another anecdote tellingly adapted from
Obenchain family lore. Unlike Aunt Jane's mother, the Major's mother, Elizabeth Obenchain, had given her husband, brother, and sons
exclusively to Confederate service. Alone with five young children in
the summer of 1864 and anticipating a search of her Virginia home by
approaching Federals, she had hidden her oldest son's store of gun-
powder in a nearby churchyard. That night, she was alarmed to see
enemy campfires burning near the place of concealment. Fearing that
the powder might be ignited, injuring the soldiers and inciting them
to burn the town in revenge, she crept into the encampment, shadowed by a frightened but loyal housemaid, and retrieved it. In Lida's
version, Elizabeth Taylor (lately of "Sally Ann's Experience") accom-
plishes the same feat, but in the company of a rheumatic old male
slave who says nothing and offers "no manner o' protection." Her sole
motivation, furthermore, is a desire to spare women like herself even

though they are on opposite sides of the conflict. Elizabeth acted, Aunt Jane recalls, after "she thought how every one o' them soldiers lyin' there asleep had a mother and maybe a wife and a sister that was prayin' for him. And all at once somethin' said to her, 'Suppose it was your boy in that sort o' danger, wouldn't you thank any woman that'd go to his help?'" Women were justified in so reframing the duties of citizens, Lida seemed to say, as long as they were denied the full rights of citizens.[7]

In July 1909, two months before "In War Time" appeared in the *Cosmopolitan,* the *Louisville Courier-Journal,* Lida's nemesis in her fight to promote suffrage, noted that *Aunt Jane of Kentucky* was in its fourteenth edition and that a second book was forthcoming. Over the past two years, the *Cosmopolitan* had carried eight more of Eliza Calvert Hall's stories, which, together with "In War Time," were about to be published by Little, Brown as *The Land of Long Ago.* The photograph accompanying the *Courier-Journal* item, however, hinted at the weariness that shadowed Lida's success. She appeared thinner and more angular than in her youth, her face and graying hair reflecting the many stresses that now attended her at age fifty-three. One was menopause, experienced near the time of *Aunt Jane of Kentucky's* debut, which was followed, as she indicated in her interview with Ewing Galloway, by an extended period of fatigue and ill health even as she maintained her publication schedule in the *Cosmopolitan.*[8]

Another was the resumption of both her suffrage activity and her entreaties to Laura Clay to forgive her waning capacities. As in the previous two years, Lida did not attend the KERA's annual meeting, in November 1908, but the delegates again praised her work and re-elected her as press superintendent. Her financial worries had lessened enough that she offered to forgo her five-dollar monthly salary and even forwarded one dollar in the name of each of her children to the NAWSA's Susan B. Anthony Fund; still, her cries for a respite from press work grew more insistent. To her relief, Laura offered to take it over herself, at least temporarily, even as she assigned Lida yet another task. A committee of the NAWSA headed by Carrie Chapman Catt had begun a drive to petition Congress for a federal constitutional amendment guaranteeing woman suffrage. Late in 1908 the committee set up its headquarters in New York and began the work of writing letters, distributing petition forms, and recruiting state organizations to collect, count, and return signatures. Knowing that Lida would have read about the "big petition" in the *Woman's Journal*, Laura sent her the forms along with some KERA membership cards and asked her to do what she could in Bowling Green.[9]

Despite its preference for achieving suffrage at the state level, the KERA had never withheld support for a federal amendment, and neither Laura nor Lida balked at the petition's call for unqualified woman suffrage. Although Lida protested that she was too worn out to enroll new members or canvass door-to-door, she tried to enlist the help of the city's WCTU chapter and one of its more progressive women's clubs. Bowling Green also held prospects for securing, in accordance with Mrs. Catt's request, as many signatures as possible from college presidents and faculty. Lida sent a copy of the petition to Ogden College with the Major and another copy to Potter College, whose dean, Mrs. Carrie Burks Mitchell, was already an active KERA member. Mary Dishman, a local public school principal, signed the petition and agreed to circulate it, as did J. Lewie Harman, vice president of the Bowling Green Business University, who had sold the Obenchains their house. Although Henry Hardin Cherry, president of the Western Kentucky State Normal School, would prove to be a supporter, Lida had to delay approaching him because of a smallpox quarantine.[10]

The response to her efforts was disappointing. The Major returned the petition from Ogden College bearing no signatures but his own, and the ladies of the WCTU were unsympathetic to a cause they believed to be ahead of its time. Lida forwarded their president's reply to Laura Clay, explaining that "she is an uneducated woman, and all the members of the Union are like her." The other clubs and schools did not return their petitions, and Lida admitted that she was simply too tired to pursue them. In the throes of "a nervous breakdown from overwork," she was nevertheless apologetic about giving up her duties as press superintendent. Transferring her newspaper list to Laura, she promised to resume the work if she could; in the meantime, she would maintain relations with a friendly Bowling Green editor and encouraged Laura to pursue the Louisville papers.[11]

Lida's greatest source of stress, her domestic life, quickly overcame the minor relief she experienced after dropping press work. Despite the success of *Aunt Jane of Kentucky*, she was not able to

claim any of the perquisites of a "literary lady" during the production
of her second book; unlike Laura, she lacked both a stenographer and
the use of her own typewriter. She had also been unable to secure
the work space that she had hoped to acquire in her Chestnut Street
house. "One thing that increases my difficulties is that I have no room
of my own," she complained to Laura, "and writing in the confusion
of family life is one of the things that has worn my nerves out." Less
remediable than these practical difficulties, however, was Lida's continuing determination to oversee the emotional and financial welfare
of those around her. "I can't stop being a mother, or a housekeeper
and I *must* write and support the family," she told Laura. Although the
sting of the Major's demotion was probably still fresh, her declaration
was curious given her children's ages; Cecil was only fourteen, but
Margery was grown, Alex had already left home, and Tom, completing his junior year at Ogden College, was preparing to do the same.
Perhaps the prospect of her children's independence had left Lida
fearing old age and the loss of her maternal identity; even as a young
mother writing poetry, she had glimpsed a time when long Sunday
afternoons tending a fretful baby would seem a welcome alternative
to a quiet, orderly Sabbath spent in an empty nest. In February 1906,
Munsey's Magazine had published another poem, "Motherhood,"
in which she envied a bird's successive broods and nature's seasonal
powers of regeneration:

> But for me the deepening shadow of years,
> The time of the failing breath!
> To the mothers of men one spring, and then
> Comes the winter of age and death.[12]

The parade of time, with its rewards, compromises, and regrets,
was a prominent theme in *The Land of Long Ago,* published on September 18, 1909, and dedicated to Lida's children. Although its tenure
on *Bookman's* most-popular list was shorter, from September through
the following January, reviewers agreed that its wholesome appeal
matched or surpassed that of *Aunt Jane of Kentucky.* The *Hartford
Courant* pronounced Aunt Jane "a real personage in American literature," the *Philadelphia Press* praised the "sweetness and sincerity"
of her recollections, and the reviewer for the *New York Times* was

charmed by the manner in which she arrived "in front of the story she started to tell" after "skirmishing around all through the neighborhood and finding little incidents and making acute little comments, none of which the reader would want to miss." Even more recognizably than she had in her first collection, Lida drew upon family legend, county lore, and her own memories of Bowling Green's people and places to give Aunt Jane's stories the pleasantly meandering quality to which her admirers were now accustomed.[13]

Two of the stories, in fact, added a physical aspect to Aunt Jane's wandering. Instead of storytelling on her porch or in her kitchen, she takes her visitor on "A Ride to Town," during which every house, store, farm, and natural feature, even the road itself, evokes a memory. In "Aunt Jane Goes A-Visiting," she recounts a recent excursion to see her granddaughter, Henrietta, in Lexington. Both experiences bring Aunt Jane face to face with modernity but she greets change, whether in the form of the new four-story buildings around the town square or the activism of Henrietta's women's club, as natural and even welcome. Custom defended for its age alone inspires no reverence in her: "I've noticed that when a thing always has been, most likely it's a thing that ought never to 'a' been," she observes. Although the narrator sees the permanence and security of her old home as the reason Aunt Jane can love rural life "without hating its antithesis," her serenity derives more from an appreciation of continuity. "We're lookin' at the same things, honey," she tells her friend during their ride to town, "but you see jest one thing, and I'm seein' double all the time." Just as she conjures up the outlines of the early courthouse square behind its new architecture, so does she glimpse the private toil of their grandmothers behind the public work of Henrietta's finely dressed clubwomen.[14]

The *Woman's Journal* greeted *The Land of Long Ago*, like *Aunt Jane of Kentucky*, as an addition to the broader gospel of women's rights. Recommending some of its stories for readings at suffrage clubs, the editors offered a free copy of the book, worth $1.50, to anyone procuring two new subscribers. Particularly noted was "An Eye for an Eye," a restatement of Lida's grim association of marriage with repetitive and thankless domestic labor. *Aunt Jane of Kentucky* had addressed the subject not only in "Sally Ann's Experience" but in "Sweet Day of Rest," a story about the hollowness of the Sabbath for women whose cooking and child-care duties never abated. In the latter tale, Milly Amos is able to laugh at her plight, but the long-married wife in "An Eye for an Eye" is not so resilient. Hannah Crawford begins secretly to sabotage her husband Miles's farm work, pulling down fences, hiding tools, and spilling bags of seed. When caught, she breaks down, laughing and crying, rocking back and forth, and muttering the Old Testament edict she has heard in a recent sermon: "An eye for an eye and a tooth for a tooth." Miles, she explains, "has been undoin' my work and givin' me trouble for thirty-five years, and I've wished many a time I could pay him back."[15]

Fortunately, she is tended by a sympathetic doctor who, rather than sending her to the asylum, treats her according to her own prescription. He orders Miles to turn the cows out of the pasture and installs Hannah there, beneath a shade tree with some "old comforts and a piller," to gaze up at the sky for the remainder of the day. Left to herself, Aunt Jane remembers, Hannah not only rested but found that "lookin' up at the sky was like lookin' into deep water, and sometimes she'd feel as if her soul had left her body and she didn't know whether she was still on this earth or whether she'd died and gone to heaven." Intuitively, this plain woman seeks spiritual knowledge by looking upward, beyond the domestic chores and religious orthodoxy that have kept her looking downward and inward.

Aunt Jane frankly regards the sermon that so disturbed Hannah as regrettable and even unwholesome; other biblical themes, while perhaps less memorable, would have been "jest as true and a heap more comfortin'." With similar outspokenness, "An Eye for an Eye" reverses the traditional assumption about marriage; rather than the state commonly thought necessary for a woman's emotional health and satisfaction, it becomes an affliction that renders her "crazy as a loon." For Hannah, furthermore, the cure is out of reach. "I can't do what I used to do. . . . There's a change come over me, and I ain't the woman I was a year ago," she admits before going out, literally, to pasture. The unorthodox therapy revives her in the short term, but her husband's awkward attempts to be more considerate have little effect, and she dies without ever recovering fully from her breakdown.

Just as Hannah searched the sky for escape, Lida looked for alternatives to the fate of the worn-out wife that, Aunt Jane and the story's narrator agree, "life repeats with endless variations." Given her female characters' limited circumstances and the social conventions of their time, the most obvious solution was beyond practical consideration. Another story admits the possibility of burdens so great that a wife might be justified in leaving her husband, but once vows have been exchanged the bride's obligation, as a mother tells her newlywed daughter in "The Marriage Problem in Goshen," is to "make the best o' your bargain." Such advice was consistent with Lida's view, which, like that of many southern suffragists, favored more carefully considered decisions to marry over more liberal divorce laws.[16]

Unfortunately, even judgments made in the utmost good faith were no guarantee against sudden catastrophe or a husband's human failings. Lida's creative response to this dilemma—encouraged, perhaps, by editorial promptings for inoffensive, marketable fiction—was to take refuge from realism in sentiment and melodrama. In "The Reformation of Sam Amos," Milly Amos's unselfish devotion supplies the moral example her husband needs to stop drinking, an outcome that Lida herself had once dismissed as a contrivance of romantic literature. In "The Marriage Problem in Goshen," Aunt Jane thinks carefully about the question of how much a woman ought to stand from a husband. Although she has faith that even the "marryin' and partin' and marryin' again" somehow work together for good, she ventures dreamily that "if folks could only love each other the way me and Abram did they'll never want to part."[17]

In two stories, Lida's turn to sentiment was so abrupt as to change the entire tone of the preceding narrative. "An Eye for an Eye" moves quickly from Hannah's decline to her kind doctor's courtship of a well-off young lady. When his family suffers financial reverses and he realizes that he cannot give her the material comfort she enjoys in her father's house, he breaks their engagement, and propriety forbids her to declare her willingness to marry him anyway. The two unwed lovers live out their lives as spinster and bachelor, side by side but apart, aged by time as they would have been by marriage but happy, Aunt Jane insists, because they are blissfully untouched by disillusionment. Telling her listener of Hannah's indifference to her husband's ministrations, Aunt Jane had observed, "It's hard to make a thing end right, honey, unless it's begun right." In the case of the doctor and the woman he is too poor to support, beginning right means not beginning at all.

In Lida's most melodramatic tale, "The Courtship of Miss Amaryllis," the charming and beautiful young lady of the title becomes engaged to the dynamic Hamilton Schuyler, but a foolish misunderstanding causes each to doubt the extent of the other's devotion. He assumes that she will come to his family estate, Schuyler Court, after their marriage, while she rather petulantly declines to live anywhere but at the Cedars, her father's house. The test of wills keeps them apart for five years, until Schuyler Court is destroyed in a fire. Hearing of the loss, Miss Amaryllis, who by now has inherited the Cedars and lives there alone, sends Hamilton the deed and vacates what is now his house. After a frantic search, Hamilton finds her at a cousin's home and, in a whirlwind ceremony, marries her.

When the narrator asks to hear how they lived happily ever after, Aunt Jane regretfully disappoints her expectation that good fortune will follow such a perfect resolution. The next winter, Miss Amaryllis dies after delivering a stillborn baby. Mother and child are buried together in an ivy-covered coffin, she in her wedding dress, their grave lined with cedar and pine to hide the cruelly frozen ground. Insane with grief, Hamilton suffers until spring when he rides away, vowing to find her as he had once before, and eventually dies in a far-off country. Despite the biblical teaching that marriages do not exist in heaven, Aunt Jane hopes that such unions as these transcend death and that somewhere the family is together again.[18]

With *The Land of Long Ago* suggesting that the best marriages existed in the supernatural, in the memories of widows or in the fantasies of spinsters and bachelors, its author likely was filled with misgivings as she turned to preparations for the wedding of her oldest daughter. On April 26, 1910, twenty-two-year-old Margery Obenchain married twenty-eight-year-old Val Graham Winston, whom she had probably met during her winter sojourns in Dallas, where both her brothers were now working. A small circle of family and friends witnessed the Episcopal Church ceremony, read at the Obenchain home from Samuel Calvert's old prayer book. Fifteen-year-old Cecil played the violin, accompanied on piano by sixteen-year-old Henry "Hugh" Underwood, the son of Lida's cousin Emma Underwood. Lida wore, in her own dismissive terms, a "gray rag," while Margery's dress was made from material sent by her uncle Edward. Repeating a military tour in the Philippines, Edward himself had married four days after *Aunt Jane of Kentucky* was published, but his sisters had yet to meet his wife.[19]

Margery's move to Dallas after the wedding left only Cecil at home with her parents, but fortunately the youngest child soon found herself enjoying a more pleasant and informal domestic atmosphere. With her siblings gone, the customary "grim, mournful" family breakfast yielded to individual convenience; even the Major, who was first to rise, proudly exercised the new skill of preparing his own meal from ingredients Cecil laid out for him the evening before. As she developed into a clever, vivacious young woman intent on her musical studies in both violin and voice, Cecil's interests allowed her to appreciate Lida's talent even if she expected life to offer her a much more congenial blend of art and love. At sixteen Cecil not only had gathered "all of Margery's old beaux and plenty of her own," according to her mother, but was declaring her intention to marry as soon as she turned seventeen.[20]

One of Cecil's more impulsive acts at this time involved the original manuscript of "Sally Ann's Experience." Lida appeared not to have treated it as a valuable artifact; the first eight pages, in fact, had long ago been lost. During one of her early romantic attachments, however, Cecil made a gift to the young man of the remainder. Her gesture was not insignificant in light of the story's ongoing popularity. After the publication of *Aunt Jane of Kentucky* and with some coaching from the *Cosmopolitan,* Lida had discussed a grant of dramatization rights to various artists including Clara Lipman Mann, a well-known stage actress and playwright. In summer 1910, Little, Brown issued another fifty thousand copies of the story in a form more durable than the pamphlet that had been offered as a bonus to purchasers of *Aunt Jane of Kentucky.* Bound in hardcover with a condensed and revised version of Lida's 1908 essay, "Why I Wrote 'Sally Ann's Experience,'" the little volume reminded the *New York Times* of President Roosevelt's recommendation that it be used as a tract in families afflicted with selfish or thoughtless husbands. Noting its suitability as an inexpensive gift (the *Woman's Journal* offered a copy to its current subscribers for fifty-five cents), the *Times* trusted that the book would find its way into the hands of many such men.[21]

While *Sally Ann's Experience* revived Lida's indictment of the "spirit of the old English common law," its illustrations were more evocative of the gentle fables of the Old South made popular, particularly in the North, by authors such as Joel Chandler Harris and

Thomas Nelson Page. Both Beulah Strong, the illustrator of *Aunt
Jane of Kentucky,* and G. Patrick Nelson, an artist of Peter Newell's
caliber whose work later accompanied stories by Jack London and
Arthur Conan Doyle, had provided drawings for *The Land of Long
Ago,* and Nelson had also illustrated most of its stories when they first
appeared in the *Cosmopolitan.* For the new *Sally Ann's Experience,*
he supplied a frontispiece depicting Job Taylor's attempted exit from
Goshen Church, and a color cover for the book showing Sally Ann
and another woman strolling through an arbor. The contrast with Peter Newell's illustrations would have startled readers who recalled the
first published version of "Sally Ann," but not those who had seen Nelson's similar portrait of Miss Amaryllis in *The Land of Long Ago.* Like
Hamilton Schuyler's doomed love, Sally Ann is a vision of antebellum
femininity—white flounced dress, bright red shawl, black gloves, a
poke bonnet framing her pleasant countenance as she watches her
companion gather roses. The frontispiece shows her in the same dress,
the youngest and most stylishly attired member of the congregation
rather than its fearsome "he-woman." With a rather meek expression
on her face, she points downward at an empty pew as if imploring Job
Taylor, who looks not nearly as ancient or miserly as before, to behave
like a gentleman and return to his seat. Only those already familiar
with the story would have known that Sally Ann's effect on the men
far exceeded the "indirect influence" suggested by this stereotypical
southern belle.

Although sales of *Sally Ann* and royalties from *The Land of Long
Ago*—which, like *Aunt Jane of Kentucky,* soon appeared in a British
edition—should have given Lida her hoped-for chance to rest from
the labors of writing for income, she continued to worry about her
family's needs even as she dreamed of withdrawing from them to pursue her art. "When Cecil marries I am going to sell out and board and
be a real 'literary lady,'" she declared to Josie, before taking inventory
of her latest cares. Her sons were properly established in Dallas, Alex
in a city engineer's position and Tom in insurance and real estate, but
settling them there had required enough financial assistance that Lida
had to reduce her Christmas spending for 1910; the following spring,
she even worked on a story for a contest in hopes of earning a cash
prize. Her subsidy of her older son gave extra weight to Lida's objection when Alex, like his father after the Civil War, grew discouraged

and expressed a desire to seek his fortune in Mexico. "I made him
stick in his present place and told him he had to make good in Dallas
before I would consent to another move," she wrote Josie. "He is a
rolling stone sort of boy anyway." Josie herself was visiting in Toledo,
Ohio, where their brother Edward was now living with his wife, Lucinda. Lida expressed kinship with her sister-in-law over their common inability to find good domestic help and, learning that Edward
had returned from the Philippines in poor health, vowed to "do some
back worrying on his account."[22]

Lida was also carrying out her intention, stated during her interview with Ewing Galloway, to write something other than "Aunt
Jane" stories. She had seized upon an idea when a friend, perhaps
after reading of Aunt Jane's quilts, sent her photographs of some thirty designs for a related domestic item, the coverlet. Handwoven on
the looms of ordinary, unnamed farm women as well as professional
craftsmen, some of them dated from the early years of the republic and were sturdy enough to have survived use by generations of
families. Delighted with their beauty and variety, Lida had resolved to
write a book on the subject, but what she envisioned as a pleasant exercise of her imagination lasting only a few months soon transformed
itself into a demanding research project. She toiled on through spring
1911, by now captive to both the charm of the topic and her commitment to her publisher. "Little Brown & Co are wailing for the ms. of
the coverlet book and it isn't half ready and I feel like giving up," she
wailed in turn to Josie.[23]

Fortunately for Little, Brown, Lida was also correcting page proofs
of a short novel, begun when Cecil was still an infant but taken up
again, perhaps, after three of the publishers who declined *Aunt Jane
of Kentucky* had encouraged her to pursue this literary form. At the
time she conceived the novel, Lida, at home with four children under
the age of ten, had been especially aware of the narrowness of a married woman's life in comparison to her husband's. Writing of the wife
and mother closeted in an urban house, she had likened her isolation
to that of the mountain woman "fur from the big road" whose husband never told her "nothin'." Without questioning women's primary
duty as homemakers (Lida herself would soon decline John Brisben
Walker's offer of syndicate journalism), she had complained that the
gulf between men's and women's spheres of action undermined their

capacity to maintain "that beautiful comradeship which constitutes a true marriage." Free of the soil, out in the world of "thought and action and progress," a husband's horizons expanded while his wife's intellectual powers and moral influence contracted. Building upon this theme, Lida's novel sounded an alarm for modern marriage even as it rose to the defense of the woman "fur from the big road."[24]

Published on May 6, 1911, *To Love and to Cherish* was dedicated to admirers of *Aunt Jane of Kentucky* and included some mild rural dialect but, unlike Aunt Jane's tales, moved quickly to the "p'int." As background, the reader learns only that its principal character, Reuben Ward, has left humble origins to study law, then returned home to claim Mary, the mountain girl who has waited for him. They have now loved each other for ten years, Reuben finding his conventional expectations of her—as she cooks, sews, gardens, and cares for his three children—completely fulfilled, and Mary, having walked the straight path from her father's home to her husband's, proud in the knowledge "that she has accomplished that for which she was born." Her faith in Reuben has animated him through a series of professional and political accomplishments until, at last, he finds himself about to be nominated by his party for certain election to the governorship of his state.[25]

To Reuben's surprise, when he triumphantly shares the news with Mary, she bursts into tears. "I ain't fit to be a governor's wife," she sobs. "I'd do anything on earth for you; but this—I believe it would kill me. I ain't got the education nor anything a governor's wife ought to have, and I'd just be a disgrace to you." She tells him that he must go to the capital alone while she remains at home in their mountain village with the children.[26]

Reuben at first dismisses her fears as a judgment of him. "If I'm fit to be governor, it stands to reason that you're fit to be a governor's wife," he protests. Mary, however, possesses neither the social graces of a gentlewoman nor the traits of mind and will that, in her husband's case, have compensated for his lack of polish. She sees that Reuben's origins have become the backdrop for his life's journey, the foil to his future, while she asks only that the days to come repeat those of her simple rural past. "Now, mind, Reuben, it's all settled," she repeats firmly. "You've got to take the nomination and I'm goin' to stay right here."[27]

The impasse prompts Reuben to a vigorous inner dialogue in search of a solution. Mary, he soon realizes, is captive to her environ-

ment. His "primal egotism" has left him inattentive to the process by
which life has loosened his "fetters of birth and custom" while binding
hers ever tighter; and yet, he reflects, he would never have loved Mary if
she had been a political woman, like the wife of his party's chairman—
shrewd, refined, childless, skilled at manipulating people and circumstances—and such a woman, in any event, would never have married
the young "Reub" Ward. In both her willingness to see him become
governor and her inability to imagine herself as a governor's wife,
Mary has not failed him—and he must not fail her.[28]

Concluding that his wedding vow "to love and to cherish" obli-
gates him to defend his wife from "the selfish encroachments of his
own nature," Reuben secretly withdraws his name from consideration.
When Mary reacts to his apparent loss of the nomination with genuine anguish, he tenderly assures her that so long as he has her and
the children, he ought to be—and is—satisfied. "Besides," he adds
meekly, "it'll all be the same a hundred years from now."[29]

"The ending of the story is idyllic, not tragic," wrote the reviewer
for the *New York Times,* but the *Louisville Post* was more perceptive,
noting the "touch of certain doubt, which darkens, a little, the glory
of the close." Lida, indeed, plants the seeds of sorrow in this homely
reconciliation. How long, she asks, before Reuben experiences the
"recoil of emotion" that he courts by having surrendered his chance
for greatness? How long before a journalist or gossip makes his secret renunciation known to Mary, destroying the very happiness it was
meant to save? What has happened to transform Mary's traditional,
supportive feminine role into a destructive force? How has she become, in the judgment of the party chairman's wife, who coldly de-
duces the reason for Reuben's political self-immolation, one of those
"good women" who "do as much harm in this world as the wicked
women"?[30]

To Love and to Cherish offered no answer to the question of what
husbands and wives like Reuben and Mary might do, for themselves
and each other, to avoid such a fate. In the meantime, however, the
author could not resist awarding a kind of revenge to this humble wife
"fur from the big road." If, as a condition of his love, Lida seemed
to say, a man limits a woman to qualities that make her unfit to accompany him to a larger life, he sets the stage for his own defeat.
In this light, Mary's most valued feminine attribute, her self-sacrifice

("You've got to take the nomination and I'm goin' to stay right here"), actually succeeds as self-protection ("I'd do anything on earth for you; but this—I believe it would kill me"). She may be unlettered and provincial, but by her admission of her inadequacies Mary declares her individuality, forcing Reuben to recognize "the wholesome truth that two can never be one."[31]

Mary has another reason for clinging to the environment in which the qualities Reuben has loved can flourish. "It won't be half as hard for me" to stay, she tells him, "as it would be to go with you."[32] Even if the man she loves abandons her, she has a better chance of surviving in the mountains than of negotiating the urbanism, careerism, and masculinism of the modern world. Though fast becoming a relic and destined to be overcome by those forces, Mary's world, indeed, retains power as a place of simple beauty and maternal strength, one to which women and men alike longed to retreat. Aunt Jane's admirers already understood this, and so would the readers of Lida's next book.

12

A Woman Spinning and Weaving

The dignity of toil is theirs,
The patience over-long,
And labor that, through storm or calm,
Keeps still its purpose strong.
   —May Stanley, "To Eliza Calvert Hall on Her
      'Book of Hand-Woven Coverlets'"

AFTER LIDA GAVE UP her duties as KERA press superintendent, Laura Clay quickly found a replacement in Dr. Louise Southgate, a Covington physician, teacher, and public health advocate. In early 1910 Margaret Weissinger, a niece of the senator who had sponsored the 1894 married women's property bill, succeeded Dr. Southgate and accomplished a feat that had regularly eluded Lida. Miss Weissinger's efforts, reported Laura, were finally gaining a hearing for the suffrage cause in the "hitherto difficult to reach" Louisville newspapers.[1]

The *Courier-Journal* had, in fact, recently endorsed school suffrage, but this concession was largely a tribute to the work of another women's association on behalf of educational reform across the state. Much larger than the KERA, the Kentucky Federation of Women's Clubs represented eighty-five organizations with over 9,500 individual members and, after a period of cautious support, had grown more vocal on behalf of the school vote. Lida's suffrage colleague in Bowling Green, Carrie Burks Mitchell, was serving as a vice president when the federation took the lead in 1908 to bring a bill before the General Assembly that would allow literate women to cast ballots in school elections.[2]

The bill failed, as did a second one introduced two years later, but other developments in 1910 suggested that the women's movement was regaining momentum. In March, the General Assembly passed legislation giving mothers equal rights with fathers to guardianship of their minor children. Membership in the KERA surged past one thousand, and the Federation of Women's Clubs edged closer to an endorsement of full suffrage as the most expedient method for accomplishing its goals. On a national level, Washington State enfranchised women, the first of many suffrage parades took place in New York City, and the editor of the *Ladies' Home Journal,* who had paid handsomely to reprint "Sally Ann's Experience," allowed a major article in favor of woman suffrage to appear in its pages.[3]

In late October 1911, Louisville was the host city for the annual meetings of both the NAWSA and the KERA. Laura implored Lida to attend the conventions, agreeing that the experience would supply good atmosphere for a suffrage story Lida was writing. Laura also assured her that she could find quiet lodgings in one of the boarding-houses recommended by the *Woman's Journal.* The NAWSA meeting itself promised to be an unquiet affair. For the past two years personal rivalries, administrative difficulties, and the uneven leadership of president Anna Howard Shaw had fostered tension among board members. In 1909 the organization had moved its headquarters from Ohio to New York City, and Laura's position on the board soon drew her into conflicts that sprang up in the new office over the division of executive powers and responsibilities. In defiance of Anna Howard Shaw, she voted in favor of contracting with Alice Stone Blackwell, publisher of the *Woman's Journal,* to make the paper the NAWSA's official organ. Living far from New York, Laura and three other non-resident officers also complained when headquarters staff failed to keep them informed about financial matters, including the conditions under which wealthy socialite Alva Belmont was subsidizing the rent for their Fifth Avenue office. Distrust only grew when the New York officers proposed amending the NAWSA's constitution to require monthly board meetings except in July and August. The practical effect, Laura claimed, would be to minimize the influence of officers

and candidates from the West and South who would be unable to
meet the expense of travel to so many meetings.[4]

Lida shared Laura's concerns about the eastern faction of the
NAWSA, agreeing that "if the powers of that board are ever turned
over to a few northern women it will be a disaster." She longed to be
present at the convention in order to cast her vote on questions facing
the membership and finally to meet some of the individuals whose
names she had seen so often in the *Woman's Journal*; at the same
time, however, she pleaded the effects of the breakdown she had suffered four years earlier and the unlikelihood of a complete recovery.
"As long as I live," she explained to Laura, "I have to write a book every year to keep my royalties up to the point where they will support
the family, besides keeping house and cooking."[5]

Lida nevertheless managed not only to attend the convention but
to draw from it a renewed sense of mission despite the NAWSA's treatment of Laura Clay. The delegates reached a compromise on the issue
of board meetings, but the eastern faction ensured that Laura, speaking for the South and West, was denied each of four offices for which
she was nominated. One of the successful candidates, a Kentucky native who had not even agreed to stand for office, was mortified to learn
that her name had been used to defeat Laura. Sophonisba Breckinridge, a University of Chicago scholar and Progressive who was herself unlikely to manage regular attendance at meetings in New York,
offered to resign, but Laura was gracious in defeat. Cheered by the
recent suffrage victories in Washington and California, she hoped that
Sophonisba's election would encourage the NAWSA to underwrite a
new campaign in Kentucky for a state constitutional amendment.[6]

One of the other women present at the convention was Sophonisba
Breckinridge's sister-in-law and close friend. Distantly related to Laura through their common ancestor Henry Clay, Madeline McDowell
Breckinridge chaired the legislative committee of the Kentucky Federation of Women's Clubs and had begun to campaign for the vote
as an outgrowth of her extensive humanitarian and reform activities.
Working out of Lexington, where her husband, Desha Breckinridge,
was the progressive editor of the *Herald,* thirty-nine-year-old "Madge"
belonged to a generation bringing fresh vitality to the suffrage movement. Where Laura had pursued the vote as a just end in itself and
as the measure most critical to legal and political equality with men,

Madge and her colleagues subordinated this strategy to a newly powerful expediency argument linking suffrage to the broader agenda of Progressivism and, in particular, to the "moral housekeeping" that women might apply to civic disorders such as child labor, impure food and drugs, inadequate schools, and urban blight. To her credit, Laura, now sixty-two, concluded that these younger reformers deserved the chance to bring their political skills to the organization she had led for the past twenty-three years. Immediately following the tumultuous NAWSA convention, she convened the KERA's annual meeting and secured amendments to its constitution that would limit the terms of its officers and make 1912 her final year as president.[7]

As part of her plan to boost the KERA's ranks to ten thousand by 1914, Laura also began advising Lida, who had enthusiastically requested two hundred blank membership cards, on local organizing. To appear more inclusive, she recommended, Lida should name her suffrage league the Warren County Equal Rights Association rather than the more locally named Bowling Green Equal Rights Association, and should encourage both women and men to join. On November 6, 1911, Lida hosted her first meeting—after which, she reported, she unwittingly stirred up a "hornet's nest" of injured southern pride. Among the five people in attendance was a young woman from Virginia who taught at the Western Kentucky State Normal School. She carried with her a membership card signed by a male colleague, but he had altered the wording of the pledge to commit himself only to school and municipal suffrage. Lida considered destroying the card because, she reasoned to Laura, if the KERA was to claim ten thousand members who endorsed full suffrage, that statement must be "absolutely true." She determined instead that the more polite course of action would be to return the card and encourage the signer to support the Kentucky Federation of Women's Clubs. Unfortunately, the woman who had first delivered the card took offense at this display of "bad manners," which, she was heard to claim, "could never have occurred in Virginia." Worried that the incident would put her at odds with the entire Normal School, Lida sought guidance and consolation from Laura. "I can't stand quarrels," she moaned.[8]

The controversy, however, soon faded, and over the succeeding weeks Lida carried her cards everywhere in order to obtain signatures. By the end of the year, she had forwarded forty-six to Laura and

promised that almost as many had been distributed and were awaiting collection. She had tied together the cards signed by a husband
and wife, she pointed out, in order to demonstrate that suffrage had
caused no discord within those families. She had also deposited copies of the *Woman's Journal* in the YMCA reading room and asked two
bookstores to offer it for sale. With her characteristic mix of perseverance and gloom, Lida was heartened by her accomplishments but
looked forward to the day when she could end such work for the sake
of her frayed nerves.[9]

Greater success followed when Madge Breckinridge, the woman
Laura Clay had in mind to succeed her as KERA president, achieved
the victory for which the Federation of Women's Clubs had been
working in earnest for several years. Having gained the endorsement
of both the state Republican and Democratic parties, a school suffrage bill finally passed and was signed into law on March 12, 1912.
Although restricted to women who could read and write—a response to the same fear of black voters that had precipitated the 1902
repeal—the measure now applied statewide. Madge was elated but
quickly agreed with the KERA that the question of full suffrage, constitutionally guaranteed so as not to be subject to ordinary repeal,
ought to be laid before the next session of the General Assembly.[10]

Welcoming the school bill's passage as a step toward the "right
protective of all other rights," Lida initiated the local campaign by
requesting that Laura add Bowling Green to her itinerary of speaking
engagements for April. In the familiar tone she had adopted after the
reform of property laws, she also lectured those who had been mere
spectators to the most recent struggle, urging them to express proper
gratitude to the Federation of Women's Clubs and the KERA by registering for the school vote. "I have always said that women are 'The
Ungrateful Sex,'" she editorialized in the local newspaper, "and the
proof is that when one of the most precious things on earth, a right, is
offered to them, they either refuse to take it or they take it without a
word of thanks." The August election for district trustees seemed to
justify her cynicism. Her own ward made the best showing, but in all a
mere forty-seven women voted—a newspaper carried the story under
the headline "Woman Suffrage Failure"—and the following September Lida was embarrassed to advise Laura that only eight women in
Bowling Green had remitted their fifty-cent dues to the KERA.[11]

Lida had been late in forwarding her membership report because she was completing a project that had been known to Laura since they had arranged her speaking engagement the previous April. Laura had assured her anxious hostess that she need not worry about the state of her housekeeping, since she would be too interested in hearing about Lida's writing to notice whether the coal soot was as bad in Bowling Green as in Lexington. To illustrate the subject of Eliza Calvert Hall's latest book, however, Lida would have readily drawn her guest's attention to a few of her more prized household furnishings. On the back of one of her easy chairs was a handwoven coverlet, extensively darned and patched but boasting pleasantly soft colors and an elaborate design known as "Tennessee Trouble." Draped over a sofa in her parlor was another coverlet in brown and ecru christened "Double Muscadine Hulls," perhaps because it represented that tough-skinned variety of grape among its kaleidoscopic patterns. The display of yet another coverlet, in shades of pink with a pattern of spheres arranged in seven rows and columns, would have allowed Lida to tell the story of how she rescued "Forty-nine Snowballs" from its fate as a potato cover and horse blanket.[12]

Since conceiving her idea for a book on coverlets a few years earlier, Lida had undertaken an impressive amount of original research. In pursuit of both representative and rare specimens, she had corresponded with city and country folk in the mountains and lowlands of Kentucky as well as with coverlet owners in Ohio, Illinois, Massachusetts, Tennessee, and New York. Particularly helpful was William Wade, a Pennsylvania collector who had given her "Double Muscadine Hulls" and may have been the source of the thirty photographs that originally attracted her interest, since Lida described him as the individual "who first made known to me the beauty of the hand-woven coverlet." She also benefited from the expertise of institutional leaders in the decades-old arts and crafts movement, dedicated to preserving skills such as spinning and weaving for aesthetic, educational, and economic reasons: Fireside Industries at Berea College, established after the school's president invited Appalachian families to sell coverlets to offset their children's tuition; Allanstand Cottage Industries, a shop opened by a missionary in Asheville, North Carolina, after she received a coverlet as a gift; and the Hindman Settlement School of Knott County, Kentucky. The teachers at Hindman may have helped

Lida to meet a local weaver whose recipes for making dye, recorded in her mountain dialect, could have come from Aunt Jane herself. From the mountains, too, came several examples of "drafts," rolls of paper or cloth with markings resembling primitive music scores that transmitted to successive generations the instructions for reproducing a "kiver."[13]

Lida had also conducted research much closer to home. Friends grew accustomed to her salutation, "Have you an old coverlet? Do you know anybody who has one? and do you know the names of any coverlet patterns?" Whether or not they could oblige, her neighbors assisted Lida in her field work with other, sometimes more reluctant sources—the county's tobacco farmers. By 1911 Bowling Green was home to two tobacco buyers' warehouses, the older of which was located only a few blocks southeast of the Obenchain home. Beginning in November of each year, farmers would haul their crop to one of these locations to be weighed and sold. A traditional method of transport involved packing the leaves in large casks, but smaller growers commonly hauled their tobacco loose, tied only in bunches for easier handling. If they were well-off, they covered the loaded wagon with a tarpaulin for the journey to town; if not, they used a more economical substitute such as an old carpet, a quilt—or a coverlet.[14]

Lida herself described the gauntlet they ran upon reaching Chestnut Street. Some might be enlisted only in her political cause—one December day, she reported to Laura, eight farmers passing her house on their way to market had become the audience for her first impromptu suffrage speech—but others would be recruited to her literary cause:

> As these wagons trail by my house, a cry goes up from some watcher: "There goes a coverlet!" I rush out signalling to the man on the wagon and begging him to let me see that old coverlet, while passers-by stare amazedly at the sight of a bareheaded woman standing in Kentucky mud or melting snow, imploring a tobacco farmer to sell her a ragged, filthy bedcover.[15]

Alternately, Lida would ask to borrow the coverlet in order to have it photographed. Sometimes the farmer would give his cheerful promise—

"Yes, ma'am, I'll bring it to you jest as soon as I sell my terbacker"—only to vanish and deprive her of a coveted specimen. If she mourned the ones that escaped, her successes were equally memorable. A neighbor's telephoned warning one January day—"There are two coverlets coming your way"—resulted in the loan of "a 'Blazing Star,' dark as the winter sky, longer and broader than the wagon, and so thick and heavy that it required a man's strength to fold it and carry it to the photographer." Another farmer temporarily parted with "Downfall of Paris," a coverlet woven three generations earlier to commemorate Napoleon's defeat. Subsequently cut up into numerous pieces, it had been sewn back together to provide a cloak for the "vile weed."[16]

The product of Lida's labor, *A Book of Hand-Woven Coverlets,* was published in October 1912, and dedicated to William Wade. Illustrated with sixty-four plates, sixteen in color, it catalogued some 350 coverlet designs with names ranging from the prosaic ("Locks and Dams," "Rattlesnake Trail," "Hen Scratch") to the floral ("Granny's Garden," "Fig Leaf," "Flowers of Lebanon") to the sentimental ("True Lover's Knot," "Soldier's Return") to the celestial ("Rising Sun," "Sea Star"). Some of them ("Philadelphia Pavement," "Irish Chain," "Sugar Loaf") had their counterparts in quilt designs, while others ("Flourishing Wave" and "Floating Wave," "Wheel of Time" and "Wheel of Fortune") were variations of the same design, their names modified over time or geographical location.

Dutifully listing, ordering, and classifying, Lida followed the investigative rules of Victorian science, but the book was at its most engaging when she used her imagination, as tobacco farmers used coverlets, as a mantle thrown over her raw bundles of data. While she included the work of professional weavers and slaves among her examples, she was most concerned to identify the craft with ordinary women whose names were largely unrecorded and whose features she took pleasure in recreating. She visualized a "happy-faced woman, who wore gray-colored muslins" and sang at her loom as the weaver of the cheerfully colored "Tennessee Trouble," and the maker of the weighty "Blazing Star" as "tall, muscular, broad-shouldered, stern of face and manner, with iron-gray hair drawn tightly back from her face." Given that coverlets, like quilts, spoke to many of her past meditations on woman's fate, Lida lost no opportunity to animate these domestic artifacts with the souls of their creators. Coverlet designs that portrayed political or

military events—"Battle of Richmond," "Washington's Victory," "Lafayette's Fancy"—swelled her suffragist's pride, for they showed that
the fires of patriotism had always burned brightly in the female heart.
"As you ponder each historical picture," she observed, "you see in the
background a woman spinning and weaving," a citizen far worthier
than the modern-day Daughter of the American Revolution or Colonial Dame who disdained such homely renditions of flags, eagles, and
mottoes. So defensive was Lida of this political sensibility that she was
willing to forgive four sisters who, loving justice more than beauty,
had cut up and divided a coverlet pictured in one of her photographs,
each preferring a part of the family heirloom to surrender of her equal
right to inherit the whole.[17]
     The rest of the book, nevertheless, stood strongly in favor of pres-
ervation. Like the quilt of Aunt Jane's patterned after an ancient Flo-
rentine mosaic, Lida recognized in the colonial coverlet the seeds of an
artistic spirit that had matured in the finest American sculpture, painting, and literature. Equal, if not superior, to its value as an art object
was its significance as the text of an otherwise forgotten life—of the
European-born foremother, the unlettered mountain woman, or the
first wife who died too early. The chic, worldly great-granddaughter
who banished her family coverlets to the attic dishonored the memory
and values of such women as much as the farmer who sacrificed their
artistic expressions of love to commercial purposes. Though she held
the next generation accountable for neglecting this maternal legacy,
for Lida the torn, stained tobacco coverlet, "still beautiful, still dignified in the midst of its humiliation," was particularly symbolic of its
maker's unsung nobility. Observing in wonder that the average specimen was sturdy enough to outlive the weaver despite only minimal
care, Lida venerated the coverlet as a perfect foil for so much else
about a woman that "perished with the using."[18]
     Priced at $4.00, A Book of Hand-Woven Coverlets was far more
costly than Eliza Calvert Hall's "Aunt Jane" books ($1.50) or To Love
and to Cherish ($1.00), and the reluctance of retailers to order large
numbers of copies caused both author and publisher some concern
about its financial prospects. After she had corrected the proofs, Lida
assisted in writing advertising material and, to foster interest in the
book, contracted for two magazine articles—one of which, a lengthy
illustrated piece in McCall's, confirmed that she had absorbed as

much knowledge of quilt patterns, probably through her mother, as coverlet designs. Fortunately, her treatment of a largely unexamined topic, together with the readability of her digressions into folklore and fancy, drew the appreciation of both general and specialist review- ers. *Literary Digest* judged *A Book of Hand-Woven Coverlets* to be a significant work, *Outlook* found it a "treasure-house," and the *Nation* particularly applauded its recovery of the histories of itinerant profes- sional weavers in several Kentucky counties. The *Craftsman*, a major voice of the arts and crafts movement, reproduced eight of the book's illustrations in its review. Its editors praised Lida's ability to combine the practical and poetic, to adorn plain facts and technical details with Aunt Jane–like touches of philosophy, romance, and humor.[19]

The notice in the *New York Times* was brief, but earlier that year the paper had reported on Berea College's role in expanding the market for handwoven goods and on the success of other coopera- tive ventures that sold products with a homemade cachet. Although First Lady Ellen Wilson created additional public interest after she engaged mountain weavers to redecorate a room in the White House, the *Times* would later note that a teacher at the Mechanics' Institute in Rochester credited Eliza Calvert Hall with the numerous inquiries the school had received from educators, businesswomen, and mem- bers of the public. Some of them had been inspired to create new coverlets while others saw their old ones in a fresh light. Alice Van Leer Carrick, herself a writer and lecturer on antiques, rhapsodized about her own small collection after the book helped her to under- stand its true significance. Unlike conventional reviewers, she also hailed the feminist spirit with which Lida had enlivened the results of her research. "Nobody can properly understand or really 'see' cover- lets until they have read this book, this wonderful, radiant, *marching* book," she proclaimed. "Why, you'd know that the woman who wrote it believed in other women, rejoiced in the earnest beauty of their work, even if you had never read 'Aunt Jane of Kentucky.'"[20]

Aunt Jane, indeed, had assured the members of her granddaugh- ter's club that the work of every generation of women, whether raising a large family or "hatching up" reform bills for the legislature, had the effect of bettering humankind. Where Aunt Jane regarded her contri- butions as largely complete, however, Lida did not yet hold thoughts of retiring her pen. Completion of *A Book of Hand-Woven Coverlets*

had left her exhausted—"It is all I can do to stand up under my burdens," she sighed to Laura—but she looked forward to beginning her
next project, a suffrage play. Shortly before the 1912 presidential election and against Laura's advice, she also joined the Progressive Party.
Theodore Roosevelt and his followers had included suffrage in their
platform, and while Laura apparently agreed with the NAWSA's Anna
Howard Shaw that such liberality was only a device to gain votes in the
West, Lida was less concerned with the question of motive. "Whether
the leaders are sincere or not," she wrote Laura apologetically, "they
have forced every party to take up the question of woman suffrage
and I 'jined' out of gratitude for this."[21]

Laura herself had just spent six weeks in Kansas, participating in
what would prove to be a successful campaign for a suffrage amendment to that state's constitution. Soon after her return, the KERA
convened its annual meeting in Lexington and entered a new era with
the election of Madeline McDowell Breckinridge to the presidency.
After some hesitation, Madge had agreed to stand for the office and
soon proved herself a capable successor to Laura. Claiming "no reason that we should make a funeral of it," she quickly introduced some
livelier methods for attracting attention to the cause such as parades,
hikes, automobile tours, and suffrage booths at fairs and other public
events. While Laura found these tactics somewhat less cerebral than
she would have preferred, she took up her new role as the KERA's
corresponding secretary and Madge's lieutenant with loyalty and renewed vigor.[22]

Lida, too, began to work with Madge after they both spied the
ever-growing constituency just beyond her front door. With an enrollment of more than fifteen hundred students, the Western Kentucky
State Normal School had purchased the campus of Potter College,
where Margery and Cecil had studied. The Normal School's president,
Henry Hardin Cherry, admired Madge and had tried to schedule her
to speak before a group of educators during the 1908 school suffrage
campaign. After Madge became KERA president and established a
committee to award ten-dollar prizes for the best equal rights essays
written by students at institutions of higher learning, Lida secured
Cherry's consent to the participation of the Normal School. Their
conversation about Madge, however, produced what Lida feared was
yet another breach of decorum. Remembering, perhaps, the tempest

over the altered membership card, she took immediate and clever remedial action. "I hope you did not get the impression last night that I was trying to make arrangements with you for Mrs. Breckinridge to address the students of the State Normal," she wrote Cherry. Knowing perhaps that either she or Carrie Mitchell might oblige, two students had approached her to request a suffrage speaker. "I mentioned the fact that we were expecting Mrs. Breckinridge but Mrs. Breckinridge never speaks except by formal invitation," Lida explained, "and I would never ask any one to extend an invitation to any of our suffrage speakers." Thus prompted, Cherry immediately extended to Madge "a formal and urgent invitation" to address his students at the opening of the spring term. Though unable to make a definite commitment, Madge was far less reticent than Lida in suggesting an intermediate course of action. "Won't you please, please have Mrs. Mitchell or Mrs. Obenchain address your thousand students," she replied. "I cannot bear to have them go away to their homes without hearing a speech on Suffrage and each one supplied with a piece of literature to take home with him or her." Unaware that the essay prize had already been discussed, she also promised to "write Mrs. Mitchell about this and won't you have a conference with her at once?"[23]

Besides acting as liaison for the essay competition, a role she would fulfill for the next several years, Lida continued to assist the KERA's past president with more conventional methods of agitation. On April 19, 1913, Laura's new lecture tour again brought her to Bowling Green as Lida's guest. At sixty-four, Laura was still accustomed to speaking up to four times a day and readily accepted two engagements Lida arranged for her, one at city hall in the afternoon before a group of clubwomen and another that evening at the courthouse. After the second meeting, Lida collected $2.50 to support the KERA's purchase of stock in the now-renamed *Woman's Journal and Suffrage News* and added $1.00 of her own toward this special project.[24]

As Laura concentrated her efforts on public speaking and organizing county suffrage leagues throughout the state, Lida turned next to gathering support for another petition to the U.S. Senate. She had targeted the professional men of town including the mayor, she informed Laura, but because she was suffering from eye problems, which her doctor had attributed to "an over-worked brain," the Major himself actually gathered the sixteen signatures. Lida nevertheless recovered sufficiently by November to attend another KERA annual meeting in Louisville, where she read one of her stories as part of the first night's program, and heard Madge Breckinridge and Laura Clay report on a productive year and outline the agenda for 1914.[25]

Two weeks later, Madge traveled to Washington, D.C., where, speaking to both the NAWSA's annual meeting and a committee of the House of Representatives, she called for a suffrage amendment to the U.S. Constitution. On a parallel course, her organizational skills and innovative methods, which included the hiring of a full-time (male) field secretary, had made possible the first serious attempt to secure an amendment to Kentucky's constitution. Over the past year, the KERA's ranks had increased almost 150 percent to 4,272, and while members were not obliged to pay dues, significant voluntary contributions had swelled its budget. Consequently, when legislators convened in Frankfort in January 1914, the KERA launched an intense campaign of public speeches, distribution of literature, and lobbying, the highlight of which was an address to a joint session of the General Assembly by Madge Breckinridge and Laura Clay.[26]

Although the House handily defeated the suffrage amendment, Madge had set the KERA on an irreversible path of growth. By the end of 1914 its membership would exceed 10,500, with 87 of Kentucky's 120 counties claiming fully or partially organized suffrage leagues. As president of the Warren County League, Lida perhaps could imagine that her long and often lonely crusade would soon end. At the same time, she could be confident that the continued popularity of *Aunt Jane of Kentucky*, as well as her determination to publish regularly in its wake, had earned her a place among the state's literary notables. During her lecture tour, Laura was pleased to report, women had reacted with great interest to the attractive circulars for *A Book of Hand-Woven Coverlets*, and she frequently found herself responding to the public's curiosity about her friend, "Mrs. Eliza Calvert Hall."[27] For Lida, as for Laura, the work that consumed her would soon be transformed by events that were, at best, bittersweet. "I can't stop being a mother, or a housekeeper," Lida had written, and, contrary to the forecasts of anti-suffrage doomsayers, neither the ballot nor a literary life would tempt her to shirk those duties.

13

Riding to Town

A woman who understands her duty can attend to the affairs of the
house in which she lives and at the same time play a citizen's part
in the management of her larger home.

—Lida Calvert Obenchain

"I RECKON KENTUCKIANS are the biggest fools in the world
when it comes to their own state," Aunt Jane once told her visitor.
"Sam Amos used to say that if you'd set a born-and-bred Kentuckian
down in the Gyarden of Eden he'd begin to brag about his farm over
in the blue-grass." A trip away from home, she acknowledged, was
useful for giving her a topic of conversation without having to think
back forty years, but she had returned from a visit to her granddaughter unshaken in her conviction that "this old house and this old farm
is the only place that could ever be home to me."[1]

Lida, too, was doubtful that the attractions of the wider world
were superior to those just outside her door. Writing to Josie, she
wished that Edward's wife in Ohio could see their state in the bloom
of spring. "I know this is the garden spot of the earth," she boasted,
and when she looked across the hills and valleys from the steps of
Henry Hardin Cherry's Normal School auditorium, she found herself
wondering "why anybody wants to go to Texas or anywhere else when
they can stay in Kentucky." With three of her four children living in
Dallas, however, and continued public interest in Eliza Calvert Hall,
Lida had begun to accommodate the necessity of travel.[2]

Fortunately, her youngest daughter was willing to play the role of companion and enthusiast. In 1904 Cecil had led her reluctant mother through the wonders of the St. Louis World's Fair, reacting with rapture to the exhibits, demanding popcorn, candy, and "other trash," and keeping her on the grounds after dark in order to watch the fireworks. "I am having a pleasant time," Lida had admitted to Josie, "but I shall be glad to get home." Less taken with some of the exhibits than with the gardens outside the buildings, she had urged her sister to attend before the flowers faded and with them the "glory of the fair."[3]

Early in 1913 Cecil, almost eighteen, accompanied her mother to New York City for the annual dinner of the Kentuckians, a social and heritage-minded club established nine years earlier by several prominent expatriates. The group's plan to recognize writers who had contributed to the state's literary fame was appropriately timed. Over the previous fifteen years, ten books by Kentuckians had appeared on the national best-seller list, and others, such as *Aunt Jane of Kentucky* and Annie Fellows Johnston's *Little Colonel* series, could be said to have reached at least one million readers. Louisville possessed a thriving literary community whose members alone had produced four best-sellers between 1902 and 1907. That so many of these authors were female had prompted the Kentuckians to invite women for the first time, but Lida, preoccupied with the exertion of the trip, was not disposed to dwell upon this singular honor. "The great dinner comes off tonight," she rather nervously wrote her mother from the Plaza Hotel, "and I don't think we shall tarry long after that." The previous evening, February 11, she and Cecil had celebrated her fifty-seventh birthday at the home of Walker Hines, a railroad lawyer and Ogden College alumnus. At the Kentuckians' dinner, Lida shared the speakers' table with such other notables as Alice Hegan Rice, whose *Mrs. Wiggs of the Cabbage Patch* had also earned President Roosevelt's praise, geography scholar Ellen Churchill Semple, playwright Ann Crawford Flexner, and Fannie Caldwell Macaulay ("Frances Little"), whose novel *The Lady of the Decoration* had been the top fiction seller for 1907, the year of *Aunt Jane of Kentucky*. Among the male honorees were Lida's old friend Robert Burns Wilson, General Basil W. Duke, the Civil War historian and veteran of Morgan's Raiders, and Irvin S. Cobb, a contributor to the *Cosmopolitan* and other magazines, who had recently published his first collection of "Judge Priest" stories. During his after-dinner remarks, Cobb's wit struck a sour note with

Lida. "In Kentucky we don't admit that women are our equals; we insist that they are our superiors," he chivalrously declared. "What on earth made you talk belated foolishness like that?" Lida scolded him afterward. "Aw, I'm a suffragist," was his meek reply, "but a fellow's got to say something at a dinner." As anxious, perhaps, to reform such attitudes as to maintain her standing among this group of authors, Lida looked forward to returning home and to work.[4]

New York, nevertheless, was a necessary element in Lida's ongoing plans to dramatize some of her earlier stories. Soon after *Aunt Jane of Kentucky* was published, she had attempted to market both "Sally Ann's Experience" and another of its chapters, "Milly Baker's Boy," and resumed her efforts to adapt "Sally Ann," with even more of a suffrage slant, after it reappeared in book form. She had also hoped for an opportunity to dramatize *To Love and to Cherish* but came nearer to success when her stage version of "The Courtship of Miss Amaryllis" drew the interest of the dean of New York producers, David Belasco. As her mother's traveling companion, Cecil recalled meeting "the great little genius" twice and hearing that the play was "just what he was looking for." The outbreak of war (or so they were told) soon ruled out production for the 1914 season, but Cecil continued to believe that the touch of sincerity she had glimpsed behind Belasco's "smoothness and slickness" was a sign that the project might some day be realized.[5]

Although she had traveled there at least once before, Texas only began to interest Lida after she and Cecil arrived in mid-July 1914 to await the birth of Margery's first child. The expectant grandmother was pleased to find that the pregnancy was progressing normally, Tom and Alex were happy in their work, and a newspaper reporter was waiting to interview Eliza Calvert Hall. For a woman with a lifelong aversion to coal soot, the city's use of natural gas for heat and light was a delightful change—"that means clean houses, clean air, clean clothes, clean hands, clean everything," Lida reported to her mother. From the porch of Margery and Val's Dallas apartment, she watched as abundant rain brought out roses, fruits, and wildflowers, and two weeks into her stay Lida had found nothing significantly lacking about Texas except the quality of its tomatoes. "The longer I stay here," she confessed, "the better I like the place and the people."[6]

A few weeks later, on August 28, Margery gave birth to a son, Val

Calvert Winston. The availability of a doctor for her daughter and a German nurse for the infant prompted Lida to contrast her own experience with more modern ways of childbirth, but she and Cecil remained for several months to lend additional assistance to the family. Lida did not depart for home, however, before drawing the attention of Dallas society for both her literary and suffrage work. She gave a reading from *Aunt Jane of Kentucky* at an event hosted by the Dallas branch of the American Pen Women and shared speaking duties with Madge Breckinridge at a luncheon inaugurating the latest campaign of Texas suffragists for an amendment to their state's constitution.[7]

Margery may have accompanied her mother back to Bowling Green or followed soon after, for "little Val" was only a few months old when his doting grandfather was photographed gently hugging him in front of the Obenchain home. At seventy-three, nevertheless, the Major, with his full white hair, moustache, and goatee, still unaccustomed to removing his jacket, had lost none of his starchiness. The next summer, after Alex had returned from Texas for road engineering work in Kentucky, he showed his underdeveloped sense of humor during an exchange between his opinionated wife and laconic older son. Tiring of a lecture from Lida on the evils of cigarettes, Alex declared, "Yes, I have a bunion on my left foot caused from smoking!" To Cecil's great amusement, her father, overhearing, earnestly corrected him: "No, my son, a tight shoe caused your bunion." When the Major planned a trip to Texas for little Val's first birthday, Cecil observed that despite an absence of forty years, he was expecting to find everything unchanged. If, in fact, he was disappointed, at least one location might have struck him as familiar. Lida, no doubt convinced by her own visit of the necessity for larger quarters, had arranged to have a house built in Dallas for the Winstons and twenty-four-year-old Tom. With its gambrel roof, second-story dormers, and Ionic-columned portico, the new cottage was strikingly similar to the house in Bowling Green that *Aunt Jane of Kentucky* had bought.[8]

Except for one more story in the *Cosmopolitan*, Aunt Jane herself had not been heard from since *The Land of Long Ago*, but rarely did mention of the other work of Eliza Calvert Hall omit a reference to her best-known character. This fond association not only kept *Aunt Jane of Kentucky* in the public imagination—the book would reach a twenty-second edition in 1916—but identified Lida, even as she faced the mobility and haste of modern society, with the values of her elderly storyteller: simplicity, rootedness, wisdom born of common sense, and most important, memory. "That's why I can write," Lida told her Dallas interviewer. "I remember everything." The watchfulness that compelled her to raise a "point of honor" with young women who casually appropriated the gains of the suffrage movement had been carried forward into her most recent book; writing of old family coverlets that "drifted down to us of the present day to be held in honor or cast aside in dishonor," she confronted their new owners with the same question: "*Have you forgotten? Have you forgotten?*"[9]

Although her methodology had been wearying, Lida's remembrance of coverlets drew her further into the study of the plain people of her own and surrounding states. Besides gathering quilt names and patterns, she examined another unheralded aspect of mountain culture—the art of basketry. She began to collect examples and to speak on the subject, an activity that, like her coverlet work, brought additional publicity and economic benefit to weavers throughout the southern mountain region. One such "basket talk" also precipitated Lida's first significant out-of-town travel without her daughter's company. In October 1915, while Cecil waited anxiously, "Mama" traveled alone to Troy, Ohio, where she addressed the Altrurian Club, gave interviews to Dayton newspapers, and attended a dinner and luncheon in her honor before returning safely home four days later.[10]

Despite Cecil's worries, Lida's stamina and confidence had seemed to grow since her completion of *A Book of Hand-Woven Coverlets*, a gain made clear not only in her public speaking but in her writing. In the foreword to *Hand-Woven Coverlets*, she had predicted her return to short fiction, admitting that she was not in the habit of subordinating her imagination to facts; rather, she regarded a fact only as a "slender thread" on which to string the beads of her fancy. Resuming this pleasant chore in earnest after her trip to New York, by July 1915 she had completed the last story for a new collection, which Little, Brown scheduled for publication the following spring as *Clover and Blue Grass*. Although she had used the title phrase in two "Aunt Jane" stories, and the book itself was to include a reprint of her nineteenth and last such tale (the fourteenth to have appeared in the *Cosmopolitan*), Lida had composed its five other chapters without bringing her famous narrator out of retirement. By the time of her solo visit to

Ohio, she was even planning her next project, a collection of essays "classifying men according to the way they love."[11]

During this period, in fact, two men had become significant players in Lida's creative and intellectual life. The first, John Wilson Townsend, was a member of the editorial board of the *Lexington Herald* and among the honorees at the Kentuckians' dinner in New York. A Harvard graduate and briefly a professor of English, Townsend had also worked as an editor of publications for the Kentucky Historical Society. After writing several books and pamphlets on his state's political and literary heritage, he had recently published what would become his signature work, *Kentucky in American Letters 1784–1912.* Before making the selections for his survey, Townsend had assigned himself the task of examining every book by a Kentuckian or about Kentucky. Although he and Lida first corresponded just prior to the publication of *Aunt Jane of Kentucky,* her success in the intervening years had earned her a place among some two hundred writers, out of a pool of more than one thousand, whom Townsend chose to profile in his book.[12]

Much as Lida had found in her investigations of quilts and coverlets, Townsend's work did not cease with the publication of *Kentucky in American Letters.* In addition to planning a dictionary, which would collect his biographical and critical research on every author, he continued to pursue copies, especially first editions, of the works he had uncovered. Lida joined his network of informants, sending him the privately printed work of local scribblers and locating books by and about the Kentucky Shakers. When he came to Bowling Green in summer 1915, they visited the nearby Shaker colony, then in the last years of its existence, which she remembered from her childhood. Their shared interest in Shaker literature gave them a ready topic of conversation, and their more personal exchanges deepened Lida's affection for Townsend, who was only three years older than Alex. "You have a place in my mother-heart," she wrote him after his departure.[13]

The occasion for Lida's sympathy was Townsend's courtship of a young woman named Grace Cole and his inability to overcome their mutual uncertainty about their prospects as husband and wife. In Lexington earlier that summer, probably in connection with a basket talk, Lida had dined with Townsend and learned an awkward truth to which neither had referred since: he had already been married once and divorced. While such knowledge could diminish Lida's estimation of character, she made an exception for Townsend, encouraging him in reserved but sincere terms to win over his "Golden Girl" with an unequivocal declaration of intent. She and Cecil even teased him about the possibility that his reticence would become the subject of a chapter in her next book, "The Loves of the Wise." When, a few months later, Lida read the notice of his impending marriage, she hid her doubts about his aptitude as a husband and congratulated him for securing "a home, a mother and a wife, three things that are better than all literary fame."[14]

As Cecil, too, assisted in Townsend's search for rare publications, her fondness for him created an intimate circle of daughter, mother, and collector. Now twenty and still intent upon a musical career, Cecil herself had been confidently at leisure in matters of the heart. Rather than fulfilling her vow to marry at seventeen, she had begun a long-term engagement to Glenn Reams, a Tennessee native close to Townsend's age, who was pursuing a medical degree in Nashville. Echoing Thomas Calvert's meditations of sixty years earlier, Cecil declared to Townsend that in dissipating much of the "glamour," her lengthy engagement would help her to avoid disappointment over a husband's inevitable failings and provide a more sensible foundation for marriage. In the meantime, she found her relationship with Townsend "wonderfully congenial," confiding that she could have loved him had they met earlier. Like Lida, Cecil admonished him to marry Grace, but her letters remained cheerfully beckoning, full of candid asides and displays of an open and affectionate nature even as she admitted to episodes of "unintentional inaccuracy"—saying things that "ain't so." Her violin performances in local churches and musicales were unremunerative, she sighed, but she found it impossible to withhold her talent from residents of a town in which she was well known and liked. If study and practice sometimes put her in the "dumps," music remained essential to her sense of well-being. One afternoon, she wrote Townsend, she and her violin had stolen away to the kitchen, the most private part of the house, and "loved each other for three hours." Even in Texas, she could not refrain from singing arias or scales while keeping house for Margery and sewing clothes for her little nephew.[15]

It was Cecil's proximity to Eliza Calvert Hall, however, that best sustained the connection with her "dear John." Answering his request for a picture of Lida, she sent one in which the subject's expression betrayed her aversion to being photographed but which had been Cecil's keepsake for the past three years. "Whenever I was away from home," she explained, "that picture went with me & was kissed good-night each night." The promise of an even more significant gift followed when Cecil confessed to Townsend that she yearned to recover the manuscript of "Sally Ann's Experience," which she had given to her old boyfriend, in order to donate it to his collection. "It's such a famous little story," she reminded him, "that I know you would keep & prize the manuscript." Only a week passed before she gathered the courage to send a note to the young man asking for its return, and only a month before the "precious" copy, except for its eight long-lost opening pages, was on its way to Townsend.[16] As she had the first time, unfortunately, Cecil would come to regret this latest disposition.

For her part, a bemused Lida conveyed Cecil's wish to receive a letter from Townsend during a visit by Glenn—"Why is it that a girl likes to torture her lover?" she asked, observing that, notwithstanding her most recent writing project, a woman's ways in love were as inscrutable as a man's. In addition to the youthful romances around her, the books that she and Townsend were now exchanging had given Lida ample raw material for her fiction. Acknowledging his offer of a rare Shaker work, she promised to return it when she had "read it and taken the heart out of it for my own use."[17]

During these same months late in 1915, Lida was conducting a similar, mutually beneficial traffic in history and literature with a second male friend. After graduating from Notre Dame, Otto Rothert had worked in his father's Louisville tobacco business and as a hotel clerk and journalist. In 1904 he inherited a 2,600-acre estate in western Kentucky's Muhlenberg County and began to cultivate what he modestly described as his hobby, local history. His investigations soon acquainted him with the relative lack of conventional sources for such work: a handful of books, legislative records, scattered newspaper files, a few pamphlets commemorating criminal trials or political controversies, and the publications of the state historical society and of Louisville's Filson Club, the private historical society to which he would contribute much over a long tenure as secretary. Further inquiry, however, convinced Rothert that much of Kentucky's story, particularly the daily lives, manners, romances, and tragedies of its ordinary people, had survived in the journals of early travelers, the reminiscences of old-timers, and the work of the state's novelists, poets, and storytellers. In 1915 he wrote an extensive bibliographic essay illustrating how these writers had found their characters, settings, and plots in local tradition, and suggesting that historians draw upon such sources to construct a fuller and more engaging portrait of the state—work that would, in turn, unearth even more of its past for adaptation in fiction and poetry.[18]

Making his own contributions over the previous two years with published histories of Muhlenberg County and one of its Baptist churches, Rothert found an appreciative audience in Eliza Calvert Hall. Pronouncing his county history a "gold mine" for authors, Lida confirmed her past reliance upon such material in composing Aunt Jane's narratives; in fact, she wrote Rothert, "If Aunt Jane and I had not parted company forever, according to a solemn promise, I would be tempted to call her up and set her to talking again, for I see the germ of many a story in your two books." At Rothert's mention of Joseph Lapsley, who had preceded her grandfather as pastor of the Presbyterian church, Lida was content to recall a favorite "Aunt Jane" tale, "The House That Was a Wedding Fee." First published in the *Cosmopolitan* and included in *The Land of Long Ago*, the story was based on a legend surrounding the 110-acre farm that James Rumsey Skiles, the church's early benefactor, had deeded to Lapsley. Lida had probably learned its principal component—that the farm was a gift for Lapsley's performance of Skiles's marriage ceremony—from her uncle John Younglove, who at eighty-eight now possessed one of the longest memories and greatest stocks of hearsay of any Bowling Green citizen.[19]

Using as her "slender threads" of fact both the gift itself and the claim that the house on the property had been designed by none other than Lapsley's former classmate Thomas Jefferson,[20] Lida had strung many sparkling beads of fancy. She cast Rev. Lapsley as "Brother Samuel Wilson" and gave him a biography similar to that of her grandfather, Samuel Calvert. Skiles became Squire Meredith Schuyler, whose brother Hamilton was featured in "The Courtship of Miss Amaryllis." In "The House That Was a Wedding Fee," Schuyler has recently pledged a generous subscription for a new church building, but Brother Wilson calls upon the session to discipline him for swearing and breaking the Sabbath. Instead of appearing to answer the charges, Schuyler increases his subscription, a defiant act that forces Wilson to resign rather than accede to the congregation's willingness to exempt its largest donor from censure.

In the midst of the controversy, Schuyler again surprises the townspeople by having Brother Wilson officiate at his elaborate wedding ceremony. When the time arrives to pay the fee, he presents the preacher with the deed to Schuyler Hall and its surrounding acreage. Deaf to Wilson's protests, he declares, "There's nothing too good for a man that refuses to bow down and worship the golden calf." Schuyler then appears before the session and promises to reform his habits, leaving Brother Wilson to spend the remainder of his too-short life enjoying his new home in the country.

The story ends with Aunt Jane and the narrator visiting Schuyler Hall—in the footsteps of many others, Lida wrote Rothert, for whom it became a local attraction. Sending him a photograph of the house and a biographical sketch of James Rumsey Skiles, Lida was as attentive to Rothert's collecting efforts as she was to Townsend's. As they exchanged books and suggestions about tracing local history sources, Lida agreed with Rothert that county histories ought to be prepared and placed in every school, an opinion that echoed her father's long-ago endorsement of the same scheme in honor of the national centennial.[21]

Though they filled her mind with ideas for essays and stories, men such as Townsend and Rothert also heightened Lida's consciousness of the duties that beckoned her away from writing. Alex had left home again, moving on to road-building work in eastern Kentucky, but from Texas the news of Margery's troubles gave her mother fresh cause for distraction. "My poor little girl is almost broken down with the care of a nervous sleepless baby and I must go to her help," Lida announced to Rothert. Correcting the proof sheets for *Clover and Blue Grass,* giving lectures on weaving, and conducting research for her essays, she was also anxious to complete books on basketry and quilts but sensed that her maternal worries would exact a high artistic price. "No wonder a woman's work does not measure up to the standard of man's work," she complained. "No novelist or poet ever had to suspend his work to nurse his grand-children."[22]

Lida's other preoccupation, of course, remained the ballot. Hurrying to finish *Clover and Blue Grass*, she had promised Laura Clay to "get in some suffrage work" and renew her thirty-year-long effort to gain more local subscriptions for the *Woman's Journal*. In November 1915 she attended the KERA's annual meeting in Lexington and visited Townsend, but it was Rothert, perhaps because of his bachelorhood and independent means, who endured Lida's reproach. "Mrs. Breckinridge expects me to do a world of suffrage work," she reported afterward. "Oh! Why don't you men give women their rights? I've spent enough time in suffrage work to have written a long novel."[23]

Madge Breckinridge herself had done a world of work over the three consecutive terms allowed her as KERA president: the Kentucky Federation of Women's Clubs, the Grange, the WCTU, and the state American Federation of Labor as well as the state Republican, Progressive, Prohibition, and Socialist parties had now endorsed the organization's goal of suffrage. At the KERA's 1915 convention, where ninety-five delegates represented more than fifteen thousand members, the press no longer caricatured as outcasts the stylish women conducting business on the stage of Lexington's old opera house. Rotating out of the office of president, Madge became chairman of another campaign to bring a suffrage amendment before the General Assembly. On March 8, 1916, the measure passed in the Senate by a wide margin but, under pressure from the Democratic governor and Kentucky's congressional delegation, failed to emerge from a House committee. Objecting to their interference, Madge warned the congressmen that in the absence of a federal amendment she would simply reintroduce the bill at every subsequent session.[24]

Later that month, Lida rejoined Madge and Laura Clay in Louisville for the National Congressional Campaign Conference of Kentucky. Sponsored by the KERA and the Louisville Woman Suffrage Association, the meeting brought together leading suffragists in the state and across the country, including NAWSA president Carrie Chapman Catt. Mrs. Catt planned to hold similar conferences in other cities to address a question that, by 1916, had become critical to the national body's future: whether it should continue to coordinate the achievement of suffrage on a state-by-state basis or devote its resources to securing a federal constitutional amendment. As chairman of her congressional district, Lida was responsible for recruiting delegates from each county to consider the issue but did not appear herself to have a settled opinion; forwarding a copy of the two-day-long program to a colleague in nearby Russellville, she merely urged her to send a representative to "what will be the most interesting convention ever held in Ky."[25]

For Laura, however, the conference highlighted her growing unease over the NAWSA's failure to accommodate southern women's strategies for gaining the vote without threatening white political supremacy in their region. Even as the conference began, suffragists in Washington were anticipating defeat in their efforts to bring a federal "Susan B. Anthony amendment" out of the Judiciary Committee and before the House, but Laura believed that it was doomed in any event because of the impossibility of ratification in the South. Earlier that year she had lobbied for her own United States elections bill, a compromise federal measure that would allow women to vote for members of Congress only and leave undisturbed the states' rights to determine qualifications, apart from sex, in other elections. Laura even spoke to the Louisville conference on behalf of the bill, but it attracted little enthusiasm. She was encouraged when both the Democratic and Republican party platforms for 1916 endorsed suffrage by state action, but as the year progressed Mrs. Catt would steer the NAWSA toward exclusive pursuit of the ultimate prize: a federal constitutional amendment.[26]

Before leaving Louisville, Lida met Otto Rothert for lunch and promised to send him a copy of *Clover and Blue Grass,* now scheduled for publication in September. The next day, she arrived home to find that the Major had become ill. At first, his condition did not appear serious enough to postpone her plans to visit Margery in Texas or to interrupt her creative work. Both Rothert and Townsend had loaned her interesting books, one of which had given her a "brilliant idea" for a short story; she was also researching an essay on John Milton and pondering how she might pay a literary tribute to the late Robert Burns Wilson. Even the prospect of Cecil's marriage to Glenn, who was graduating in June, did not distract her. "I am begging them to elope and be done with waiting," she confessed to Townsend.[27]

The Major, however, soon developed jaundice, and his condition worsened. Lida still hoped that he might recover, but by early May his doctor determined that he could be treated only with surgery, which,

at seventy-five, he would be unable to tolerate. Lida quickly apprehended not only the gravity of the diagnosis but her consequent duty.
"I am dropping suffrage work, *everything*," she notified Rothert, "and
trying to get ready for the work of nursing my husband through a long
illness."[28]

By July, the Major's doctors had concluded that liver cancer would
end his life before the close of summer. "All my suffrage work has
come to a stop, and all other work too," Lida confirmed to her colleague in Russellville. As she concentrated on his care, like so many in
her circumstances she reflected on the brevity of existence and on the
irony of death's arrival just as humans, through the wisdom of years,
began understanding how to live. At the same time, she could not
resist casting her glance toward the future. Using the brief intervals
available to her to work on the pile of unanswered correspondence
and unfinished manuscripts on her table, she realized, with some relief, that she would not collapse under the strain of the Major's final
illness.[29] Like Aunt Jane, who had outlived most of the characters in
her stories, she knew this tale would end at the "buryin'-ground"; still,
the work of the last few years had given her hope that "there's a plenty
more to be told over on the other side."

14

"Be Glad You Are Not a Woman"

> Alas! The stream turned from its course cannot at once forget the
> old channel and the old banks.
> —Eliza Calvert Hall, "Millstones and Stumbling-Blocks"

WILLIAM ALEXANDER OBENCHAIN died early in the morning
of August 17, 1916. Later that day, while Cecil slept and Lida waited
for Alex's train to arrive, she finished a letter to Otto Rothert. She had
been prepared for the end. "I have watched the Major die by inches
for five months and a half," she wrote, "and I am glad his release has
come." Margery and Tom were unable to travel from Texas, but the
Major's brother, Francis Obenchain, was expected from Chicago in
time for the funeral. Although the Major favored cremation on economic and sanitary grounds, his family buried him the next day in his
Confederate army uniform.[1]

The local newspaper gave Ogden College's "grand old man" a solemn tribute, praising his wisdom, gentlemanly manner, and dedication to teaching. When his club reconvened in the fall, the members
published their own appreciation in the newspaper and presented a
copy to his widow. Lida herself wrote a respectful memorial for Ogden College's fall bulletin and yearbook. While she, too, emphasized
the Major's unswerving devotion to his profession and found his lasting monument in the training and achievements of his students, she
reminded his admirers that this man who "plodded patiently" to his

classroom year after year had expected to become a great lawyer and that his choice to teach had rested on a foundation of "bitter and life-long self-denial." Had he been able to read his own eulogy, the Major might have shrunk from the aura of defeat surrounding this grim characterization. He had, after all, answered the call of duty, overcome thwarted ambition, given his talent to a noble cause, and by earning a place in the hearts of his students, lengthened his usefulness by the term of their lives. Like that of the authors she had once praised for channeling their creativity into the service of reform, he might have asked his wife, was his not "immortality enough"?[2]

For Lida, nevertheless, the familiar quarrel between duty and ambition resurfaced in the months following the Major's death. Her first obligation was to carry out the terms of his will, which, with the exception of some Confederate mementoes bequeathed to his sons, generally allowed her to divide his personal possessions among the children as she saw fit. Within three weeks of the funeral, she had devoted five long days to dismantling his vast book collection, "separating the wheat from the chaff and getting rid of the latter" while retaining some volumes for herself, the children, and the Major's friends. She asked both Otto Rothert and Francis Obenchain's daughter Jeannette, a teacher at the University of Chicago, to help her obtain valuations for the rare items, which she planned to sell on the children's behalf. Adding urgency to the divestiture of these material encumbrances was Lida's anticipation of a prolonged, perhaps even permanent, stay with Margery, whose health was now recognizably unsound. As she prepared to surrender to the "sin of unselfishness" and defer all immediate plans for herself—"God only knows when I will be able to do any writing," she moaned to Rothert—she held fast to the belief that a new and productive phase of life was still within her grasp. "I am full of hope and courage," she continued, "and feel sure I can do my best work in the next few years, if fate will only give me half a chance. Be glad you are not a woman."[3]

Almost overlooked in Lida's distribution of the Major's books was the publication of her own, *Clover and Blue Grass,* in the third week of September 1916. Having objected unsuccessfully to one of the stories as "not in harmony" with the rest of the contents and postponed publication for several months after the target date of spring 1916, Little, Brown had finally issued the book, dedicated to young Val Win-

ston and to Edward's four-year-old daughter Martha Calvert, with a
suitably picturesque cover and frontispiece but otherwise devoid of
illustrations. Although reviewers found its single "Aunt Jane" story
sufficient to recommend the volume to Eliza Calvert Hall's public,
Clover and Blue Grass made only one appearance on *Bookman's* list
of most popular new releases.[4]

Its five other chapters, nevertheless, were some of Lida's best.
The Land of Long Ago had been a companion volume to *Aunt Jane of
Kentucky,* but *Clover and Blue Grass,* despite its idyllic-sounding title,
was more the sequel of *To Love and to Cherish.* As that book's ending
foretold, maintaining the traditional feminine connection to home, nature, family, and memory had now become complicated by new defini-
tions of womanhood. For the variously situated women of *Clover and
Blue Grass,* this fact of modernity constitutes both a stepping-stone
and a millstone, a source of female progress and of defeat.

One of the stories, in fact, returned to Reuben and Mary Ward's
dilemma, only to place it in the hands of another couple who work
in partnership to effect a different outcome. In "One Taste of the
Old Time," David Maynor's luck as an inventor has taken him and
his wife Sarah from a small cottage in a nearby mill district to a well-
appointed brick house in town. Sarah, however, is miserable. As a cottage dweller, she remembers, "I'd get up in the morning, and I knew
just exactly what I'd have to do, and I knew I could do whatever I had
to do." In her new home, she feels useless and out of place—socially
inadequate, estranged from her old friends, and intimidated by her
two servants.

Her husband, Sarah discovers, is also dismayed at the peculiar
burdens of wealth. Knowing that they cannot reverse course—their
old cottage, in fact, is about to be torn down by its new owner—David
first tries an analytical approach, suggesting that they seek out other
friends and servants, but Sarah's emotional refusal quickly inspires
another plan. He buys the lumber of their demolished cottage, recon-
structs it near its old location, restores its plain furnishings and small
garden, and takes Sarah there. Husband and wife spend a peaceful
week keeping house for themselves, renewing old friendships, and
enjoying the "paradise of the worker."

When David tells Sarah that they must return to town so that he
can prepare for a business trip, he is surprised to find her calm and

even cheerful at the prospect. Before long, she quietly claims dominion over the servants, takes up the duty of social calls, and joins the
local women's club in order to seek legislation to improve the conditions of the mill workers in her old neighborhood. The critical moment in her transformation comes when, anticipating David's return
from his trip, she buys commercially cultivated roses to adorn both
the house and herself rather than the simple blossoms she once would
have plucked from a backyard garden. Their week spent away from
home, Sarah explains to her admiring husband, has shown her that
having fulfilled the duties of poverty, they must now assume the duties of wealth. Though she is pleased to keep their restored cottage,
she hints strongly that another visit will not be necessary.

Like Sarah, the wife in "Mary Crawford's Chart" has a generous
and empathetic husband to support her when technical innovation,
in the form of a dressmaker's chart bought from a "raw city fellow,"
turns her life upside down. The shortage of such men both in and
outside fiction, however, does not deter the middle-aged spinster in
"Old Mahogany." Samantha Mayfield becomes the sole survivor in
a house filled with her mother's ancestral collection of china, silver,
and mahogany furniture but takes no comfort in this material and
psychological inheritance.[5] Instead, she briskly sells almost all of the
home's furnishings and junk, even the roots from its ancient garden,
to a wealthy, fashion-conscious neighbor for whom the old, emptied
of its associations with past owners, becomes new again. "I'm not attached to my old furniture; it's been attached to me," Samantha assures her delighted purchaser. She uses some of the money to buy
modern yellow oak furniture, which, along with the "new-fashioned"
flowers in her garden, symbolizes her fresh start in life. With the
rest of the proceeds, she plans to travel, for she is "jest as tired of
Goshen"—its old roads, fences, farms, "yes, and the old people,
too"—as she had been of her old mahogany; and, she declares, she
will marry "if I should happen to find a man that'd match up with
my new furniture."

While Samantha is able to separate her identity from a home that
has become barren and obsolete, the principal character of "Millstones
and Stumbling-Blocks" cannot. As a result, in Lida's most heartbreaking tale of female sacrifice, Margaret Williams and her home face ex-
tinction together. Margaret discovers that her daughter Anna Belle

and her suitor Henry are pining away in their mothers' houses rather
than marry and leave the two widows alone. The realization quickly
sends her on a visit to Henry's mother, Mrs. Martin. Their children
would deny it, Margaret tells her, but "we're stumblin'-blocks in their
way, and they're waitin' for us to die." She proposes to move in with
Mrs. Martin and deed her own house to Anna Belle and Henry, who
can then marry in the knowledge that their mothers will have companionship. Convinced that she too must "get out of the way" of her
child's happiness, Henry's mother agrees.

Without even feigning protest, Henry and Anna Belle accept
Margaret's gift. After the wedding, the two mothers sit on the porch
of their shared house, somewhat bewildered by the consequences of
their self-abnegation. Their new arrangement is polite but awkward,
and their resolution never to quarrel for fear of upsetting the children suggests that it will remain so. Later, in her room for the night,
Margaret weeps in despair, overcome by the sight of her most treasured family furniture in this unfamiliar setting and a strange yard
outside her window. With the "hand of Change . . . tearing at every
root and tendril" of her heart, she can only hope for strength in her
daughter's parting words: "You are the very best mother in the whole
wide world."

While Margaret becomes the best mother at the precise moment her realm is extinguished, in the other stories of *Clover and
Blue Grass* the maternal state is already diminished or nonexistent:
Sarah Maynor is childless, Mary Crawford has only stepchildren, and
Samantha Mayfield has as little need for babies as she has for the
old cradle she sells her neighbor. Symbolic of their displaced fertility
is the women's attenuated relationship to nature: Margaret loses her
home's comfortably overgrown yard, Mary Crawford lies exhausted
in the middle of a bountiful spring day, and for Sarah and Samantha
flowers become commodities, as consciously uprooted as their owners. Where indeed among these characters, who are both reformed
and deformed by progress, is the "natural" woman? Whatever prospects she faces, each has exchanged a powerful archetype of femininity for something far less determinate. The stage has been set for
the requiem that is *Clover and Blue Grass*'s final chapter—probably
the one that Little, Brown found not in harmony with the others but
which Lida, in any event, called her "very best story."[6]

The heroine of "One Day in Spring" is neither an old woman whom time has bypassed nor a wife whose traditional home is being transformed by modernity; rather, she is a throwback to the sentimental feminism that dominated the literature of Lida's childhood: young, innocent, and apparently docile, she nonetheless harbors an innate superiority capable of eclipsing the power of every man around her.[7] Miranda Crawford, a Kentucky farm girl, helps her mother keep house for her father and younger brothers. In a scene reminiscent of one of Lida's Ivory soap poems, she sits in a dingy bedroom, homesick—that is, sick of home—a bucket and soap by her side, wondering where to begin her share of the spring cleaning. Suddenly, into the open window come the tidings of the new season: a fresh breeze, lambs bleating in the distance, greenery everywhere. These perceptions send her into an Aunt Jane–like "flash of consciousness": "The woods in spring," she whispers to herself, instinctively answering their call.

Bolting past her startled mother and out of the house, Miranda spends the day wandering through forest and pasture, on a journey back through her childhood (in an echo of "The Gardens of Memory," she associates picking wildflowers with her father's company) to her primal home in the bosom of the "Great Mother." The goddess Nature, indeed, becomes the object of her worship; inspired by the beauty around her to sing a hymn to the afterworld's "land of pure delight," she concedes the pagan view that such a paradise lies right before her in the springtime woods. Late that afternoon, finding a small clearing—"a sort of fairy ring"—she lies down to rest under a tree, a bunch of violets clasped in her hand.

Before long, a man striding through the woods encounters her sleeping form. His consternation quickly turns to embarrassment when he senses that he has walked into a setting no less intimate than her bedroom. Retreating a respectful distance, he appoints himself a secret sentry but also becomes something of a voyeur to this mysterious union of nature and the feminine. He keeps watch for other intruders until Miranda wakes, then follows her at a distance until she is almost home. Returning to the spot where she slept, he pockets the withered violets that prove he has not been dreaming.

Once home, Miranda cheerfully resumes her duties, but her experience of the "great, deep peace of the woods" has given her an au-

thority that belies her servile status. She makes amends to her weary
mother by cooking dinner and promising to start her cleaning chores
the next day, and rekindles the affection of her equally weary father by
securing his promise to walk with her in the woods as they had when
she was a child. Without even knowing it, she has also pacified the
man who saw her sleeping and who sits awake that night, still pondering his strange encounter "face to face with the True Romance."

Though Lida denied to John Wilson Townsend that she had ever
addressed the topics of "spring" or "Kentucky" in verse, "One Day
in Spring" was perhaps her most deliberate attempt to infuse her
prose with the poetic quality that she believed had given *Aunt Jane
of Kentucky* its lasting appeal. The "gift of rhythm and rhyme" itself
had largely deserted her in recent years, but Lida, like her old editor
Richard Watson Gilder, continued to regard poetry, with its appeal
to the soul rather than the intellect and its concern with truth rather
than facts, as the province of the genuine artist. Since the success of
"Sally Ann's Experience" she had periodically declared her intention
to publish her own poems in book form even though the rewards,
as other Kentuckians had learned, were severely limited. When he
died, her friend Robert Burns Wilson was struggling to support a wife
and daughter on a small literary income, and Lida herself would purchase one of his paintings to help pay his funeral expenses. The fate
of Madison Cawein two years earlier was no less discouraging. While
the Louisville native had earned international acclaim for his nature
poetry, its outdated mythological and spiritualist content never engaged more than a small circle of readers, and at the time of his death
Cawein was receiving private relief from the Authors Club of New
York. Lida nevertheless defended Cawein's "thoroughly orthodox
taste," which "could not tolerate free verse or any of the other modern absurdities that masquerade under the name of poetry." Although
Americans' post–Civil War fascination for communing with the dead
had long ago fallen out of fashion, she also took seriously the claim
that he had written his poems "under spirit influence."[8]

If Lida looked to tradition to set the standard for poets, she was
less conservative in the matter of freedom for the novelist. Late in
1916 she joined other members of the Authors' League of America in
signing the Dreiser Protest, a campaign led by that scourge of Puri-
tanism, H. L. Mencken, against the censorship of Theodore Dreiser's

novel *The Genius*. Lida also sent Mencken a slightly revised version of an essay she had written years earlier deploring "Comstockery," the overreaching crusade against obscenity sanctioned by federal law since 1873 under pressure from Anthony Comstock's New York Society for the Suppression of Vice. Although Mencken declined to publish it because the books she cited had by then sunk into obscurity, he praised the quality of Lida's argument and suggested that she forward the essay to Dreiser himself. She promptly did so but, like her old poems, believed that it could still be published as part of a collection and accordingly asked Dreiser to return it after he had read it.[9]

Among the material enjoined by the Comstock Law as obscene was literature on contraception and abortion, a prohibition that Lida would have found especially objectionable, given her complaints about the effect of constant childbearing on a woman's welfare. The "main p'int," Aunt Jane had told her granddaughter's friends, was "the way you love your children, not how many children you have. And further than that," she had continued, "there's such a thing as a woman havin' so many children that she hasn't got time to be a mother, but that's a p'int that men don't consider." In October 1916, when Cecil left for Dallas to bring back Margery and little Val for a visit, Lida's concern that such a fate awaited her oldest daughter must have been palpable, for Margery, still unwell, was now pregnant again.[10]

Even as the prospect of another grandchild accelerated Lida's plan to go to Texas, Cecil was also giving her mother little reason to remain in Kentucky; by April 1917 she and Glenn had decided to marry the following October and settle in Nashville. Lida's first obligation was to tend to Margery, but she now envisioned herself making two new homes, one near each of her daughters. Consequently, before leaving for Texas in early May 1917 to await the delivery of Margery's baby, Lida put her Chestnut Street house up for sale. "I leave with a heavy heart," she confessed to Otto Rothert, "but the change is inevitable."[11]

Arriving in Dallas to find its amenities intact—"I never saw anything more beautiful than the wild-flowers of Texas," she exclaimed to her mother—Lida quickly realized that the future would remain uncertain. With the United States' entry into World War I the previous month, Glenn had volunteered for duty with the Army Medical Corps, and in anticipation of his leaving for Europe he and Cecil had moved their wedding date up to June. Not only would Lida be unable to attend, she watched as both of her sons, Alex at twenty-eight and Tom at twenty-five, sought to follow Glenn into military service. "All my plans are overturned and I have ceased to make plans. I have no idea where I shall be this time next year," Lida complained to her mother. Only a month after departing, her thoughts returned to Kentucky and to her beloved garden from which, she hoped, she could at least obtain some flowers for transplant to Texas. "Maybe," she even speculated, "I shall some day drift back to Bowling Green and take possession of my old home."[12]

Margery's daughter, also named Margery, was born on June 8, 1917. When the nurse left after two weeks, Lida inherited her duties along with those of keeping house, supervising the cook, and making sure that little Val, a lively boy almost three years old, did not manhandle his baby sister or learn too many "ugly tricks" from the cook's six-year-old son. Although she doubted that Margery would cope without her, the unsettled living conditions in a house with an infant left Lida anticipating Glenn's posting overseas, after which she could join Cecil and find some time for writing. Only eight days after the birth of "little Margery," Cecil and Glenn had married in Bowling Green at the home of one of Lida's neighbors but had then moved to Washington, D.C., where Glenn was receiving additional medical training. When word finally came in September that he would be leaving for England, Lida boarded a train for the long ride northeast.[13]

"My blessed mother, came to us last night!" Cecil notified her aunt Josephine on September 25. They had stayed awake talking until early morning, and Cecil was arranging for a drive that day along the Potomac River. The wartime conditions that had swelled the population and prices of Washington had not dampened her enthusiasm for the city. "This is such a lovely place to write and rest," she declared, and her intention, largely realized, was to keep "Mama" there all winter. For her part, Lida was flattered by a series of callers, including a request for a sitting from Harris and Ewing, the capital's largest photographic news service, and was impressed by the good salaries she saw paid to women. In early December, when almost six hundred delegates arrived for the NAWSA's annual convention, she even attended the opening reception at the New Willard Hotel in an unsuccessful attempt to find Laura Clay. She remained torn, however, between her duty to two daughters. Margery reported that she was well, Lida assured her mother, "but I know she needs me." If, on the other hand, Cecil accepted Glenn's invitation to travel to England when conditions were safer, she would have to accompany her.[14]

Shortly before returning to Texas early in 1918, Lida assured Otto Rothert that while she had written virtually nothing since leaving Kentucky, she had gathered some material in anticipation of doing what she believed would be her best work. Unfortunately, Dallas offered even more distractions than Washington: a harsh winter had left Margery's children sick, and both she and Lida required treatment for dental problems. Little Margery, who so closely resembled her grandmother that her mother called her "Lida Calvert," was clever and sweet, but little Val was as disobedient as he was delightful, tormenting his sister by knocking her down and his grandmother by leaning over her table and singing as she tried to write. "We *must* get a nurse," Lida moaned to Josie, lamenting the servant problem in general and the shortcomings of their current domestic in particular. She managed, nevertheless, to find some recreation enjoying Margery's garden, picking wildflowers in the woods, or accompanying Tom on drives in the country, and was even able to spend a few days with Alex while he awaited his embarkation orders. After some delay in obtaining an assignment, Tom finally entered San Antonio's Camp Travis in June 1918. Alex, having already served a year, was happy in the army; he had found what he wanted, Lida conceded, even though "it is not what I want." She nevertheless pronounced both sons "fine boys"—two of her "four remarkable children"—and when Alex was promoted to his father's rank Lida sent Josie the news of "another Major Obenchain."[15]

Besides helping Margery and monitoring Cecil for signs of neediness, Lida was also concerned about her aging mother. Commiserating with her sisters over eighty-nine-year-old Margaret's frailty, she tried from a distance to contribute to her care by sending clothing and offering to pay for a nurse. When Maggie wrote of a setback, Lida was quick to pronounce it her final illness and privately caution that the difficulties of wartime train travel would prevent her from attending the funeral. Margaret, however, proved resilient. A few months later she had resumed her sewing, turning the scraps Lida sent from Tom's old neckties into pincushions; the formidable seamstress and quilter,

in fact, remained sufficiently discriminating about some of the garments that came from her oldest daughter for Lida to conclude that
nothing pleased her. A letter of Margery's nevertheless spoke to the
affection of her Texas kin for the Calvert family matriarch. "Mama
worries all the time because she is not there," Margery confided. A
photograph of the baby was on the way, she promised, together with
Margery's hope that "Greatma" would see the resemblance to both
Lida and the correspondent, who signed herself "Your loving Little
Lamb."[16]

During Lida's stay with Cecil in Washington, Margery had asked
for "Double Muscadine Hulls," the brown coverlet given to her mother by William Wade, in order to make a portière. Thanks to the ten-
ant who now occupied her still-unsold house, Lida had been able to
delay disposition of the rest of its furnishings, but fulfilling Margery's
request recalled the tedious choices she had made concerning the
Major's estate and to which she would have to subject her own belongings: separating the wheat from the chaff and disposing of the
latter. Prominent in the former category were her unpublished manuscripts and essays, currently stored in an old trunk at the house. Anxious to regain possession of these papers, Lida instructed Josie to send
them to Dallas. She indicated that the disposition of her books would
require more thought but that she intended to sell her furniture after
Cecil had taken what she wanted.[17] Given that the war had suspended
Cecil's plans as well as her own, this process promised to be far less
brisk than Samantha's cheerful divestiture in "Old Mahogany."

Even if Lida could not yet visualize her permanent home with
certainty, she was fortunate to be a resident of Texas when the legislature approved a bill granting women the right to vote in primary
elections. She had likely been following developments in the state
since her return early in 1918, when suffragists gained a place on the
agenda of a special legislative session called to consider prohibition.
The primary suffrage bill passed easily on March 26 and became law
ninety days later, sending Lida and 386,000 other women to register
in the few weeks preceding the July election. After voting, she predicted confidently to Maggie and Josie that the next legislature would
approve full suffrage.[18]

At the time Lida cast her ballot, the barriers for all American
women were steadily falling. A majority of states had enacted at least

some form of suffrage, and in fifteen of them women and men had equal access to the vote. Since 1916, Carrie Chapman Catt had continued the NAWSA's support for these state measures as part of a strategy to create favorable conditions for ratifying a federal constitutional amendment.[19] On January 10, 1918, her plan had come nearer to its final test when, with President Woodrow Wilson's blessing and by exactly the two-thirds vote required, the U.S. House of Representatives approved the Susan B. Anthony amendment.

The House vote had important consequences for the KERA. At Mrs. Catt's request, the board agreed to abandon its plan for another major, and possibly successful, state campaign while Senate confirmation of the Anthony amendment was pending. Firmly opposed to the board's decision was Laura Clay. Although she was, at age sixty-nine, the acknowledged icon of the Kentucky movement, Laura had unsettled many in the KERA with her hardening conviction that the only appropriate path to the vote was through state rather than federal action. She grew even more resentful over the lost opportunities of 1918 after the Kentucky General Assembly adjourned free of suffragist pressure, and on October 1, the U.S. Senate rejected the Anthony amendment.[20]

Like many other suffragists, nevertheless, Laura busied herself with fund-raising and food conservation measures as part of the war effort, and in Texas Lida also searched for ways to contribute that would not interfere with the care of her grandchildren. The Authors' League finally provided her with an opportunity when, in conjunction with a YMCA fund drive, she was commissioned to write a series of newspaper features on the association's work ministering to soldiers in training at nearby Camp Dick and Love Field. Uniquely, Lida's first attempt at wartime journalism achieved wide circulation, for the articles appeared in the same edition of the *Dallas Daily Times-Herald* that announced the Armistice; even the author had difficulty obtaining a copy. Although she expected that the truce would disappoint her oldest son, who had been eager to reach the front, the safe return of Alex along with two other family members recently landed in France, her brother Edward and Cecil's husband Glenn, was now assured.[21]

The war's end also presented the possibility of Lida's return to Washington and to the Library of Congress, which she regarded as a likely place to achieve some of her literary goals. Another long-delayed

ambition was to stop in Bowling Green to begin settling her outstanding affairs: in addition to the house and her personal effects left
behind, she still owned one and one-quarter acres of vacant land, inherited from the Major, in the block south of her Chestnut Street
property. Newspapers forwarded by Maggie and Josie detailing the
prospects for oil drilling in the county had given her some hope that
she could sell on favorable terms. The growth of the Texas economy,
however, also convinced her that the Major, who had liquidated his
Dallas real estate in the 1870s to reinvest in Bowling Green, had fool-
ishly given up the chance to be a millionaire.[22]

In January 1919 Lida sold her Chestnut Street home to the neighbor who had hosted Cecil's wedding, but once more she had to put
aside her travel plans. Forced to instruct Maggie and Josie from Texas on the relocation of her books, manuscripts, furniture, and other
belongings before the new owner took possession, she candidly as-
sessed the other consequences of her status as a live-in grandmother.
"For the last two years I have done little except nurse sick people
and babies," she reported to her mother peevishly, "& I think I'll get
a trained nurse's outfit and wear it the rest of my life." Although she
took delight in both children's cleverness even as little Val's misdeeds
regularly attracted a "good switching," Margery's drift in and out of
illness and the high turnover of household servants had created awkward bonds, especially with the youngest. Little Margery "thinks I am
her mother," Lida mourned to Josie, "and I don't know how I'll ever
get away from her."[23]

Late in April, with Margery's husband, Val, away on business and
the children recovering from influenza, Lida began a difficult letter to
Josie. "Don't read this to mother," she wrote across the top. Five weeks
earlier, Margery had entered a sanatorium in Kerrville, three hundred
miles away, after being diagnosed with tuberculosis in both lungs. Lida
wanted nothing about her daughter's condition to be communicated
to the curious in Bowling Green except for the doctors' opinion that
recovery was certain. Bearing sole responsibility for the house and
children during Val's five-day business trip had overwhelmed her, but
she was determined to stand in Margery's place until she recovered.
Lida's frame of mind was similar to that which she had adopted when
the Major's illness was diagnosed; while prepared to direct her sisters
and Cecil regarding the storage, delivery, or sale of her possessions in

Bowling Green, she planned to give little time to anything else except her current domestic obligations.[24]

As the months passed, Val spent even more time traveling, leaving his mother-in-law in charge of his small son and daughter. While she continued to take pride in her ability to withstand the strain of caregiving, Lida was now more conscious of having been thwarted by fate. "I seem to have started life all over again," she observed to her mother, "raising children and keeping house, when I thought I was through with such work forever."[25] One aspect of the past, nevertheless, would not be prolonged. Just as the events of 1919 were reacquainting Lida with woman's perpetual duties, they were also extracting from her the thorn of woman's perpetual disfranchisement—and offering her a chance, at sixty-three, to tell new stories.

15

Grandmother's Debut

We need some nearer, sweeter lure than heaven to keep our steps
from flagging on the long march from cradle to grave.
> —Eliza Calvert Hall, "The Horoscope"

EVEN AS SHE COMPLAINED that Margery's children were a
"stumbling block" to her work, Lida had notified her sisters in July
1918 of her first new fiction since *Clover and Blue Grass*. "I shall
have a little story in the *Woman's Home Companion*," she announced,
"but I don't know just when." Given its subject matter, the editors
had probably decided to delay publication until actual events, including a Senate vote on the Anthony amendment, could supply a happy
ending for its main character. "Grandmother's Début," nevertheless,
stood on its own as Lida's tribute to the courage and humanity of the
veteran suffragist.[1]

The story opens with Rachel Morrow's decision to accompany
her two granddaughters to the national suffrage convention in Washington. Though she is long retired, Rachel's work "doing yeoman
service for the Cause under Susan B. Anthony" has left her physically and mentally agile. She also remains strong-minded in her disdain of fashion, but grudgingly allows her granddaughters to fit her
with an evening gown and shoes, style her hair, and apply "wicked
rouge" and "frivolous powder" in preparation for the convention's
opening reception. "Grandmother is going to be a débutante," cries
the more insistent of the two girls, and the Washington event will be
"her coming-out party."

Entering the receiving line at the New Willard Hotel, Rachel is soon secretly thrilled, not only by the compliments given her new look but by the respect she draws as one who has endured "the heat and burden of the day when woman suffrage was distinctly unpopular." She grows more tolerant of the other extravagantly dressed women around her when she realizes that having proven the old theory that "suffrage would never succeed until it became fashionable," they are the heralds of victory.

Before long, Rachel is pleasantly reunited with a childhood sweetheart, Albert Everett, now a senator and known to be undecided on the pending suffrage amendment. Anxious to talk over old times, the two retreat to a corner where, as the sole object of Albert's attention, Rachel drinks in the admiration that her upright but emotionally ungenerous husband had long withheld; a suffragist, after all, is still a woman, and "every woman is at heart a girl." Only when Rachel is back in her hotel room for the night, dreamily contemplating her beautiful garments and the wave in her hair, does the thought strike her. "Good gracious!" she whispers to herself. "I clear forgot to ask Albert how he stood on the Federal Amendment!"

Together with two elegant illustrations by Alice Barber Stephens, one of the country's best-known book and magazine artists, "Grandmother's Début" appeared in the *Woman's Home Companion* only after Congress had provided the long-awaited breakthrough. The year 1919 had begun, on February 10, with another Senate defeat of the Anthony amendment, but on May 21 the House again passed it, and on June 4 the Senate finally concurred with a margin of two votes beyond the necessary two-thirds majority. Predicting quick ratification of the amendment in twenty-eight states where women already enjoyed partial or full suffrage, supporters began their campaigns to reach the required total of thirty-six.[2]

Ironically, neither Lida nor Laura Clay was disposed to celebrate this historic achievement. The day after the Senate vote, as Lida posted the letter to her mother in which she mourned her resumption of housekeeping and childrearing, Laura wrote to Madge Breckinridge, who had returned to the presidency of the KERA. Now convinced that the federal amendment was an unconscionable encroachment on the sovereignty of the states and opposed to the KERA's commitment to ratification, Laura dramatically severed her thirty-year-long ties to the organization. As most of her colleagues looked on in dismay, she and a few sympathizers formed the Citizens' Committee for a State Suffrage Amendment and declared war against the federally mandated enfranchisement of women.[3]

On June 28, 1919, when Texas became the ninth (and first southern) state to ratify the Anthony amendment, Lida was absorbed in family matters. Both sons had returned to civilian work, Alex at the State Highway Commission and Tom in the oil business, and Cecil and Glenn were in search of housing in Nashville. Most significantly, Margery had been released from the sanatorium five days earlier and settled at home in a curtained, second-floor sunroom to complete her recovery. As her period of bed rest dragged on well beyond the prescribed three months, Lida became uneasy. Watching in vain for any signs of permanent improvement that would allow little Margery and Val to reestablish some rapport with their mother, she confided again to Josie that the possibility of her own withdrawal was remote. "I don't see how I'll ever get away from these two children," she observed sadly. "They will not let me get out of their sight, and I don't see how Margery will ever be able to manage them alone."[4]

"Margery sick in bed cannot come love and sympathy Lida" read the telegram delivered to Josie on February 11, 1920. It was Lida's sixty-fourth birthday, and a telegram of congratulations from Cecil and Glenn had been followed an hour later by another bringing word of her mother's death. Lida had reacted stoically to the Major's passing, but this loss brought tears and a consoling hug from little Margery. Margaret Younglove Calvert had just passed her ninety-first birthday, and her fortitude had buoyed her oldest daughter until the end. "She is wonderful," Lida had written Josie the previous fall, asking, in the season when county fairs were opening across the state, if her mother's needlework had taken a premium. She had recently sent some freshly picked pecans and a small check for Christmas, and now sent Josie another check to help with the funeral expenses.[5]

Whatever her actual resemblance to Aunt Jane, in death Margaret Younglove of Johnstown, New York, acquired some of the attributes of the plain old woman of Kentucky. A memorial written for the local newspaper praised her "grace and simple dignity" as representative of a past age. Edward's young daughter Martha always associated her with flowers, and years later, greeting the blossoms of another Texas spring, Lida would be reminded of her mother's love for coral honey-suckles. Ed's wife Lucinda remembered Margaret in her favorite chair, with a smile on her face and a cheerful word for everyone. Although Lucinda's fondness for sitting with her suggested that her conversation and stories as well as her disposition had a beneficial effect on others, ultimately too much of Margaret's own story of strength and survival had remained untold, smothered in that cloak of anonymity so long deemed appropriate for her sex. Mrs. Thomas C. Calvert, the newspaper judged with approval, had "passed unobserved" through ninety-one years, her life like "the soft flowing of gentle streams in far-off meadows," its "placid current" creating no stir.[6] This public tribute was, to borrow a phrase of Aunt Jane's, "a curious sort of a monument—'bout as perishable as the sweepin' and scrubbin' and mendin'" that encumbered women's desire to leave something permanent behind. What eventually served Margaret Calvert's memory best, in fact, was Aunt Jane's own humble recipe for immortality:

> "Some folks can build churches and schools and hospitals to keep folks in mind of 'em, but all the work I've got to leave behind me is jest these quilts, and sometimes, when I'm settin' here, workin' with my caliker and gingham pieces, I'll finish off a block, and I laugh and say to myself, 'Well, here's another stone for the monument.'"[7]

Not long after the telegram bearing news of her mother's death, Lida received a document marking the end of another chapter in her life. With a federal suffrage amendment close to becoming the law of the land, the NAWSA had undertaken to honor the presidents of state organizations and other outstanding women who had labored for the ballot. The arrival of her Distinguished Service Certificate turned Lida's thoughts back to Kentucky and to the debt she owed her co-workers. As early as 1911, when Laura Clay was urging her to attend the state and national conventions in Louisville, she had reflected upon the role the KERA had played in her accomplishments. That year, readers had purchased some twelve thousand copies of the hardcover edition of *Sally Ann's Experience*, and Laura had been touched when Lida sent her an autographed copy. "But for my work in the Ky. E.R.A.," she had acknowledged graciously, "Sally Ann's Experience

would never have been written, [and] if Sally Ann's Experience had
never been written, I would never have been the author of *Aunt Jane
of Kentucky*, so my share of literary fame and fortune rest [*sic*] on my
belief in woman suffrage." Almost nine years later, wishing to share
credit for the NAWSA certificate, Lida again hailed Laura's role in
singlehandedly "blazing the suffrage trail through the wilderness of
Kentucky." Both Laura and Eugenia Farmer, she recalled, had first
set her feet on the "path of duty," then kept her "coward soul" from
leading her astray at a time when the cause was distinctly unfashion-
able.[8]

Lida also referred, albeit indirectly, to Laura's stubborn rejection
of the final act in the suffrage drama. Denying charges of racism and
excessive legalism, Laura had waged a desperate campaign to derail
the KERA and revive a state suffrage bill, but she had stopped just
short of opposing her own enfranchisement when, on January 6, 1920,
the Kentucky General Assembly ratified the Anthony amendment.
Lida, too, professed to be unhappy with the manner in which the
women of Texas had gained the ballot. After granting the vote in primary elections, the legislature had approved a suffrage amendment
to the state constitution, but it had been defeated in a referendum.
"Then the legislature set aside the will of the voters," Lida complained
to Laura, "by ratifying the Federal Amendment. I don't like to get a
right thing in the wrong way."[9]

Laura's response was heartfelt, both in her return of Lida's compliments—"Without a receptive spirit on your part, Mrs. Farmer and I
might have labored in vain"—and in her gratitude for Lida's apparent
disapproval of the way in which suffrage, in Laura's words, was "being
pushed" by "that hideous Anthony amendment." Raising the banner
of states' rights, however, was probably less important to the author
of "Grandmother's Début" than propitiating a woman she respected
as the greatest of Kentucky suffragists, one whose faith and laughter,
she remembered, could "blow my doubts and fears away." Lida made
clear, in fact, that she had no time to rejoin any branch of the struggle;
seeming to agree with Laura that the federal amendment was politi-
cally tainted, she had promised Ellis Meredith, the Colorado suffragist and Democratic Party organizer, that she would editorialize against
women using their votes to reward Republicans but had not been able
to accomplish even that.[10]

More distressing for Lida than the use of party politics to gain
justice for women was the likelihood that this new era would give her
no greater peace of mind than she had possessed as a young mother
without political or legal rights. Although her own health was good,
Margery's, she now believed, would never be fully restored. Adding to
her sense of uncertainty was Cecil and Glenn's departure from Nashville for Toledo, Ohio, where their marriage was beginning to founder.
"The world seems to me topsy-turvy now," Lida reflected to Laura.
Observing that the creator of optimistic Aunt Jane had never been an
optimist herself, she was more doubtful than ever that life's "jumble
o' quilt pieces" would someday resolve itself. "I sometimes think,"
she ventured gloomily, "that we are at the end of this era and there is
nothing but chaos and black night beyond."[11]

Though she still pined for Kentucky and its people, after her
mother's death Lida renewed her efforts to sever her material ties to
Bowling Green. She and Edward deeded their interest in Margaret's
home to Maggie and Josie, and she instructed Josie to continue disposing of her furniture. When oil drilling began in earnest that spring
and ignited a minor real estate boom, Lida was also tantalized by the
prospect of selling the land she still owned near her former home
and reinvesting the money in Texas. She was determined, however,
to optimize her timing and not do "a right thing in the wrong way"; if
she could find a buyer who would undertake to construct an attractive
house on part of the one-and-one-quarter-acre parcel, she calculated,
the rest could be broken up and sold as building lots for enhanced
prices.[12]

Enlisting a local real estate firm to solicit offers, Lida disqualified speculators and transients as purchasers and demanded to know
both the identities and intentions of all interested parties. She asked
Josie to provide her with more detailed intelligence, including any
hint of "crooked dealings" on the part of the realtors themselves.
Although Josie was privately convinced that hurried sales would be
unwise because future improvements in sewage and water systems
would enhance the land's value, she loyally attempted to guard her sister's interests through long-distance and often fruitless negotiations.
When an agreement to sell two lots to a member of the Underwood
family was about to collapse, Lida finally dispatched Tom to Bowling Green with a power of attorney to complete the transaction. Lida

both praised and paid Josie for her business aptitude, but their experience revived the sisters' distasteful memories of an earlier time. "It seems to come natural to men to do dishonest things," Lida declared. "We are not in a position, however, to say anything about dishonesty when we remember what our own father did."[13]

In her effort to make sense of a topsy-turvy world, particularly one over which illness was now casting a permanent shadow, Lida made the Calvert men the villains of another narrative. When doctors first diagnosed Margery's tuberculosis, she wrote Josie, they determined that it had been incubating for three years; a year later, she told Laura Clay that Margery had had the disease her entire life. Although she was not yet willing to surrender Margery's children to the same diagnosis, their sickliness only confirmed Lida's sense that a conspiracy of heredity was to blame. She outlined this theory to Edward's wife, probably in response to Lucinda's condolences for her mother's death. Combining the subjects of tuberculosis treatment and family history, she claimed that before dying of the disease, her grandfather Samuel Calvert had infected his entire family, and her father, Thomas, had in turn infected his. Edward was tempted to admonish her but ultimately confided his irritation only to Maggie. "Apparently Lida's old mania for jumping at conclusions about diseases & medical treatments grows with age," he observed from his latest military posting at Fort Robinson, Nebraska. "I can not see how a person of ordinary intelligence could write thus, thinking it would serve any good purpose." Given that over the years Ed had been far less solicitous of her and Josie than Lida, Maggie was not as likely to find fault with her older sister; nevertheless, advancing age would only increase Lida's enthusiasm for doctoring her loved ones.[14]

When Tennessee's ratification on August 18, 1920—only the fourth by a southern state—ensured that the Anthony amendment would become the Nineteenth Amendment to the U.S. Constitution, Lida seemed barely to notice. In the months afterward, she was preoccupied with the usual cares: buyers for her remaining lots were scarce, Margery lingered in her sickroom, and like her sisters, Lida experienced the burden of storing family possessions after Alex removed himself from the house but left his "plunder" behind. She longed to send for the rest of her books from Bowling Green and attend to the delayed matter of a stone for the Major's grave, but heaviest on her mind was a crisis that, like Margery's illness, threatened to fuel gossip in her hometown. That summer, she had begun urging Cecil to leave Glenn, whose war service, Lida believed, had caused him to become mentally unstable and a threat to her safety. When Glenn himself abandoned Cecil early in 1921, Lida joined her in Toledo, where together they feared the possibility that he would commit suicide. Although Cecil was initially reluctant, Lida convinced her to come to Dallas, where Alex had offered to share an apartment with her.[15]

Glenn soon returned to Toledo and, finding Cecil gone, instituted divorce proceedings against her on the grounds of abandonment. Lida was miserable over the scandal, but both she and Cecil enjoyed a pleasant respite when, on November 30, 1921, thirty-year-old Tom wed Scotta Goodwin, the well-to-do daughter of a Dallas businessman. Both Scotta and her widowed mother were refined but unpretentious, and Lida was delighted with the marriage. A few minor domestic improvements also helped to sustain her: Tom's moving out of the house made more room for her books and pictures, another of her lots was sold, she had found a capable servant, and Margery, though weak, was holding her own in the manner of her Younglove grandmother.[16]

Responding to a Christmas greeting from one of her suffrage colleagues sixteen months after ratification of the Nineteenth Amendment, Lida reflected only briefly on the cause to which she had dedicated so much of her intellectual energy. In Boston, Alice Stone Blackwell was at work on a biography of her mother, Lucy Stone, but on holidays the former editor of the *Woman's Journal* regularly remembered her talented contributor. "It is you who have 'spread the light' your entire life," Lida demurred in reply to Alice's praise. "My candle burns very dim nowadays and is hidden under the bushel of domestic cares and worries." Her general state of mind, together with an appreciation of the broader tasks ahead, disinclined her to self-congratulation. "Well, the ballot is won," she remarked simply to Alice, "but now comes the work of educating women to use it and getting women into every department of government. May you live long to work for this!" A year later, after new sorrows had dimmed her candle still further, Lida was more certain of the meaning the cause held for her. As much as it had taxed her nerves, making the case for the vote, with all of its unassailable logic and transparent nobility, had given her life a clarity and direction that she had not since enjoyed. "Those were glorious days when we were fighting for justice," she observed. "I believe I enjoy a fight more than the victory that ends the fight."[17]

As Alice would subsequently learn, Lida's relish of women's hard-won gains and her particular fondness for expressing it as a question—"*Have you forgotten?*"—did not cease to fuel her literary ambition. For the time being, however, she was conservative, though by no means dilatory, in her writing. Unsure of how to respond creatively to an unsettled future, she had turned to the recovery of some of her past work. She informed Otto Rothert that after many years of prose composition she had rediscovered the "gift of writing in rhythm and rhyme" and was applying it to some of her old, unfinished poems. Several months earlier, the *Dallas Morning News* had reprinted a twenty-five-year-old poem she had composed after a friend remarked ruefully upon the inner critical voice that so often brought her self-doubt and worry. Asked to meditate on the uses of such an "enemy," Eliza Calvert Hall had vowed in verse to evade "his carping reach" through a life of positive thoughts and unimpeachable acts:

And of my enemy I thus shall make
A beacon light to guide me to my goal,
A faithful guardian of my house of life,
A spur and whip to urge my laggard soul;
And tho' our strife may never have an end,
I yet may call this enemy my friend.[18]

Lida also placed another story in the *Woman's Home Companion* that starkly demonstrated her ability, as she had explained to Laura Clay, to write optimistically of the world while expecting only "chaos and black night" outside her own door. Dating possibly from the "brilliant idea" she had conceived in 1916 after John Wilson Townsend asked her to review a book on astrology, "The Horoscope" again featured the illustrative artwork of Alice Barber Stephens. The story told of an aging farm wife, Amanda McDavid, who applies for a horoscope through the mail. Full of flattery and the usual predictions of new friends and financial windfalls, it concludes: "Keep a stout heart, and all will be well. Your last days will be your best days." The oracle proves to be correct, not because of the influence of the stars but because of the change it brings to Amanda's attitude; preparing herself for the best rather than the worst, she becomes the author of her own good fortune.[19]

Lida soon enlisted Tom's new wife to type some of her poems and completed another short story, which Cecil regarded as one of her best. To her relief, she also sold the last of her Bowling Green lots in February 1922. The proceeds, while adequate, had not justified the Major's investment, and he received another posthumous scolding for these "foolish" purchases even as Lida placed a carefully deliberated order for his gravestone. After concluding, perhaps, that neither she nor the children were likely to join him, she had rejected a family monument in favor of a single stone with a simple inscription: name and dates, followed by "His work remains." She then directed her sisters to send more of the Major's remaining personal effects, particularly his books, to Alex. A bibliophile like his father, Alex had rented a house near Lida's and now had room, she wrote Maggie, for some of the "rubbish" still being stored in Bowling Green.[20]

Lida's quarrel with the material trappings of life had begun with her suffragist's disdain for women who concerned themselves more with fashion and furnishings than with securing their legal and political rights. Her sense of oppression was particularly acute during the "silly excitement" of Christmas, with its obligatory "orgies" of consumption driven to new heights by her grandchildren's demands for "useless toys." The holiday season of 1922, however, promised a much deeper unhappiness, for Margery was eating little and was no longer responding to any treatment. By Christmas Eve her doctor had informed the family that the end was near, and Lida, increasingly distraught over her daughter's suffering, wrote Josie that "we hope he is right."[21]

When thirty-five-year-old Margery Obenchain Winston died on the morning of January 20, 1923, Lida claimed to have been spared the severe grief she had expected. Thankful instead for the release of yet another loved one, she professed a spiritualist faith that Margery remained "alive and well and near me all the time" and vowed to do everything for her grandchildren that their mother would have done. Within a month she was fulfilling her promise and consolidating her

maternal authority, giving some of Margery's clothes to Maggie and
Josie, planting a new garden, teaching the children during the day,
readying them for their father's arrival home at night, and worrying
about where best to raise them in order to keep them from developing tuberculosis. Grief over her firstborn, nevertheless, soon found its
expression in regret and recrimination. She had not wanted Margery
to marry Val, she insisted to Josie, and declared to Otto Rothert that
not only should her daughter never have had children but were she
herself to "come back to this earth in another incarnation I would
never be a mother again." Margery's death had rendered her "a pessimist forever," completely alienated from the philosophy of her most
famous character. "'Aunt Jane' is an optimist," Lida mourned, "but
her creator has lost all faith and all hope."[22]

"I have an enemy," Eliza Calvert Hall had written twenty-five
years earlier, and her despair over Margery's fate was his worst strike
to date—yet, as Lida also revealed to Rothert, both personal and au-
thorial pride still simmered behind the veil of a mother's depression.
Two years earlier, Rothert had strengthened her determination to collect and publish her verse after he sent her a copy of his biography of
Madison Cawein. Reminding him of her intention, asking for an up-
date on literary activities in her home state, and conveying some other
positive news—Cecil was rebounding from her troubles, and Tom and
Scotta had become the parents of a son—Lida assured Rothert that
in spite of her cares the Texas climate was keeping her in excellent
health and equal to any task that the future might impose.[23]

Lida also sent her friend the text of a poem that linked her both
to him and spiritually, she hoped, to the subject of his biography. A
recent first-prize winner in a contest sponsored by the Louisville
Arts Club, "The Pack" was based on a story Rothert had once told
her about Madison Cawein's unfulfilled ambition to capture the
gruesome climax of a foxhunt in verse.[24] The dilemma of the prey,
as well as that of the poet unable to realize his vision, were topics
especially suited to a woman who, over the past several years, had
seen the suffrage battle won but the rest of her ambitions driven
into a corner. With so many of the "hounds of life"—"Despair and
Sorrow and Failure and Loss"—on her trail, flight held no victory,
Lida wrote, for they could be neither outwitted nor outlasted. Contemplating the reflex of the hunted animal as tooth and claw met

its flesh, she found compelling evidence, indeed, that the only true glory lay in the fight:

> Grant me the courage of that dumb beast
> The courage a man may lack
> To turn and make a hopeless stand
> And die with my face to the pack.

16

A Hard Worker All Her Life

Now, shut your eyes and let the sun and the wind take care of you.
—Eliza Calvert Hall, "An Eye for an Eye"

ONLY TWO WEEKS AFTER boasting to Otto Rothert of her robust health, Lida entered Baylor Hospital for treatment of bronchitis. For all concerned, the illness was something of a blessing. Lida found that the ministrations of a modern health care institution agreed with her and was satisfied to remain there until fully recovered. With a good nurse looking after the children, Val continued his frequent business travel, and Cecil, on whom the principal burdens of her mother's convalescence might otherwise have fallen, was able to attend to her own work. Upon her return to Dallas after the end of her marriage, she had used a loan from Val to open a teahouse. Decorated with roses from Lida's garden and an "Aunt Jane of Kentucky" poster designed by Mary Wickliffe Covington, a Bowling Green artist, the business had become popular with other transplanted Kentuckians and served to supplement Cecil's income from music.[1]

Margery's death, however, had set significant change in motion. Lida was not given much longer to complain about her grandchildren's chronic colds and weakness, for by Christmas 1924 ten-year-old Val and seven-year-old Margery had moved to a new home. Their father had quickly remarried and, to Lida's indignation, did not encourage them to memorialize their dead mother or to maintain more than casual contact with her family. Val's pursuit of a new life also created a rift between Alex, who defended him, and Tom, who did not. Holding

Val solely to blame for these "disgraceful" family squabbles, Lida was confident that her grandchildren would reassert their loyalty to her once they were older.[2]

Cecil, too, had grown restless. Late in 1924, she decided to close her teahouse to assume similar but more demanding duties in the Northeast. Her cousin Hugh Underwood, a U.S. Military Academy graduate and now an instructor, had been charged with reorganizing the West Point Army mess and had recruited her on a temporary basis to oversee meal preparations and train permanent staff. While she disliked being away from Lida and missed the rest of the family, Cecil soon grew fond of her work, with its opportunities for regular travel to New York City, and of West Point, which raised thoughts of her uncle Edward and of her father's days as a military cadet in Virginia.[3]

Though permanently settled in Dallas, Tom was preoccupied with a young family and a new career in the securities business; consequently, when Cecil left for West Point, Alex moved back in with Lida and seemed to inherit by default the role of her everyday companion. He told Cecil that he was comfortable with the arrangement, but it was likely doomed from the start. At thirty-six, Alex remained a "rolling stone," captive to what a friend later called his "haunting restlessness." Having given up his state highway job for work at a private construction company, he nevertheless talked of leaving Texas as soon as he completed his latest road engineering assignment. If Alex was content to minimize both his professional responsibilities and his personal entanglements, living with his mother would have been difficult in light of her marked ambivalence toward these tendencies. Lida confessed to Otto Rothert that she was distressed by her eldest son's drift into "old bachelorhood," but at the same time—thinking, perhaps, of a second divorce in the family, another relocation or more grandchildren to raise—she claimed to "dread marriage far more than death." Whether he decided simply to follow his inclination or, as Cecil later charged, grew weary of Lida's criticism, Alex soon left to resume employment with the state in Wichita Falls.[4]

Finding herself alone again, Lida was anxious about the future— "I wish some fortune teller could tell me what I ought to do," she lamented to Maggie—but was far less gloomy than she had been when sick relatives and unsatisfactory servants monopolized her time. Intent upon bringing order to her house by making needed repairs, disposing of unwanted clutter (including Cecil's abandoned tearoom furniture and china), and recovering possessions of greater value, especially books, from Bowling Green, she also indulged more frequently in long walks, gardening, bread making, and writing. Not the least of her goals was to atone for the time lost nursing Margery and her grandchildren by completing a book on basketry that she had begun before leaving Kentucky. Like *A Book of Hand-Woven Coverlets*, the project required a foundation of primary research to support her flights of imagination, but in Texas she could not find any practitioners of the craft outside schools. With only her own collection of baskets and weaving samples dating from the days when she lectured on the subject, she longed for renewed access to Bowling Green, where she suspected that many interesting specimens lay unappreciated in the homes of her friends. As custodian of the Calvert family inventory, Josie received prompt instructions to look through the house. Where was the little card basket, Lida asked, that stood on their mother's parlor table when they were children? Could she obtain a photograph of one of the old-fashioned basket wagons that used to come to town?[5]

Even as she wrestled with the problem of distance, Lida must have been encouraged when her long-standing interest in the crafts associated with Kentucky's mountain people drew a generous response in her adopted city. In June 1925, at a reception given in her honor by a group of Dallas women who had roots in Kentucky, she spoke about the Pine Mountain Settlement School, established in 1913 to serve an isolated area of Harlan County, and offered samples of the students' handiwork. So inspired were the seventy-two women in attendance that they immediately formed the Dallas Kentucky Club, not only to honor their native state but to establish and maintain a scholarship fund for the benefit of the Pine Mountain school. Within a year, the club hosted its first major event, a reception for four hundred with music, readings, and a promise to render even greater service to the mountain children.[6]

Lida also expected her work on basketry to complement *A Book of Hand-Woven Coverlets*, still in print after more than a decade and prompting collective responses similar to that which had greeted her appeal on behalf of the Pine Mountain School. The previous year, a group of Chicago women had organized the Colonial Coverlet Guild of America to catalogue, photograph, and encourage the preservation of these "American tapestries." Recognizing the support she had received from the guild's adoption of *A Book of Hand-Woven Coverlets* as its "official book," the author accepted an invitation to speak at a luncheon given by the president in her honor.[7]

Lida's trip to Chicago in November 1925 was part of a lengthy journey that reunited her, in some cases after many years, with friends and family. Accompanying her to the Coverlet Guild luncheon was her niece, Jeannette Obenchain, whom she had probably last seen at the St. Louis World's Fair more than twenty years earlier. Journeying further north, she then spent a pleasant few days in Appleton, Wisconsin, where Edward was now stationed. Brother and sister had not seen each other for eighteen years, but Ed largely confirmed Lida's protestation of good health; other than one or two missing teeth and her measured way of ascending a staircase, he detected remarkably little change in her appearance or constitution. As she neared seventy, however, Lida may have acquired some additional Aunt Jane–like traits with which to charm her hosts. His mother-in-law, wrote Ed to his sisters, had so enjoyed sitting and listening to Lida talk that she had "wept copiously" when they parted.[8]

Lida spent the remainder of the year with Cecil, who was finishing her work at West Point, then returned to Dallas early in 1926 without making a stop in Bowling Green. Newly conscious of her distaste for winter weather and coal-burning cities, she was anxious to resume work in her garden and tend to the house in which her own roots were now irretrievably planted. While she assured her sisters that she was trying to weed out the contents of its seven rooms and reported that Tom had convinced her to write a will, Lida otherwise denied any preoccupation with death except as it vaguely time-limited her intention "to do some good work." Having wished for astrological guidance after Alex left, she concluded, too, that the stars were on her side: she could continue with her poetry and basketry projects as well as the seemingly endless disposition of her books and furnishings stored in Bowling Green because, she wrote her sisters, "the fortune tellers and palmists all say I am going to live way into the eighties."[9]

Age, nevertheless, conspired more frequently to circumscribe Lida's existence. After leaving West Point, Cecil resumed teahouse work and persuaded her mother to make one more trip north, a fifty-hour train ride to Connecticut, in late 1928. While the fall scenery of

New England made the journey worthwhile, Lida declined to remain through the winter; she retreated again to the sanctuary of her Texas garden, where she could gather roses and daffodils by the armful, experiment with corn, beans, and turnips, and cultivate her increasing resistance to further travel. Only when Maggie suffered a severe bout of rheumatism did she loyally volunteer to come to Bowling Green to help Josie care for their sister. Fortunately, the crisis passed and Lida was able to confine her assistance to sewing nightclothes, earnestly second-guessing Maggie's physician, and prescribing home remedies ranging from mineral water to tomato juice with salt and lemon to Campbell's soup. Relieved at the news of Maggie's improvement, she confessed that even the thought of making a journey sickened her.[10]

Advancing years also brought Lida the opportunity to become a subject of study when Sophie Lee, the daughter of an old suffrage colleague, wrote her master's thesis on Eliza Calvert Hall. While Lida responded graciously to her request for assistance, the timing must have given her pause. She had long known of the public's continuing love for *Aunt Jane of Kentucky*—"It is curious how that book lasts," she observed to her sisters—but with her now-completed basketry book not yet placed with a publisher and her volume of poems still a work in progress, she had little to relate about the future or even the recent past. Her retrospective for Sophie was nevertheless courteous and professional; omitting the personal troubles that might have excused her declining productivity, she concentrated instead on the prized blooms in her writer's garden—her first poem for *Scribner's*, "Sally Ann's Experience," *A Book of Hand-Woven Coverlets*, and *Aunt Jane of Kentucky*. Assessing the rest of the undergrowth, Lida recommended that Sophie weed out "inferior verse" from Eliza Calvert Hall's "real poems" and largely disregard her suffrage articles because they were "of no importance from a literary point of view."[11]

If she directed Sophie to presume, as she had long ago in her essay on Charlotte Perkins Stetson, that writing done for a purpose ultimately did not qualify as art, Lida still prized the intellectual legacy of the suffrage movement. Reflecting on the years they had spent making their case for the vote with evidence from history, literature, and scripture, she asked Alice Stone Blackwell to recall the identity of the Ivy League professor who had once used Alice's *Woman's Journal* editorials as "perfect specimens of logic." The battle that she had savored more than the victory, moreover, continued to spark her imagination in ways she was comfortable disclosing only to a contemporary. Having declared to Sophie that a copy of "Grandmother's Début" was "not worth looking for," Lida revealed to Alice that she had written yet another woman suffrage story and was also at work on a lengthy article about the cause. Although a literary agent had returned the story on the grounds that its subject was passé, and Lida acknowledged that her chances of publishing the article were slim, she intended to persevere; Alice's forthcoming biography of her mother, she added, would give her some of the necessary factual background.[12]

Even before Lida finished reading *Lucy Stone: Pioneer of Woman's Rights*, however, Alice found herself in a position similar to that of a Goshen elder forced to hear Sally Ann's experience—except that race, not gender, was the source of Lida's strenuous objection. Years earlier, she had drawn a distinction between the right to vote and the right to govern, suggesting that the latter was more properly entrusted to a small, educated class of men and women. After a decade in Texas, her position had metastasized into a strident defense of the South's racial caste system. Like most northerners, she charged, Alice was naïve about the fundamental differences between whites and blacks, and too uncritical of the legacy of the antislavery movement. Lucy Stone's work for woman suffrage and property rights had been heroic, but Lida was appalled to read of her association with abolitionists such as William Lloyd Garrison and Wendell Phillips, men whose "insane hatred of the south and insane love for the negro" had sparked the Civil War and, a generation later, still inspired pernicious campaigns for the social equality of blacks and whites. "We don't propose to be ruled by negro legislatures," she informed Alice, "even where negroes are in a majority." In a twenty-page screed that appropriated the rhetorical skills she had used in support of suffrage to the cause of white supremacy, Lida countered Alice's mention of "lynching horrors" with graphic tales of black men's sexual crimes against white women that, in her opinion, warranted extreme measures. Likening the South itself to these violated victims, Lida ignored the connection between lynching and the cult of male chivalry, which had traditionally idolized women but restricted their rights as the price of protecting them from life's dangers, both real and imagined.[13]

"But enough of this. Of course we are friends and always will be,"

Lida reminded Alice, urging her not to waste her ailing eyesight on a letter of rebuttal—and having faith, perhaps, that Alice would respect her readiness to argue even when she had no chance of persuading. As a further gesture of respect, she asked Alice to send her some literature on socialism; while her own reading on the subject had left her suspicious that the creed was "very much like the efforts of the reconstructionists to turn society bottom side upwards," she seemed prepared to keep an open mind.[14]

It was to such a woman, solicitous but intransigent, intellectually acute but reactionary, that her youngest daughter returned late in 1931. Since leaving her job at West Point, Cecil's efforts to make a living in the restaurant and hospitality business had given her only a moderate sense of accomplishment, while her hopes for a second marriage that might realize her "ideal of friendship, companionship and love" had remained unfulfilled. During one Connecticut winter she had suffered what she described as a severe nervous breakdown, a state that wrenched her thoughts back to the past and especially to its losses and disappointments: her father's illness and death, Margery's sad fate, and her own dream of becoming a famous violinist. Although her emotional health stabilized, the Depression eventually eroded her business prospects, and she spent two months visiting friends before arriving back in Texas with a companion, Harry Barker, who intended to study painting at the Dallas Art Institute.[15]

Whether out of financial or emotional need, Cecil had also begun to write articles and stories, an undertaking that gave her fresh ambition even as it held over her the standard of her mother's success. A year and a half before returning to Dallas, in fact, Cecil had attempted to repossess a talisman of that success, asking John Wilson Townsend to oblige her by returning the manuscript of "Sally Ann's Experience." When she gave it to him fifteen years earlier, she explained, she had been too young to appreciate its significance within the family and now wished to add it to her own collection of books and papers. As the months passed and the manuscript did not appear, Townsend's obfuscation on the question of its whereabouts only aggravated Cecil's regret. Suspecting that he had sold it and wondering if it could be traced, she was hurt by his cavalier approach to the custody of her gift. "If it means so little to you that you don't even know where it is," she had chided him, "then do find it & let me have it." Her entreaties continued, apparently in vain, until the summer before her departure for Texas.[16]

Though pleased to have Cecil's company again, Lida had spent most of the year in relative self-sufficiency, speaking on coverlets at the Dallas Museum, helping to judge entries in a local quilt contest, gardening, baking bread, sewing for her sisters, entertaining old acquaintances from Kentucky, and even enjoying an occasional visit from Margery and Val, who were now teenagers. Several months after Cecil's arrival, however, Lida suffered the most serious illness she had ever experienced, an attack of neuritis, rheumatism, or both that left her with pain and stiffness in her shoulders, arms, and legs. The extraction of several teeth added to her discomfort, but she was determined to overcome what she regarded as a temporary setback. By early 1933, she was again spending hours in her garden and boasting to her sisters of the doctor's finding that she had the constitution of a seventeen-year-old girl.[17]

For Cecil, unfortunately, the experience of her mother's infirmity and its aftermath was shattering. The woman in whom she had witnessed a growing strength and emotional steadiness over the past decade had not only aged suddenly but was greeting her diminished activity and independence with a bitter contrariness. "She is like a five year old child—a very rebellious child," Cecil complained to Maggie. "Nothing pleases her and by not expecting any appreciation, I am not hurt or disappointed. It has taken all of the patience at my command to help her, and still does." Homesick for New England, rendered at times physically faint by stress and finding her attempts to cook meals, keep house, and write fiction either criticized or ignored, Cecil retreated to her typewriter in a mood of angry detachment, as fascinated as she was infuriated by Lida's temperament. Under the guise of making "a study of her character for future writing," she identified her mother as the villain in a series of sensational tableaux that she recalled for Maggie: Lida hating her father for his financial misdeeds, showing utter contempt for the Major, not wanting to bear any of her children, poisoning her household with a "nightmare of restrictions and needless quarrelling," making Margery's life "pure tragedy," hating Val, quashing Cecil's musical aspirations with her "sick anxiety," alienating Alex with her nagging, and finally, conducting a "life long revolt" against the world. "Don't misunderstand me, I am not bitter,"

Cecil loftily assured her aunt. "I see the good qualities in everyone
and have only admiration for people who take up the burden of life
and carry it to its weary finish."[18]

Cecil's uniquely harsh outburst reflected not only her fragile
mental state but the frightening solitariness of her own burdens as
caregiver. Her brother Alex was nearby, having moved from Wichita
Falls to Fort Worth, but his determination to conceal a growing de-
pendence on alcohol had only widened the distance he kept from
his mother and siblings. Tom and his wife had also been unhelpful,
but Tom began to pay closer attention when word reached him of
Cecil's denigration of their family life to some of Lida's friends. Assuming that his sister had also unburdened herself to her aunts, he
quickly protested to Maggie that his childhood memories had been
happy ones; his parents had accomplished much with little, and Cecil had the least right to complain because, as the youngest, she had
most benefited after Lida's books became successful. Praising his
mother's ability to manage a house and four children while still finding time to write, Tom dismissed Cecil's outspokenness as the flaw
of someone whose parents had been entirely too lenient rather than
too strict.[19]

Cecil nevertheless gained a respite in October 1933 when Tom
conveyed their mother to the popular health facilities at Marlin, some
120 miles south of Dallas. Lida had avoided travel earlier that year,
declining invitations from the Colonial Coverlet Guild in Chicago and
the Presbyterian Church in Bowling Green, which was planning a
centennial pageant featuring "Aunt Jane" vignettes, but Marlin's hot
mineral springs offered the possibility of relief for her rheumatism.
Although the three-week program of baths and other treatments did
not completely eliminate the stiffness in her muscles, ten days after
returning home she had an operation that gave her another chance to
demonstrate her fortitude: at the age of seventy-seven, she had her
tonsils removed.[20]

Only when Lida judged the health of her writing career did she
lapse into the gloom she had so often expressed earlier in life when
family duties taxed her physical strength. Now, the culprit was not domestic drudgery but the Depression, which she blamed for her failure
to market her basketry manuscript as well as a stack of poems, stories,
and plays. "I am utterly useless," she complained to Alice Stone Black-

well, mourning her lost influence with publishers and producers as a sign of mortality more sobering than old age. Exclusion from the arena of public discourse had also inflamed one of her long-held grievances, namely the unacknowledged debt that younger generations of women owed their suffragist foremothers. Perhaps Cecil, with her bobbed hair, divorce, artist boyfriend, and well-employed typewriter (she had recently sold two articles), stoked her mother's resentment even as she brooded over her own unappreciated labor; in any event, Lida was determined to apply her pen to the task of reclaiming the moral high ground. As if it were a surprise weapon to be fired at complacent audiences in the manner of Sally Ann's experience, she disclosed to Alice her "secret plan" for a "scenario," perhaps even a Hollywood screenplay, depicting her sex's progress from ancient times to the present and giving particular attention to the struggle for suffrage. Convinced that young women must be "shown the depth of the pit out of which they were digged," she envisioned a production that would, through its clear-eyed "picturesqueness," guarantee remembrance of those who had wielded the shovels.[21]

No sooner had Lida outlined this ambition than writing itself became more painful and difficult. Although she had first experienced minor stiffness in her right hand four years earlier, not until mid-1934 did advancing arthritis compel her to draw upon Cecil's typewriting skills to maintain her correspondence. As the condition rapidly settled in her knees as well as her hands and she became more dependent, the role of nurse again fell to her daughter. Cecil's earlier revolt against her mother's decline, however, seemed to have spent itself, leaving in its place only a numb sadness. "None of it seems real—mother's distressing condition and the whole changed aspect of life," she wrote to Maggie and Josie. As she read to Lida on their back porch and cared for her, alone at first—her friend Harry Barker was now studying art in Taos, New Mexico—and then with the aid of a practical nurse, Cecil mourned her lost fantasies of the future. "The hopes and dreams were that Harry and I would have a home in the country," she confessed to her aunts, "that Mother would be with us in health and that life would go on pleasantly. But it wasn't in the cards!"[22]

Lida, too, seemed to become less headstrong, but pain and loss of mobility did not dull either her intellect or her senses. Summoning the effort now required to complete a letter in her own hand, she commiserated privately with Alice Stone Blackwell, who was herself in ill health. "I rebel against my own misfortunes and I am equally rebellious over yours," Lida declared, objecting characteristically to the dearth of rewards given two such hard workers in the twilight of life. At the same time, with the roses in her garden blooming more bountifully than ever and the mockingbirds singing night and day, she allowed a drop of optimism to soothe her unrest. Never having reflected much on the nature of God, she had lately assured herself that this "Power"—which she imagined "as Huxley did—'the infinite and eternal energy from which all things proceed'"—would ultimately "have care for the men and women who try to make this earth what it ought to be." Though she wished, like Aunt Jane, that she might never become too old to work, Lida permitted herself, in the manner of one of her fictional farm women, to stop work for a moment and look up at the sky.[23]

On August 20, 1935, Tom and his wife took Lida by train to Wichita Falls, where she entered a private hospital to receive specialized treatment for her arthritis. Two months of heat wraps on her hands and arms and injections in her joints brought little improvement. When she became depressed, Tom considered complying with her request to be taken home. It was Lida, nevertheless, who lifted Cecil's spirits when she arrived at the hospital in the middle of a December night after a long bus ride from New Mexico, where she had spent the past month. She surprised her mother, who sleepily asked the nurse if she had dreamed hearing the sound of her child's voice. They talked at length, then Cecil went to Dallas to retrieve some more of Lida's clothes. By the time she left again for Taos, her mother was "smiling and hopeful of plans for the future," and even followed up their visit with a letter insisting that she was free of pain and expected to walk again. Tom, too, noticed Lida's steadier penmanship when she wrote to him expressing her belief that the treatments were starting to take effect.[24]

On the morning of December 18, Lida woke with a sore throat and fever, but downplayed her symptoms to Tom when he visited the next day. In the early morning of Friday, December 20, however, her doctor telephoned to warn that her condition had worsened. As Tom and his wife hurried back to Wichita Falls, Lida slipped into unconsciousness. A few hours later, she died. At seventy-nine years and ten months, she might have demanded that the fortune tellers account for their predictions that she would live far into her eighties, but Tom was more conciliatory when he notified his uncle Edward, his aunts Maggie and Josie, and Cecil. "She had suffered long," he assured them, "and I don't think she minded going." [25]

Epilogue

Next to layin' the body in the ground, child, this foldin' up dead
folks' clothes and puttin' 'em away is one o' the hardest things
people ever has to do. It's jest like when you've finished a book and
shut it up and put it away on the shelf.

—Aunt Jane

THE DAY AFTER HER DEATH, Lida was memorialized in a simple ceremony amid tributes of poinsettias and lilies. Although she
had made known her wish to be cremated, Tom arranged for her to
be buried in Dallas's Grove Hill Cemetery near Margery. Cecil was
not present; reluctant to oblige his sister to retrace a journey she had
made only days earlier, Tom had refrained from telephoning, and his
telegram did not reach her in time for her to attend. Alex, too, was out
of reach but intentionally so; over the past year he had been drifting
through Texas and the Southwest, dividing his time between work and
drink. Only months earlier, he had gone missing for several days from
a job in Phoenix, and Tom's inquiries in Fort Worth had uncovered
the extent of his brother's addiction. Although Alex had reestablished
contact with Cecil at the time she last saw Lida, he had not taken the
opportunity to visit his mother.[1]

As the Bowling Green newspaper eulogized Lida for her contribution to Kentucky literature, the city where she had resided for some
twenty years also remembered her as one of its own. The Dallas Kentucky Club, of which she was honorary president, promptly renamed
its Pine Mountain Settlement School fund the Eliza Calvert Hall

Obenchain Scholarship. In his column for the *Dallas Times-Herald,* editor Tom C. Gooch applauded the artistry Lida had brought to her treatment of coverlet weaving as well as to the fiction that had earned a president's praise. After the years she had spent courting newspaper opinion, however, what she would have found most gratifying was his praise of her call for suffrage at a time when relatively few had championed the cause. Taking up Lida's battle standard—*"Have you forgotten?"*—Gooch reminded his readers that as long ago as the 1880s, "Mrs. Obenchain was demanding equal rights for women," asking "not for glory for her sex but for simple justice." He was careful to add the usual qualifier—"Being cultured and well educated, she was not the militant kind of suffragist"—and preferred to credit the students of the Major's small college with inspiring Lida's sympathy for the humbler elements of society. Nevertheless, he attributed her influence not only to a strong personality but to a forceful intellect— to her head as well as her heart—and declared that "a great woman" had been lost to Texas and the nation.[2]

While Gooch hailed the manner in which Lida gave voice to ordinary folk struggling to realize their aspirations, others associated her only with the sunny contentment of her most famous literary creation. "And so, the Author of lovable 'Aunt Jane' passed away," a colleague of Beulah Strong, Lida's illustrator, wrote to Maggie on hearing the news. "The pity of it, that people who give the world so much delight, must be taken away!" Thirty years after its publication, she could think of few acquaintances who had not read *Aunt Jane* or been rendered "happier for having known the exquisitely optimistic, friendly old lady." A schoolteacher friend of Alex's, convinced that Lida's own "happy philosophy" radiated from her books, was struck by the contrast between his mother's giftedness, which seemed to have rested lightly upon her shoulders, and the chronic melancholy she saw in Alex.[3]

Indeed, after Lida's death, those most needing shelter in the garden of the plain old woman of Kentucky remained in the wilderness. "Why can't we be happy in such a lovely world?" Lida had asked Alice Stone Blackwell in the last spring of her life. Keep cutting and sewing, Aunt Jane might have interjected, and in time all the pieces of the puzzle will be in the right place—but for Cecil, the most important piece had now vanished. "Nothing will ever be the same again, for want of Mother to share it," she mourned to Josie the following summer. Cecil had just ended her ill-advised sojourn in New Mexico and returned to Dallas, where she masked a deepening depression with the charm and vitality known to her friends. As she grew lonelier in a house filled with Lida's books and papers, neither her memories nor her writing could console; that Christmas, after replying to well-wishers who had been unaware of Lida's death, she was helpless to muster her thoughts for the long letter she yearned to send her aunts in Bowling Green. When the pack of hounds finally overtook her, it gave almost no warning. Cecil spent the evening of February 11, 1937, pleasantly, entertaining neighbors on what would have been her mother's eighty-first birthday. The next afternoon, leaving the house warm and her dinner prepared on the stove, she took a street-car downtown to the Tower Petroleum Building, opened a window on an upper floor, and stepped out.[4]

Less than two years later, Alex's troubled life also came to an end. After falling in love with a married woman, he had fled to Sicily Island, Louisiana, and found work on a plantation. There, he had impressed the owners with his talent, culture, and sensitivity, but unsettled them with his alienation, lack of purpose, and tendency to blame his family for a host of unmet needs. He spoke often, nevertheless, of his Kentucky home, of his beloved sister Margery and her children, and of his mother's writing. "He was very proud of her ability as an author," remembered his schoolteacher friend.[5]

Late in November 1938 Alex's body was discovered in the woods near Alexandria. Although a coroner's jury ruled that the gunshot wound and other injuries he suffered had been inflicted by another hand, Tom had little doubt that the cause of his brother's death was suicide. Alex's life had long been unraveling, he gingerly explained to his aunts, but at least he had attempted to conceal his habits, especially from Lida. Declaring to Maggie, by contrast, that his younger sister had "caused more trouble to Mother and everyone else than you could ever imagine," Tom then turned to the bleak task of sorting through the contents of Lida's house, hastily packed and stored after Cecil's death.[6]

From the house where they had spent most of their lives, seventy-eight-year-old Maggie and seventy-four-year-old Josie Calvert also took stock, weighing Tom's revelations about the recent past with happier memories solicited from and shared with others. Heedless of the restraints of age and distance, the two sisters entered into a generous and thoughtful exchange with the Louisiana family that not only had befriended Alex but subsequently grown close to Tom. They even sought to comfort Tom's sixteen-year-old son in a letter that his father, still reluctant to detail the circumstances of Alex's death, intercepted. Although Tom's relationship with his niece and nephew had been complicated by his estrangement from their father, Margery and Val, now college students, received affectionate letters and small gifts from their great-aunts in Bowling Green.[7]

Like one of Lida's old coverlets, the strands of the family were worn and frayed, but they held. From Dallas, young Margery took up her pen and wrote shyly at first, not quite sure how to begin her story. She asked Maggie and Josie to tell her more about themselves and about the mother who had died when she was only five. She told them of her boyfriends, including the one she considered "special" and would soon marry. Although she possessed little by which to remember the Calvert women, she had some books—*Aunt Jane,* naturally, being her favorite—and a picture in her mind, which Lida had impressed upon her since childhood, of the unsurpassed beauty of their Kentucky garden. She also had a hope chest, for which she had begun to piece a quilt.[8]

Appendix

Calvert Family Members

Thomas J. Hall (1775–1859)
m. Emma Wallis (d. 1849)

  I. Eliza Caroline Hall (1804–71)
    m. 1825
    Samuel Wilson Calvert (1796–1837)

    A. Thomas Chalmers Calvert (1826–98)
      m. 1855
      Margaret Younglove (1829–1920)

      1. **Eliza "Lida" Calvert** (1856–1935)
        m. 1885
        William Alexander Obenchain (1841–1916)

        a. Margery Obenchain (1887–1923)
          m. 1910
          Val Graham Winston (1881–1951)

          i. Val Winston Jr. (1914–88)
          ii. Margery Winston (1917–2002)
            m. 1939
            Sydney O. Bonnick Jr. (1915–2001)

   b. William Alexander "Alex" Obenchain Jr. (1888–1938)

   c. Thomas Hall Obenchain (1891–1970)
      m. 1921
      Scotta Goodwin (1892–1979)

      i. Thomas Hall Obenchain Jr. (1922–2002)

   d. Cecilia "Cecil" Obenchain (1895–1937)
      m. 1917
      Glenn H. Reams (1889–1971)

 2. Mary Calvert (1858–1902)

 3. Margaret "Maggie" Calvert (1860–1947)

 4. Josephine "Josie" Calvert (1864–1956)

 5. Edward Calvert (1870–1957)
    m. 1907
    Lucinda Neely (1872–1961)

    a. Martha Calvert (b. 1912)

B. John Griffin Calvert (1827–29)

C. Emmons Whitfield "Joseph Whit" Calvert (b. 1828)
   m.?
   Martha Smith (1840?–80)

D. Emma Hall Calvert (b. 1829)

E. Sarah Amanda Calvert (1832–86)

F. Henry Baxter Calvert (1834–55)

Younglove Family Members

David Younglove (1754–97)
m. 1779
Anna Nancy Failing (1759–87)

I. Isaiah Younglove (1783–1843)
   m. 1806
   Susannah Yanney (1787–1841)

   A. Joseph I. Younglove (1818–94)
      1st m. 1847
      Sarah A. Morehead (1831–82)

      1. Emma Younglove (1857–1933)
         m. 1877
         Robert Underwood (1844–1907)

         a. Henry "Hugh" Underwood (1893–1960)

   B. Mary Younglove (1823–55)

   C. John E. Younglove (1826–1917)

   D. Margaret Younglove (1829–1920)
      m. 1855
      Thomas Chalmers Calvert (1826–98)

      1. **Eliza "Lida" Calvert** (1856–1935)

   E. Jane Younglove (1831–61)

   F. Five others

Notes

Abbreviations Used in Notes

Bennett Dep.	Esther Bennett Deposit, Laura Clay Papers, Margaret I. King Library, University of Kentucky
CFP	Calvert Family Papers, Calvert-Obenchain-Younglove Collection, Kentucky Library, Western Kentucky University
COR	Cecil Obenchain Reams
EC	Edward Calvert
ECH	Eliza Calvert Hall
Fuller	Paul E. Fuller, *Laura Clay and the Woman's Rights Movement* (Lexington: University Press of Kentucky, 1975)
JC	Josephine "Josie" Calvert
JEY	John E. Younglove
JIY	Joseph I. Younglove
JWT	John Wilson Townsend
JWTC	John Wilson Townsend Collection, Library Special Collections, Eastern Kentucky University
KFW	*Kate Field's Washington*
Knott	Claudia Knott, "The Woman Suffrage Movement in Kentucky, 1879–1920" (PhD diss., University of Kentucky, 1989)
Ky. Lib.	Kentucky Library, Western Kentucky University
LC	Laura Clay
LCO	Lida Calvert Obenchain
LCP	Laura Clay Papers, Margaret I. King Library, University of Kentucky

Lee sketch	Autobiographical sketch written by Lida Calvert Obenchain for Sophie Lee, [1929], SC 792, Kentucky Library, Western Kentucky University
MC	Margaret "Maggie" Calvert
MYC	Margaret Younglove Calvert
NAWSA records	National American Woman Suffrage Association Records, Manuscript Division, Library of Congress, Washington, D.C.
NYT	*New York Times*
OFP	Obenchain Family Papers, Calvert-Obenchain-Younglove Collection, Kentucky Library, Western Kentucky University
OMP	Lida Calvert Obenchain Miscellaneous Papers, Filson Historical Society, Louisville, Ky.
OR	Otto Rothert
ORP	Otto Arthur Rothert Papers, Filson Historical Society, Louisville, Ky.
ORMP	Otto Arthur Rothert Miscellaneous Papers, Filson Historical Society, Louisville, Ky.
PCSM	Presbyterian Church of Bowling Green Session Minutes, Kentucky Library, Western Kentucky University
SC 77	Manuscripts Small Collection No. 77, Kentucky Library, Western Kentucky University
SC 261	Manuscripts Small Collection No. 261, Kentucky Library, Western Kentucky University
SC 578	Manuscripts Small Collection No. 578, Kentucky Library, Western Kentucky University
SC 792	Manuscripts Small Collection No. 792, Kentucky Library, Western Kentucky University
SWC	Samuel Wilson Calvert
TCC	Thomas C. Calvert
THO	Thomas Hall Obenchain
UC	Underwood Collection, Kentucky Library, Western Kentucky University
WAO	William A. Obenchain
WJ	*Woman's Journal*
YFP	Younglove Family Papers, Calvert-Obenchain-Younglove Collection, Kentucky Library, Western Kentucky University

Prologue

1. "Sweet Day of Rest," in ECH, *Aunt Jane of Kentucky* (Boston: Little, Brown, and Company, 1907), 103 (epigraph); LCO to OR, June 14, 1921, ORP. She made the remark after reading Rothert's biography of the poet Madison Cawein.

2. William S. Ward, *A Literary History of Kentucky* (Knoxville: University of Tennessee Press, 1988), 55.

3. Elizabeth Ammons, *Conflicting Stories: American Women Writers at the Turn into the Twentieth Century* (New York: Oxford University Press, 1991), 3.

4. Elaine Showalter, *Sister's Choice: Tradition and Change in American Women's Writing* (Oxford: Clarendon Press, 1991), 161. See, for example, ECH, *Aunt Jane's Album* (San Pedro, Cal.: R. and E. Miles, 1980); Patricia Wilens, *Friendship Quilting* (Des Moines, Iowa: Meredith Corp., 1990); ECH, *A Quilter's Wisdom: Conversations with Aunt Jane,* with an introduction by Roderick Kiracofe (San Francisco: Chronicle Books, 1994); Margret Aldrich and Whitney Otto, *This Old Quilt: A Heartwarming Collection of Quilts and Quilting Memories* (Stillwater, Minn.: Voyageur Press, 2001). The sisterhood of quilters has never completely forgotten Aunt Jane; see Carrie A. Hall and Rose G. Kretsinger, *The Romance of the Patchwork Quilt in America* (Caldwell, Idaho: Caxton Printers, 1936), 17 (thanks to Steph Mc-Grath, senior curator, DuPage County Historical Museum, for bringing the "Aunt Jane" quote therein to the author's attention); Marguerite Ickis, *The Standard Book of Quilt Making and Collecting* (New York: Greystone Press, 1949, repr. Dover Publications, 1959). Lida's study of coverlets has also recently been reissued; ECH, *A Book of Hand-Woven Coverlets* (Rutland, Vt.: Charles E. Tuttle Company, 1966); ECH, *The [sic] Book of Handwoven [sic] Coverlets* (New York: Dover Publications, 1988).

5. Miriam Houchens, "Amazing Best Sellers by Kentucky Women Writers," *Filson Club History Quarterly,* vol. 41, no. 4 (October 1967): 353–56; Judy Elsley, "Uncovering Eliza Calvert Hall," *Encyclia: The Journal of the Utah Academy of Sciences, Arts and Letters,* vol. 68 (1991): 155–72; Judy Elsley, "Lack of a Separate Purse: Eliza Calvert Hall's *Aunt Jane of Kentucky,*" *Legacy: A Journal of American Women Writers,* vol. 9, no. 2 (1992): 119–27; ECH, *Aunt Jane of Kentucky,* ed. Melody Graulich (Albany, N.Y.: NCUP, Inc., 1992); ECH, *Aunt Jane of Kentucky,* with a foreword by Bonnie Jean Cox (Lexington: University Press of Kentucky, 1995). On a more popular front, see the transcript of the KET (Kentucky Educational Television) Bookclub's 2001 discussion of *Aunt Jane of Kentucky* at www.ket.org/content/bookclub/books/2001_jun/transcript306.htm/ [accessed December 15, 2005]. In August 1986, Rita Kohn and Marita Brake premiered a one-woman play, *Aunt Jane Remembers,* at the StoreFront Theater in Havana, Illinois. The playwrights Norma Cole and Naneki Elliott adapted three "Aunt Jane" stories into a one-act play, *Just Desserts,* which has been performed for

schools, conferences, and women's groups since 1997; see www.nanekielliott
.com/play.html [accessed March 26, 2007]; see also Norma Cole and Naneki
Elliott, *Just Desserts* (Woodstock, Ill.: Dramatic Publications, 2000).

6. Even after the 1890s reform of married women's property laws, a
Kentucky wife's conveyance of her land was null and void unless her husband
joined in the deed; not until 1942, seven years after Lida's death, was a deed
signed by a wife alone sufficient to pass title, subject only to her husband's
joining in to release his right of curtesy. The legal inability of a wife to act as
surety for her husband persisted until 1974.

7. "My Mail-Bag," *KFW*, October 17, 1894, 244.

1. Fighting and Preaching

1. "Milly Baker's Boy," in ECH, *Aunt Jane of Kentucky*, 109 (epigraph).

2. Calvert Family Genealogy Notes, CFP. At least two other Elizas appear in Lida's family tree. Eliza Caroline Hall's mother, Emma Wallis, had
a sister named Eliza. Emma's brother, John Fielding Wallis, had a daughter,
Ann Eliza, who accompanied her widowed father when he took a position
on the first faculty of the University of Alabama at Tuscaloosa in 1831. Ann
Eliza was said to be the university's first coed because Fielding Wallis had
his colleagues tutor her after she graduated from the Alabama Female Academy; James B. Sellers, *History of the University of Alabama* (Birmingham:
University of Alabama Press, 1953), 1: 45–46.

3. Calvert Family Genealogy Notes, CFP; LCO to Mrs. William J. Potter, October 5, 1933, OFP; "The House That Was a Wedding Fee," 42, and
"The Reformation of Sam Amos," 214, both in ECH, *The Land of Long Ago*
(Boston: Little, Brown, and Company, 1909). A transcript of a letter from the
War Department in the Calvert Family Genealogy Notes reports no military
record of a "Samuel Wilson Calvert" but confirms that a "Samuel Calvert"
served in the West Tennessee Militia during the War of 1812. The likelihood
that she was descended from two "fighting parsons" seems to have pleased
Lida; in "The House That Was a Wedding Fee," she also alludes to Eliza
Caroline Hall's great-uncle, James Hall, a Presbyterian minister who left his
pulpit to serve in the Revolutionary War.

4. SWC Journal, December 30, 1821, CFP; James H. Moorhead, "The
'Restless Spirit of Radicalism': Old School Fears and the Schism of 1837,"
Journal of Presbyterian History, vol. 78, no. 1 (Spring 2000): 22; Joseph T.
Fuhrmann, *The Life and Times of Tusculum College* (Greenville, Tenn.:
Tusculum College, 1986), 27–28. The effects of the Civil War forced rival
Greeneville and Tusculum colleges to merge in 1868.

5. SWC Journals, October 6, December 13, 1821, July 15, August 7,
1823, CFP; Fuhrmann, *Tusculum College*, 21, 33.

6. SWC Journals, October 26–November 11, 1824, March 6, 1831;
SWC, "A Book Containing Questions, Notes & Essays on Important Subjects in

Theology," November 23, 1824, CFP. Samuel did not graduate from Greeneville College; the trustees in fact awarded no degrees between 1822 and
1825; Fuhrmann, *Tusculum College*, 32.

7. SWC Memoranda, 1825–37, CFP. Samuel records the birth of
"Thomas Chalmers Hall," although "Hall" does not appear in any other family references to Thomas's full name.

8. Ibid.

9. SWC Journal, January 27, 29, 30, February 1, 1831, CFP. Samuel refers to the school for which he was soliciting support as the "M. L. Academy,"
which may have been the Manual Labor Academy, an institution near Spring
Hill, Tennessee, on the Maury County–Williamson County line.

10. SWC Journal, February 2, 6, 1831, CFP; PCSM, October 27, 1831.

11. Jere Nelson Fitts and Thomas Newton Moody, *Joseph B. Lapsley:
From Rockbridge to Warren* (Bowling Green, Ky.: J. N. Fitts, 1994); John B.
Rodes, "The Story of Bowling Green, Kentucky and the First Presbyterian
Church," unpublished manuscript, 1939, John B. Rodes Collection, Ky. Lib.,
9, 11.

12. SWC Journal, December 9, 1831, CFP.

13. Rodes, "First Presbyterian Church," 12, 17, 21; Warren County, Ky.
Deed Book 10, 276. During the Civil War, Lapsley and two of his children
were moved to a site in Bowling Green's Pioneer Cemetery where, according
to legend, his pulpit once stood.

14. SWC Journal, August 21, December 7, 1835, CFP; ECH, "House
That Was a Wedding Fee," 46.

15. SWC Journal, October 14, December 8, 29, 1835, CFP.

16. Obituary of Samuel W. Calvert, *Cincinnati Journal & Seminary*, n.d.,
transcript, CFP. Although most accounts insist that Samuel's funeral was the
first in the new church, Lida's sister Josephine could not verify this when
providing information for a 1935 newspaper series on Bowling Green's early
history. At least one church history states that Eliza's father preached at the
funeral, but the presiding minister appears to have been Rev. John W. Hall,
a Tennessee colleague of Samuel's who later became president of Miami
University; see PCSM, February 22, 1833, June 17, 1837; Elnora B. Simons
to JC, April 6, 1905, CFP.

17. Rodes, "First Presbyterian Church," 13; *Ky. Acts* 1833–34, ch. 317.
The list of subscribers for the church building can be found in Elsie Burmeister Cooke, *A History of the Presbyterian Church, Bowling Green, Kentucky* (Bowling Green, Ky.: First Presbyterian Church, 1983), 14–16.

18. TCC to MYC, May 19, 1878; D. H. Davis to MC and JC, April 19,
1899, CFP; "Reminiscences of the Life and Teachings of Mary K. Jones
While a Resident of This City," ca. 1885, typescript, Martha Cullin Scrapbook, Ky. Lib.

19. Moorhead, "The 'Restless Spirit of Radicalism,'" 25–26; Rodes, "First
Presbyterian Church," 53–59.

20. SWC Journal, November 28, 1832, CFP; Elizabeth Cox Underwood to Joseph Rogers Underwood, April 26, 1852, UC; "House That Was A Wedding Fee," 42–43, "A Ride to Town," 30, and "The Watch-Meeting," 286, in ECH, *Land of Long Ago.*

21. D. H. Davis to JC, August 28, 1899; TCC to MYC, May 19, 1878; TCC to JC, April 2, 1874, CFP.

2. "It Did Not Look as We Had Pictured You"

1. TCC Diary, February 22, April 14, 1846, CFP.

2. Ibid., February 27, March 3, 17, 1846.

3. Ibid., March 7, 23, April 10, 20, 1846.

4. Ibid., December 31, 1851–January 18, 1852.

5. Ibid., January 1–February 8, 1852. While in Nashville Thomas had caught the eye of one young lady, Anna, whose Valentine's Day greeting pointedly informed him that she would not refuse a proposal of marriage; TCC and MYC Invitations, CFP.

6. TCC Diary, January 4, 24, 1852, CFP.

7. Fannie Segur Foster, "A Distinguished Daughter of Kentucky," *Holland's Magazine,* October 1919, 53; Elise Lathrop, *Early American Inns and Taverns* (New York: Robert M. McBride and Company, 1926), 255; Elizabeth Cady Stanton, *Eighty Years and More (1815–1897): Reminiscences of Elizabeth Cady Stanton* (London: T. Fisher Unwin, 1898), 20.

8. Moses Younglove to Margaret Younglove, February 4, 1852; Sarah Calvert Simons to TCC, December 11, 1854; Emma Calvert Tarbet to TCC, January 15, 1855, CFP.

9. TCC Diary, Friday [February 27, 1852], CFP; Elizabeth Cox Underwood to Joseph Rogers Underwood, April 26, 1852, UC; PCSM, May 2, December 13, 1852.

10. TCC Diary, January 29, 1852, CFP; Jonathan Jeffrey and Michael Dowell, *Bittersweet: The Louisville and Nashville Railroad and Warren County* (Bowling Green, Ky.: Landmark Association, 2001), 6, 8, 56.

11. TCC Diary, February 26, 29, 1852, CFP.

12. Sarah Calvert Simons to TCC, December 11, 1854; Emma Calvert Tarbet to TCC, January 15, 1855; Jane Younglove to TCC, August 11, 1855, CFP.

13. Whether Lida had a middle name is somewhat unclear. The county registry of births names her as "Eliza Calvert," as does one entry in the Calvert family Bible, but a second entry reads "Eliza C. Calvert." Later in life, her sister Margaret inscribed some family birth and death information in a datebook, writing Lida's name as "Eliza Caroline," but light pencil lines have been drawn through "Caroline," and no other evidence of her middle name can be found. See MC Diary/Datebook, CFP.

14. Foster, "Distinguished Daughter of Kentucky"; Jane Younglove Di-

ary, September 6, December 1, 1857, YFP; LCO to JC, October 4, 1933, OFP; Calvert Family Genealogy Notes; TCC to Mary Calvert, August 31, 1876; TCC to JC, March 19, 1876, CFP. Thomas J. Hall died in 1859 and was buried in Rock Creek, Tennessee. The 1860 slave census shows Thomas C. Calvert as the owner of one male, age forty-five, and one female, age thirty-three. Uncle George may be the male, since the Presbyterian Church minutes of March 19, 1862, authorize the deacons "to employ the boy George belonging to T. C. Calvert" as sexton. The identity of the female is unclear; perhaps it was Isabella Curd, although she is recorded as forty years old in the 1870 census.

15. JIY to JEY, July 15, 1864, YFP.

16. TCC to Mary Calvert, May 6, 1874; Lily Hughes Lucas to JC, October 19, December 8, 1938, CFP; LCO to JC, October 3, 1928, August 6, 1929; LCO to Hatty [Grider], October 27, 1923, OFP.

17. Warren County, Ky. Deed Book 26, 176; Bowling Green City Minutes, December 8, 1856, Ky. Lib.; PCSM, September 1859. The value of Thomas's real and personal property in 1860 would carry about $740,000 worth of purchasing power today.

18. Arndt M. Stickles, *Simon Bolivar Buckner: Borderland Knight* (Chapel Hill: University of North Carolina Press, 1940), 98, 103; ECH, "Bowling Green and the Civil War," *Filson Club History Quarterly*, vol. 11, no. 4 (October 1937): 248 (written in 1894 and published posthumously); LCO to OR, August 11, 1915, ORMP.

19. Stickles, *Simon Bolivar Buckner*, 118; W. W. Mackall to Simon Bolivar Buckner, November 13, 1861; George W. Johnson to James Hines, December 20, 1861, Hines Collection, Ky. Lib.; Deposition of TCC, November 12, 1870, Clarence Underwood McElroy Collection, Ky. Lib.; affidavit of George Lehman, *George Lehman v. United States*, Ct. Cl. No. 2310 (July 16, 1879), photocopy, Ky. Lib.; *S. D. Bruce v. T. C. Calvert*, No. 259 (indexed as No. 3570), Cir. Ct. (Warren Co., Ky., July 8, 1869). Thomas's wartime businesses were not always profitable. The beef venture derailed, he later claimed, when an army officer attempted to extort an interest in the contract in return for timely approval of payment vouchers. After the war, George Lehman (Thomas's partner in the bakery) made a claim against the U.S. government for unpaid rent.

20. Stickles, *Simon Bolivar Buckner*, 103, 120; JIY to James Younglove, April 25, 1862, YFP; Warren County, Ky. Deed Book 30, 134; "Life and Teachings of Mary K. Jones."

21. Affidavit of George Lehman, *Lehman v. United States*; PCSM, December 2, 1864; Rodes, "First Presbyterian Church," 61–64, 80, 83.

22. *Ky. Acts* 1865, ch. 1669; *Ray's Administrators v. Bank of Kentucky*, 10 Bush 344 (Ky. Ct. App. 1874) at 346–47.

23. *Ray's Administrators v. Bank of Kentucky* at 346; *United Society of Shakers v. Underwood et al.*, 11 Bush 265 (Ky. Ct. App. 1875); *Davenport v. Underwood et al.*, 9 Bush 609 (Ky. Ct. App. 1873) at 615.

24. Deposition of TCC; LCO to JWT, June 19, 1915, JWTC; TCC to MYC, August 18, 1866, CFP.

25. J. W. Calvert, "Special Statement," undated letter, apparently to MYC, CFP.

26. D. J. Williams, Residence of T. C. Calvert Esq., Front Elevation Sketch, CFP; J. F. Redford to Caleb Bell, June 17, 1871, Bell Family Letters, Ky. Lib.

27. *Barclay, Claypool & Co. v. T. C. Calvert, William Cooke and L. L. Cooke,* No. 344 (indexed as No. 3732), Cir. Ct. (Warren Co., Ky., October 20, 1870); *T. W. Baird v. Thomas C. Calvert,* No. 353 (indexed as No. 3596), Cir. Ct. (Warren Co., Ky., November 9, 1870); *Ray's Administrators v. Bank of Kentucky* at 352; Calvert, "Special Statement"; Warren County, Ky. Deed Book 37, 32.

28. *Louisville (Ky.) Courier-Journal,* October 17, November 4, 24, 1870; *Ray's Administrators v. Bank of Kentucky* at 347.

29. *Courier-Journal,* October 17, 1870; Petition of John L. Row to W. L. Dulaney, Judge of Warren Court of Common Pleas, November 9, 1870, McElroy Collection.

30. Deposition of TCC; *Courier-Journal,* October 17, November 24, 1870; *Shakers v. Underwood* at 615; *Ky. Acts* 1865, ch. 1669, §12.

31. TCC to MYC, [1871], CFP.

3. Exile

1. Petition for Pardon of TCC by Creditors, April 15, 1880, Governor Luke P. Blackburn Correspondence, Kentucky Department for Libraries and Archives, Frankfort, Ky.; *Shakers v. Underwood* at 269; *Ray's Administrators v. Bank of Kentucky.* Through several trials and appeals, the Shaker case generated a precedent-setting examination of the principles upon which bank directors might become liable for employee theft. In 1879, however, the parties appear to have settled the case; Thomas H. Hines to Clarence U. McElroy, January 18, 1879, McElroy Collection.

2. Calvert Family Genealogy Notes; TCC to JC, September 13, 1874; TCC to MYC, February 3, 1878, CFP; LCO to MC, December 26, 1934, OFP; "Old Mahogany," in ECH, *Clover and Blue Grass* (Boston: Little, Brown, and Company, 1916), 96, 113.

3. TCC to MYC, [1871], CFP.

4. Ibid.; Petition for Pardon of TCC by Attorneys of Bowling Green, April 15, 1880, Blackburn Correspondence; *Courier-Journal,* June 9, 1883; Charles Whittle, "Warren College," unpublished manuscript, 1924, Ogden College Collection, Western Kentucky University Archives. Thomas Calvert's correspondence gives few clues to his whereabouts. In 1875 he wrote to his daughter Mary and referred to the weather in her "part of the world," but in 1876 he complained to Margaret that he had

little news of events in her "part of the country." Two years later he mentioned reading a Chicago newspaper and told her that by "going out of the way a little" he could find some familiar faces, suggesting that he was not a great distance away. He also wrote in October of the presence of autumn leaves, which would have been inconsistent with residence in South America. A letter written to him in 1888 refers to his past business activity in Washington Territory; TCC to Mary Calvert, February 28, 1875; TCC to MYC, April 10, 1876, March 31, September 15, October 18, 1878; Levant F. Thompson to TCC, April 26, 1888, CFP.

5. J. W. Calvert, "Special Statement"; Storts School Invoices, 1871–1875, CFP; Fannie S. Wilson, "Gleanings From An Old Scrap Book: Green River Female Seminary, Bowling Green, Kentucky," unpublished manuscript, 1940, Ky. Lib. As the Shakers proceeded with their lawsuit, Joseph Whit remained under the suspicion of Joseph Underwood, president of the Bank of Bowling Green at the time of its failure. In 1874 he received a report from his son that Joseph Whit had waved an envelope full of bonds in a Louisville store; Eugene Underwood to Joseph R. Underwood, March 18, 1874, McElroy Collection.

6. Narka Nelson, *The Western College for Women, 1853–1953* (Oxford, Ohio: Western College, 1954), 5, 10, 26, 60.

7. *Western Female Seminary Catalogue*, 1873–74; M. L. [Martha] Calvert to MYC, February 12, 1874, CFP (emphasis in original).

8. Storts School Invoices; TCC to Mary Calvert, December 8, 1875, CFP. Lida may have made an abortive attempt to return to school in summer 1876; TCC to MYC, August 25, 1876, CFP.

9. TCC to MYC, February 11, 1876; TCC to Mary Calvert, September 7, 1874, May 20, 1876, CFP; Warren County, Ky. Deed Book 43, 424; Book 41, 179. At the time Margaret moved into her house, Park Street was known as Buena Vista Street. A 1909 deed confirmed an earlier settlement with Margaret, the record of which had been lost, for her dower interest in Thomas's Vinegar Hill property, by then known as Copley Knob; Warren County, Ky. Deed Book 106, 259.

10. TCC to MYC, August 25, 1876, May 19, June 28, 1878; JC Diary, November 25, 29, 1878, February 13, June 25, 1879; Mary Kendall Jones to MYC, August 23, 1876; TCC to JC, March 19, 1876, CFP; Cecil Calvert Obenchain to JWT, June 13, 1915, JWTC; unidentified biographical sketch of Mrs. Eliza Calvert [*sic*], Mackie E. Bennett Collection, Ky. Lib. This sketch was written between 1923 and 1935, possibly by Mrs. Bennett. It gives details of Lida's schools and identifies some of her students and the location of their desks, suggesting that the writer had also been a student. Although Maggie was less than a diligent scholar, Thomas in fact believed that she had the "best mind" of his five children; TCC to MYC, August 25, 1876, CFP.

11. TCC to JC, September 13, 1874; JC Diary, November 24, 25, 1878, January 21, February 2, April 11, 1879, January 10, April 3, May 28, September 15, October 5, 1880, January 31, 1881, CFP.

12. Henry C. Batts to MC, June 8, 1883; TCC to MYC, November 25, 1875, CFP. From 1871 to 1883, Thomas wrote at least 116 letters, a count that includes those he mentions having written in the text of those that survive. Although he refers to correspondence with every family member, all of the surviving sixty were written to his wife Margaret or to daughters Mary or Josie. Only one letter written to Thomas during his exile, by Josie on September 5, 1877, still exists. Having no safe place to store letters from his family, Thomas carried them in his pocket and burned all but the most recent when the bundle became too large; TCC to Mary Calvert, February 28, 1875, CFP.

13. TCC to MYC, July 8, 1875, February 11, 1876, August 12, 1877, March 31, May 19, 1878; TCC to Mary Calvert, December 8, 1875, May 20, 1876, March 10, 1878; TCC to JC, April 22, 1877, CFP.

14. TCC to JC, April 2, 1874, January 3, 1875; TCC to Mary Calvert, April 11, 1871, April 2, 1872, August 24, 1873, May 6, 1874, May 20, 1876; TCC to MYC, August 10, 1876, August 11, September 15, 1878, CFP; PCSM, July 6, November 1, 1873.

15. TCC to MYC, December 27, 1875, April 10, 1876, August 12, 1877, March 31, April 28, June 28, 1878; TCC to Mary Calvert, August 24, 1873, May 6, 1874, February 28, 1875, August 31, 1876; TCC to JC, February 8, 1876, CFP.

16. TCC to Mary Calvert, September 7, 1874, February 28, December 8, 1875; TCC to MYC, April 29, 1876, May 19, June 9, 1878, CFP.

17. TCC to MYC, July 8, 1875, January 16, March 26, 1876, June 9, 28, October 18, 1878; TCC to JC, February 8, 1876; JC Diary, December 4, 12, 28, 1878, CFP. Lida, in fact, had two dressmakers: Mrs. James Kemp, whose sons clerked at Younglove's Drugstore, and Carrie Burnam Taylor, whose firm came to employ as many as three hundred seamstresses in the service of local women and a substantial mail-order clientele. Mrs. Taylor drew on New York and European fabrics and trends for her distinctively styled garments.

18. TCC to Mary Calvert, April 11, 1871, CFP; LCO to MC and JC, September 3, 1929, OFP; Elyce Wakerman, *Father Loss: Daughters Discuss the Man That Got Away* (New York: Henry Holt, 1984), 253, 256, quoted in Donna Dickenson, *Margaret Fuller: Writing a Woman's Life* (New York: St. Martin's Press, 1993), 55. The similarities between Lida's early experiences and Margaret Fuller's are noteworthy. Fuller's father, serving in Congress, was absent for much of her childhood. To save him money, she educated her younger sister and brothers at home, and the economic upheaval caused by his death compelled her to continue teaching. Fuller's paternal uncle was even involved in the family finances as administrator of her father's unproductive estate.

19. LCO, "Education Does Not Necessarily Mean Mere Completion of School," *Dallas Daily Times-Herald,* December 31, 1922; ECH, "Second-Hand People," *KFW,* October 24, 1894, 262. The unidentified biographical sketch of Lida in the Mackie E. Bennett Collection claims that she eventually burned her diploma (presumably from the Storts school) because she decided that it "did not amount to much." While not verified elsewhere, this gesture would be entirely consistent with Lida's view of education as more than school attendance.

20. COR to MC, December 14, 1932, OFP; TCC to Mary Calvert, June 8, 1875, September 9, 1877, CFP.

21. TCC to JC, September 16, 1876; Martha Calvert to MYC, [January] 2, 1879, CFP.

22. TCC to MYC, October 18, 1878; Martha Calvert to MYC, March 23, 1880, CFP.

23. Petition for Pardon of TCC by Attorneys; Petition for Pardon of TCC by Creditors; W. H. Rochester to Luke P. Blackburn, May 1, 1880, Blackburn Correspondence.

4. The Major

1. JC Diary, September 15, 1879, CFP.

2. Arthur W. John, *The Best Years of the Century: Richard Watson Gilder, "Scribner's Monthly," and the "Century Magazine," 1870–1909* (Urbana: University of Illinois Press, 1981), x, 3, 13, 26–27, 32–33, 45, 56, 59, 173–74; Alfred Habegger, *My Wars Are Laid Away in Books: The Life of Emily Dickinson* (New York: Modern Library, 2001), 563–64, citing "The Woman Question," Josiah Gilbert Holland Papers, Box 1, Manuscripts and Archives Division, New York Public Library; "Kentucky Women Poets," *Courier-Journal,* August 16, 1931; Lee sketch. Reproducing "Galatea" (but not exactly as published in *Scribner's*) for Miss Lee, Lida attributed the "exquisite" praise to Gilder; in "Lida Calvert Obenchain," an autobiographical sketch published in *WJ,* October 14, 1899, 326, she credited Holland.

3. Eliza C. Hall, "Galatea," *Scribner's Monthly,* November 1879, 34; Eliza C. Hall, "A Lesson in Mythology," *Scribner's Monthly,* December 1879, 320; Eliza C. Hall, "An International Episode," *Scribner's Monthly,* April 1880, 952; John, *Best Years of the Century,* 67–68. Mary Mapes Dodge began writing children's stories after she was suddenly widowed; in 1873 she became the editor of *St. Nicholas,* the juvenile magazine launched by Scribner and Company that appeared on Josie Calvert's reading list. In 1883 Emma Lazarus wrote her most celebrated poem, "The New Colossus" ("Give me your tired, your poor, / Your huddled masses yearning to breathe free"). Elizabeth Stuart Phelps published her own, identically titled poetic meditation on the Galatea myth in *Harper's Monthly,* May 1883, 892.

4. Susan Coultrap-McQuin, *Doing Literary Business: American Women*

Writers in the Nineteenth Century (Chapel Hill: University of North Carolina Press, 1990), 119, 159, 170; Showalter, *Sister's Choice,* 49.

5. JC Diary, February 27, March 4, May 29, 1879, CFP. Henry Woods soon married another of Joseph Underwood's daughters, Josephine, and in 1893 Malcolm Crump married Warner Underwood's daughter Mary.

6. Warren County, Ky. Deed Book 38, 307; "'Barn' Removed after Long Years of Use," (Ogden College) *Cardinal,* October 22, 1924; Jesse B. Johnson and Lowell H. Harrison, "Ogden College: A Brief History," *Register of the Kentucky Historical Society,* vol. 68, no. 3 (July 1970): 189–220; JC to TCC, September 5, 1877, CFP.

7. Healey/Brown Family Genealogy, http://worldconnect.rootsweb .com/cgi-bin/igm.cgi?=GET&db=cjpacker&idI1112 [accessed May 7, 2003]; Diane R. Jacob, archivist, Preston Library, Virginia Military Institute, to the author, March 8, 2001; WAO, "Stonewall Jackson's Scabbard Speech," *Southern Historical Society Papers,* vol. 16 (1888): 44–45; XV Club Minutes, April 22, 1897, Ky. Lib. Ogden's professors, proudly described by an alumnus as a "rebel faculty," included the much-loved General William F. Perry, a native of Alabama and veteran of Gettysburg who taught from 1883 to 1900; Silas Bent, "Memories of Ogden Faculty of 1902," *Cardinal,* April 14, 1927.

8. XV Club Minutes, May 4, 1899; WAO, "How General Lee Made Glad the Heart of a Subaltern," *Confederate Veteran,* May 1901, 224; (Bowling Green, Ky.) *Park City Daily News,* February 12, 1987.

9. Jesse Butler Johnson, "The History of Ogden College" (master's thesis, George Peabody College for Teachers, Nashville, Tenn., 1929), 54–55.

10. "Gens. Kirby Smith and Bushrod Johnson," *Confederate Veteran,* December 1908, 639; XV Club Minutes, January 2, 1896.

11. JC Diary, March 22, April 24, June 1, 23, July 13, 1879, CFP.

12. JC Diary, August 24, 1879, July 2, 24, 1880; Genevieve Curtis to MC, September 1, 1879, January 18, 1880, CFP.

13. JC Diary, August 27, September 6, November 15, 1880, CFP. "We (the girls I mean) had the pleasure of seeing Master Hugh Campbell, Sam Stout, Emery Phillips and John Rodes receive first class paddlings," Josie wrote gleefully after a day at school. Edward's finicky appetite drew this observation: "My beloved brother, it seems, has had an exceedingly strong desire to become famous in this world. This morning he conceived a plan for fasting a week"; JC Diary, December 3, 1878, August 30, 1880.

14. Eliza C. Hall, "Compensation," *Scribner's Monthly,* October 1880, 852; LCO, "Charlotte Perkins Stetson: A Poet of Two Reforms," *Courier-Journal,* March 27, 1895 (reprinted in *Woman's Tribune,* June 22, 1895, 97); "Kentucky Women Poets"; ECH, "Felicissima," *Atlantic Monthly,* June 1881, 784; John, *Best Years of the Century,* 151; Matthew Schneirov, *The Dream of a New Social Order: Popular Magazines in America 1893–1914* (New York: Columbia University Press, 1994), 46; LCO to OR, June 14, 1921, ORP; Sophie Lee, "Elizabeth [*sic*] Calvert Hall" (master's thesis, George Peabody

College for Teachers, Nashville, Tenn., 1929). Lee quotes the original couplet in "Felicissima" as: "She plunged to pain's most dark, most sacred deeps;
/ And on her breast a pale, cold baby sleeps." Aldrich rather blandly rewrote
it: "She fathomed pain's most sacred mysteries,—/ Wan on her breast the
flower of beauty lies!"

15. Genevieve Curtis to MC, October 24, 1882, CFP.

16. TCC to JC, July 25, 1884; Henry C. Batts to MC, June 8, 1883, CFP;
Courier-Journal, August 19, 1883.

17. TCC to JC, March 16, July 25, September 25, 1884, March 25, 1886,
CFP.

18. *Courier-Journal,* June 3, 1883.

19. Biographical Sketch, Mackie E. Bennett Collection; "Great Social
Event," [*Bowling Green (Ky.) Times-Gazette,* July 15, 1885], clipping in OFP.

20. Genevieve Curtis to MC, [1885], CFP; COR to MC, December 14,
1932, OFP; "My Mail-Bag," *KFW,* October 17, 1894, 244. The poem, "Reasons," was published in *KFW,* September 12, 1894, 167.

21. Genevieve Curtis to MC, August 2, 1885, March 4, 1886, CFP; COR
to MC, December 14, 1932, OFP; "My Mail-Bag," *KFW,* October 17, 1894.

22. Edmund Wilson, *Patriotic Gore: Studies in the Literature of the Amer-
ican Civil War* (New York: Oxford University Press, 1962), 305–6; XV Club
Minutes, October 9, 1890; [LCO], "William Alexander Obenchain," *Ogden
College Bulletin,* April 1917, 4; *Park City Daily News,* February 12, 1987.
In *Writing a Woman's Life* (New York: Ballantine Books, 1988), Carolyn G.
Heilbrun discusses the tendency in biography to view women's marriages
"from the outside, using only the indications of happy marriage that romance
and the patriarchy have taught us" (95). The same can be said of courtships.
Our cultural preference is to see a starry-eyed young woman (preferably
younger than Lida's twenty-nine), hear her rhapsodic praises of the young
man, and sense the powerful sexual attraction. In the absence of such signs,
finding the language to understand and describe the resulting marriage, no
matter how long-lived, as anything other than an imperfect bargain remains
a challenge (93). In this regard, it is unfortunate that the union of Lida and
the Major is not so much explained as obscured by Cecil's later, anguished
claim that it was a foolish, even ugly mistake. Maggie Calvert's school friend
in St. Louis poses an even more curious example. An affectionate, perceptive
young woman who observed that matrimony had "the most deadening effect
on girls" and who failed to see the nobility of so "merg[ing] your life into
that of another's as to lose your identity," she became engaged to a man she
casually described as neither particularly handsome, nor wealthy, nor even
likeable. How does one judge her decision—or his? See Genevieve Curtis to
MC, December 27, 1886, CFP.

23. [LCO], "William Alexander Obenchain," 5; "Major William Alexander Obenchain," *Cardinal,* 1913; Johnson and Harrison, "Ogden College: A
Brief History," 199.

24. Cecil Calvert Obenchain to JWT, September 4, 1915, JWTC. The Major's "favorite hobby is discipline," explained the 1913 Ogden College yearbook. Under the heading "Famous Sayings by Famous Men," the 1914 yearbook offered: "Major.—'You boys need discipline.'"

25. *Courier-Journal,* December 30, 1883, July 12, 1885; ECH, "Her Choice," *Century Magazine,* January 1884, 462; Henry C. Batts to MC, [December 1883], CFP; "Great Social Event." Publication in the *Century*—formerly *Scribner's*—marked the continuation of Richard Watson Gilder's patronage of Lida. The magazine had changed its name in 1881 when Charles Scribner sold his interest.

5. Cook, Scullion, Nurse, Laundress

1. *Ky. General Statutes* 1873, ch. 52, art. II, §4.

2. William Blackstone, *Commentaries on the Laws of England* (Oxford: Clarendon Press, 1765), 1:430. In 1776, Virginia had accepted the authority of English statute and common law made prior to 1607, subject to alteration by its legislature. Similarly, in 1792 Kentucky's first constitution adopted the general laws of Virginia until specifically altered or repealed, and the 1799 constitution contained substantially the same provision. English law thus was passed down to Kentucky, albeit in a selective manner.

3. Fuller, 40; *Moreland v. Myall,* 77 Ky. 474 (1879); *Ky. General Statues* 1873, chs. 24, 48, 52.

4. John D. Johnston Jr., "Sex and Property: The Common Law Tradition, the Law School Curriculum, and Developments toward Equality," *New York University Law Review,* vol. 47, no. 6 (December 1972): 1046–50; *Basham v. Chamberlain,* 46 Ky. 443 (1846); *Uhrig v. Hortsman & Sons,* 8 Bush 172 (1871).

5. Gen. 2:24, 3:16; Johnston, "Sex and Property," 1046–47; *Ky. Revised Statutes* 1873, ch. 47, art. II, §4. All biblical references are to the King James Version.

6. *Yates' Will,* 32 Ky. 215 (1834); *Wilkinson v. Wright,* 45 Ky. 576 (1846); *Ky. Revised Statutes* 1852, ch. 106; *George v. Bussing,* 15 B. Mon. 558 (1855).

7. *Ky. Acts* 1867–68, ch. 146, §1; TCC Diary, February 17, 1852, CFP; Warren County, Ky. Deed Book 24, 316; Book 27, 566; Book 43, 424.

8. W. Lewis Roberts, "Property Rights of Married Women in Kentucky," *Kentucky Law Journal,* vol. 11, no. 1 (November 1922): 2. In one of his letters to Margaret, Thomas Calvert appeared to accuse Joseph Underwood of manipulating the laws of coverture by "compell[ing] his daughter to plead her rights as a married woman, to avoid payment of an honest debt incurred to provide clothes for herself and family"; TCC to MYC, March 26, 1876, CFP. A creditor had in fact sued Underwood's daughter Julia and her husband, John T. Cox, in connection with money advanced for the family's nec-

essary expenses. The creditor made the loan in the belief, almost certainly correct in law, that Julia's signature on the promissory note charged her trust property with payment of the debt. The Coxes appear to have disputed this, although the court record is incomplete as to their defense of the action and its outcome; see *Matthew Hare v. John T. and Julia U. Cox*, No. 2800, Cir. Ct. (Warren Co., Ky., January 12, 1861). Thomas Calvert referred disdainfully to this tactic while writing of the engagement of Julia's half-brother Robert, whom he disliked, to Joseph Younglove's daughter Emma.

9. Fuller, 2–3, 10–16.

10. Fuller, 23–27. Susan B. Anthony's three lectures in Richmond were part of a tour of Kentucky in late October 1879 that included stops in Owensboro and Bowling Green; Knott, 13.

11. Mary Jane Clay to LC, April 18, 1863, Bennett Dep., quoted in Knott, 19.

12. "Great Social Event"; *Courier-Journal*, October 25, 1885; XV Club Minutes, October 22, 1885; Warren County, Ky. Deed Book 60, 442; *Bowling Green Times-Gazette*, June 3, 1885, typescript, Ky. Lib. The Major's salary would carry the purchasing power of about $28,700 today.

13. "Great Social Event"; XV Club Minutes, March 19, 1891, October 13, 1910.

14. LCO, "Prologue to The Queen of the Birds," March 4, 1886, Schools Special File, Ky. Lib.; *Courier-Journal*, January 16, 1887; *Bowling Green Times-Gazette*, February 11, 1885. Many sources give Margery's birth year as 1886, but it appears to have been 1887. Lida wrote an article in June 1902 referring to her fourteen-year-old daughter; LCO, "A Model Commencement Address," *WJ*, June 28, 1902, 208. Margery's stated age in her obituary would also place her birth in 1887.

15. LCO to JC, August 18, 1894, OFP.

16. [LCO], "New Domestic Literature," *NYT*, October 17, 1897; LCO to LC, August 1, 1906, LCP; LCO, "Interesting Article by Gifted Writer on Subject of 'Hired Girl Problem,'" unidentified Bowling Green, Ky., newspaper article, [November 1905]; LCO to MYC, August 26, 1914, OFP; ECH, "Woman and Nature," *KFW*, August 1, 1894, 78; Foster, "Distinguished Daughter of Kentucky," 53. Biographers of Emily Dickinson and Emily Brontë have noted that they, too, excelled in bread making, considered by one 1867 household manual to be the premier domestic art; Habegger, *Life of Emily Dickinson*, 502, 605.

17. LCO to JC, August 18, 1894, OFP; XV Club Minutes, March 28, 1912.

18. Fuller, 30–34, 37–40.

19. LCO to Henrietta B. Chenault, February 20, August 25, 1888, LCP.

20. LCO, "Woman Suffrage a Principle," *WJ*, February 29, 1896, 72; *Courier-Journal*, January 9, 1887; TCC Business Papers, CFP.

21. Fuller, 37–38.

22. "Some New Lamps for Some Old," unidentified newspaper article, [1913]; Fannie Segur Foster, "Eliza Calvert Hall," unidentified newspaper article, [Dallas, August 1914], OFP.

23. [LCO], "Why Democratic Women Want the Ballot," *National Bulletin*, December 1892; Martha M. Solomon, "The Role of the Suffrage Press in the Woman's Rights Movement," in *A Voice of Their Own: The Woman Suffrage Press, 1840–1910* (Tuscaloosa: University of Alabama Press, 1991), 13; *Woman's Tribune*, March 1885, 2; LCO, "Woman Suffrage a Principle," 72.

24. Laura Ballard, "What Flag Shall We Fly?" *Revolution*, October 1870, quoted in Solomon, "The Role of the Suffrage Press," 9; Bonnie J. Dow, "The Revolution, 1868–1870: Expanding the Woman Suffrage Agenda," in Solomon, *A Voice of Their Own*, 75; Susan Schultz Huxman, "The *Woman's Journal*, 1870–1890: The Torchbearer for Suffrage," in Solomon, *A Voice of Their Own*, 88.

25. E. Claire Jerry, "The Role of Newspapers in the Nineteenth-Century Woman's Movement," in Solomon, *A Voice of Their Own*, 23; Huxman, "The *Woman's Journal*," 89.

26. Foster, "Eliza Calvert Hall." The use by women, deliberately or unconsciously, of a transformative event to embark upon a "quest plot" and thereby escape the conventional life narrative of marriage and motherhood is discussed in Heilbrun, *Writing a Woman's Life*, 48.

6. Straight to a Woman's Heart

1. Fuller, 18–19, 21.
2. "Some New Lamps for Some Old."
3. ECH, "Why I Wrote 'Sally Ann's Experience,'" *Cosmopolitan*, July 1908, 164.
4. "Some New Lamps for Some Old"; Foster, "Eliza Calvert Hall"; Foster, "Distinguished Daughter of Kentucky"; LCO to [JWT], [ca. 1907], JWTC.
5. Charles H. Crandall, *Representative Sonnets by American Poets* (Boston: Houghton, Mifflin and Company, 1890). The poems by Eliza Calvert Hall were "Her Choice," *Century Magazine*, January 1884, 462, and "One Way of Love," *Century Magazine*, May 1884, 122.
6. *Courier-Journal*, November 13, 1887; "Kentucky Women Poets."
7. "Kentucky Women Poets"; ECH, "The Unspoken Word," *Harper's*, November 1891, 918.
8. "Lida Calvert Obenchain," *WJ*, October 14, 1899, 326; "Kentucky Women Poets"; Ann Douglas Wood, "The Literature of Impoverishment: The Women Local Colorists in America 1865–1914," *Women's Studies*, vol. 1 (1972): 4, 5, 9, 17, 22; Elsley, "Uncovering Eliza Calvert Hall," 157. Among the ten sentimental writers surveyed by Wood, "Fanny Fern," Sarah Hale,

Lydia Huntley Sigourney, Elizabeth Oakes Smith, Ann M. Stephens, and Harriet Beecher Stowe all sympathized with some aspect of the women's rights movement.

9. ECH, "My Inspiration," undated clipping of poem "written for the *Intelligencer*," OFP.

10. LCO Miscellaneous Poems, OFP.

11. LCO to JC, August 18, 1894, OFP; Foster, "Eliza Calvert Hall"; ECH, "Why I Wrote 'Sally Ann's Experience,'" 165; LCO, "Women and Literature," *NYT*, January 16, 1898, sect. 2, 2; "Some New Lamps for Some Old."

12. Knott, 40; *Courier-Journal*, January 14, 18, 26, 1890; "The Constitutional Convention of Kentucky," *WJ*, March 14, 1891, 86; *Laws of Kentucky* 1889–90, ch. 293; "Letter from Kentucky," *WJ*, June 17, 1893, 190.

13. "Kentucky," *WJ*, January 30, 1892, 41; "The Constitutional Convention of Kentucky"; "Of Interest to Kentucky Women," *WJ*, July 18, 1891, 227.

14. "The Constitutional Convention of Kentucky"; "Kentucky," *WJ*, January 30, 1892, 41; *Courier-Journal*, February 10, 1892; "Equal Rights Hearing in Kentucky," *WJ*, February 20, 1892, 62–63. Kentucky had, in fact, been the first state to grant school suffrage to women on a limited basis. An 1830 law passed (but apparently never utilized) to encourage the "diffusion of education" allowed local district taxation by popular vote, and included in the franchise any widow or feme sole over twenty-one residing in the district and owning property subject to taxation for school purposes; *Laws of Kentucky* 1829–30, ch. 387. An 1838 act establishing a common school fund carried forward this right, although it appears rarely to have been exercised; *Laws of Kentucky* 1837–38, ch. 898; Knott, 196–97. In 1886, under a system of county taxation that did not apply to chartered cities, widows and spinsters having taxable property or a child or ward of school age were among the qualified voters; *Laws of Kentucky* 1885–86, ch. 1224.

15. "Kentucky E.R.A.," *Woman's Tribune*, November 26, 1891, 238.

16. E. Claire Jerry, "Clara Bewick Colby and the *Woman's Tribune*, 1883–1909: The Free Lance Editor as Movement Leader," in Solomon, *A Voice of Their Own*, 112, 123–24, 128; "Kentucky E.R.A.," *Woman's Tribune*, November 26, 1892, 238. "Why Democratic Women Want the Ballot" was published in the *Woman's Tribune*, December 17, 1892, 250, and October 12, 1895, 135, and in the *National Bulletin*, December 1892. Clara Bewick Colby suffered her own depredations as a married woman. Her husband, Leonard Colby, a charming but unprincipled character, was an officer in the Nebraska National Guard at the time of the 1890 Wounded Knee Massacre. He adopted an orphaned Lakota girl, Lost Bird, then deserted Clara for the girl's nursemaid. After he and Clara divorced in 1906, Leonard rarely met his financial obligations to either her or Lost Bird. Clara was forced to close the *Woman's Tribune* in 1909 and died in poverty in 1916; see www.sdpb.org/tv/oto/lostbird/summary.asp [accessed March 26, 2007].

17. LCO, "Why Democratic Women Want the Ballot."

18. Ibid. (emphasis in original); Dow, "The Revolution," 83–84; Huxman, "The *Woman's Journal*," 99. The characterization of woman suffrage arguments as based upon either justice or expediency is part of Aileen S. Kraditor's study, *The Ideas of the Woman Suffrage Movement, 1890–1920* (New York: Columbia University Press, 1965), 43–74, while Huxman's analysis of the rhetorical tasks facing suffrage as a social movement has provided a useful framework for the discussion in this chapter. See also LCO, "Woman Suffrage a Principle."

19. 1 Cor. 11:7–9; Eph. 5:24; 1 Cor. 14:34–35.

20. Knott, 55–56, 63–68; Gen. 1:27, 5:1–2. Knott observes that Laura and her sister Sallie used the evangelical framework while her mother and sister Mary preferred to argue for women's rights based on the American idea of individual liberty.

21. [LCO], "Woman in Politics," *Kentucky Leader*, January 10, 1895. Beginning with the nuns and female mystics of the Middle Ages, women had engaged in Bible criticism for over a thousand years. Although Lida and the Clay sisters had learned about many of the heroines of history, mythology, and literature, like other suffragists they were forced to devote time to what one historian has called a "constant reinventing of the wheel" caused by lack of access to this female intellectual tradition; see Gerda Lerner, *The Creation of Feminist Consciousness: From the Middle Ages to Eighteen-Seventy* (New York: Oxford University Press, 1993), 18–19, 166.

22. [LCO], "Woman in Politics"; Knott, 125, 133, 135.

23. Knott, 123, 137; Marjorie Spruill Wheeler, *New Women of the New South: The Leaders of the Woman Suffrage Movement in the Southern States* (New York: Oxford University Press, 1993), 48–49; LCO, "A Clerical Defamer of Women," *WJ*, January 12, 1895, 15; LCO, "The Egotistic Sex," *Womankind*, December 1896, 5; LCO, "A Higher Physical Life for Women," *Womankind*, May 1897, 5.

24. LCO, "Medical Co-Education in Kentucky," *WJ*, April 21, 1894, 128; LCO, "Real Southern Chivalry," *WJ*, September 15, 1894, 292; Wheeler, *New Women of the New South*, 6–7, 18–19; Huxman, "The *Woman's Journal*," 98–99.

25. LCO, "The Typical Woman's Page," *NYT*, November 7, 1897. The approach of a "rationalist" feminism, which pursues legal and political rights to end women's subordination, and a "romantic" feminism, which views the former as hollow without a corresponding psychological transformation, is discussed in Dickenson, *Margaret Fuller*, 133.

26. ECH, "The Sin of Unselfishness," *KFW*, March 28, 1894, 196–97 (emphasis in original).

27. LCO to OR, September 6, 1916, ORP; LCO, "The Greek Definition of Idiot," *Woman's Tribune*, August 18, 1894, 141. Lida hinted at her authorship of "Why Democratic Women Want the Ballot" by signing this article "Lida Calvert Obenchain, 'A Kentucky Woman.'"

28. ECH, "On the Duty of Calling a Spade a Spade," *KFW,* February 9, 1895, 86–87 (emphasis in original); ECH, "Second-Hand People," *KFW,* October 24, 1894, 261–63.

29. ECH, "A Forecast," *KFW,* July 26, 1893, 55; ECH, "Reasons," *KFW,* September 12, 1894, 167; "I Didn't Do It," *KFW,* October 3, 1894, 210; "My Mail-Bag," *KFW,* October 17, 1894, 244; March 2, 1895, 132; March 9, 1895, 148–49.

30. Huxman, "The *Woman's Journal,*" 105; ECH, "Second-Hand People," 261, 262; ECH, "The Opinions of 'John,'" *Womankind,* June 1896, 5; ECH, "Woman and Nature," 77; ECH, "So Fur from the Big Road," *Womankind,* August 1896, 4–5 (reprinted in *WJ,* September 5, 1896, 282).

31. ECH, "The Opinions of 'John.'"

32. ECH, "So Fur from the Big Road," 5; ECH, "The Sin of Unselfishness," 196 (emphasis added); ECH, "Second-Hand People," 263.

33. LCO, "Charlotte Perkins Stetson"; Wheeler, *New Women of the New South,* 49, 72–73; ECH, "Second-Hand People," 263. Although Josephine Henry was slight and wore glasses, Laura Clay was a sturdy, imposing woman; only her aggressive lobbying skills matched Lida's stereotype of a suffragist; see Fuller, 38.

34. ECH, "Second-Hand People," 263; LCO, "Charlotte Perkins Stetson."

35. Charlotte Perkins Stetson to LC, January 5, 1897, LCP; LCO, "Charlotte Perkins Stetson."

36. LCO, "Charlotte Perkins Stetson."

7. Money and Marriage

1. LCO to JC, August 8, 18, 1894, OFP.

2. Henry C. Batts to MC, February 20, March 4, 1884; W. B. Wylie to MC, June 9, 1894, September 18, 25 [n.y.]; Aaron H. Taylor to JC, August 2, 1894, July 8, August 27, 1895, December 26, 1898, CFP. As the letters she saved indicate, Charles Kendall Jones was still in love with Maggie in 1906, when she was forty-five and he was sixty-five; he had even held out hope that Josie might have him. See Charles Kendall Jones to MC, June 29, July 20, 1906, CFP.

3. *Laws of Kentucky* 1891–1893, ch. 205; "Kentucky Women Happy," *WJ,* June 3, 1893, 174.

4. Knott, 141; *Laws of Kentucky* 1894, ch. 76; Fuller, 46–47. For Laura Clay's account of the parliamentary proceedings surrounding passage of the 1894 property rights law, see LC to E. W. Bagby, June 18, 1914, LCP.

5. Fuller, 33, 46; "Kentucky," *WJ,* January 30, 1892, 41; *Laws of Kentucky* 1894, ch. 100; "School Suffrage Granted in Kentucky," *WJ,* April 21, 1894, 122.

6. LCO, "A Kentucky Woman on Kentucky Politics," *WJ,* April 21,

1900, 122; Roberts, "Property Rights of Married Women in Kentucky," 5. The court of appeals cases are *Rose v. Rose*, 104 Ky. 48 and *L. S. Mitchell v. J. T. Violett*, 104 Ky. 77. The cause-and-effect relationship between the KERA and the reform of married women's property law in Kentucky needs study. Surveying the mid-nineteenth-century reforms that occurred in virtually every state as well as Britain and Canada, historians have placed women's demands for equality in the context of other factors creating a favorable climate for change: the need to shield family property from a husband's creditors; the underutilization or ineffectiveness of equity in protecting wives' separate estates; women's increased family responsibilities due to divorce, custody, and adoption reforms; the growth of personalty over realty as a source of wealth; and men's growing use of incorporation, rather than confiscation, of a wife's property as a method of capital formation. See, for example, Richard H. Chused, "Married Women's Property Law: 1800–1850," *Georgetown Law Journal*, vol. 71, no. 5 (1983): 1359–1425; Carole Shammas, "Re-Assessing the Married Women's Property Acts," *Journal of Women's History*, vol. 6, no. 1 (Spring 1994): 9–30. With respect to developments in the southern states during Reconstruction, one historian has argued that equality was simply the by-product, not the object, of property law reform; legislators expanded married women's rights, erratically and ambivalently, in response to anticipated economic and social benefits rather than feminist arguments; Suzanne D. Lebsock, "Radical Reconstruction and the Property Rights of Southern Women," *Journal of Southern History*, vol. 43, no. 2 (May 1977): 195–216.

7. Nancy K. Forderhase, "'The Clear Call of Thoroughbred Women': The Kentucky Federation of Women's Clubs and the Crusade for Educational Reform, 1903–1909," *Register of the Kentucky Historical Society*, vol. 83, no. 1 (1985): 19–35.

8. LCO, "A Point of Honor," *WJ*, June 22, 1895, 194 (emphasis in original).

9. LCO to LC, September 26, 1911, LCP; "Tennessee Centennial Exposition," *WJ*, May 15, 1897, 40; LCO, "The Evolution of Justice," *Womankind*, August 1897, 8–9, October 1897, 6–7.

10. LCO, "The Evolution of Justice," *Womankind*, August 1897, 8–9.

11. Ibid., 9. See also Lida's sarcastic rendition of a husband's marriage vow in "The Rights of Wives," *NYT*, October 24, 1897, and in the *Woman's Tribune*, April 19, 1902, 59.

12. Wheeler, *New Women of the New South*, 16, 74–75, 85; LCO, "The Rights of Wives"; Mrs. David T. Duncan, "Money Matters in Marriage," *NYT*, October 31, 1897.

13. LCO, "Extravagance a Virtue," *NYT*, November 28, 1897; C. E., "The Pay of Servants," *NYT*, December 12, 1897; LCO, "On the Sins of Economy," *NYT*, December 26, 1897.

14. LCO, "The Evolution of Justice," *Womankind*, October 1897, 7;

LCO, "Suffrage Work and Other Work," *WJ*, April 16, 1904, 122–23; LCO, "Hired Girl Problem"; LCO to LC, August 1, 1906, LCP; LCO, "The Myth of Conservatism," *WJ*, January 15, 1898, 22; January 29, 1898, 38–39.

15. [LCO], "Women and Their Ideals," *NYT*, October 31, 1897; LCO, "Not a Question of Years," *NYT*, November 14, 1897; LCO, "Women and Literature."

16. Ewing Galloway, "Eliza Calvert Hall Is Seen at Close Range," *Henderson (Ky.) Daily Gleaner*, August 30, 1908 (reprinted in *Bowling Green (Ky.) Messenger*, September 3, 1908). Lida's contract with Walker would in any event have been short-lived; the syndicate folded in November 1898, a victim of increased competition from other syndicates as well as the influence of mass-market magazines. See Charles Johanningsmeier, "Expanding the Scope of 'Periodical History' for Literary Studies: Irving Bacheller and His Newspaper Fiction Syndicate," *American Periodicals*, vol. 5 (1995): 14–40.

17. EC to JC, October 3, 1897, CFP; LCO to JWT, September 15, 1915, JWTC; LCO to OR, September 20, 1915, OMP.

18. *Ogden College Catalogue*, 1886–87, Western Kentucky University Archives; *Official Register of the Officers and Cadets of the U.S. Military Academy, West Point, New York*, vol. 8 (1888): 21 and vol. 8 (1890): 15, 28; MC Diary, August 19, 1925; EC to JC, October 3, November 5, 1897, CFP.

19. WAO, "Stonewall Jackson's Scabbard Speech"; WAO, "Black Bass Fishing in New River, Virginia," *American Angler*, September 1893; XV Club Minutes, April 16, 1891, February 2, 1911; WAO, "Character Building: Mental and Moral," in *Signal Lights: A Library of Guiding Thoughts by Leading Thinkers of To-Day* (Marion, Iowa: Waffle and Maddock, 1892), 99–108.

20. COR to MC, December 14, 1932, OFP; LCO, "The Egotistic Sex"; XV Club Minutes, April 2, 1896. The XV Club's minutes of its discussion of "Woman in the XIXth Century" are interesting for the range of opinion they reflect. As secretary, the Major dutifully recorded the traditionalism of Judge Warner E. Settle ("Woman's duty is to bear & rear children, & her sphere of action is the home"), the resignation of lawyer Nat Porter ("The woman's movement is progressing, & we must either move with it or be run over"), and the reactionary views of several others, including lawyer William Dulaney ("women should be prevented from talking out at all in church") and banker J. Whitfield Potter, who "had a horror of women voting, & believed it would be a calamity when they were given the franchise in Kentucky."

21. ECH, "Why I Wrote 'Sally Ann's Experience,'" 165; Galloway, "Eliza Calvert Hall Is Seen at Close Range"; Lee sketch.

22. Schneirov, *Dream of a New Social Order*, 82, 87, 106, 269; Frank Luther Mott, *A History of American Magazines, 1741–1930* (Cambridge, Mass.: Belknap Press, 1957), 4: 482–84, 490; "Some Suggestions for Young Writers," *Cosmopolitan*, March 1899, 583.

23. Brander Matthews, "Four Ways of Delivering an Address," *Cosmopolitan*, July 1898, 334–35.

8. Sally Ann's Experience

1. ECH, "Sally Ann's Experience," *Cosmopolitan,* July 1898, 283–91.

2. The Mite Society recalls the parable of the widow's mite in Mark 12:41–44; giving her last two half-pennies to the temple treasury, she makes a contribution out of poverty more significant than those of the wealthy donors who have put in large sums out of abundance. The twelve dollars collected by the women of Goshen Church forty years earlier (about 1858) would carry the purchasing power of about $235 today.

3. A short story of Eliza Calvert Hall's, "The Look without Words," reproduced in Lee, "Elizabeth [*sic*] Calvert Hall," appeared in Cable's short-lived magazine *Symposium* (1896).

4. The literature on local color and regional writing, particularly that of women, is now extensive. A lengthy bibliography appears in "Regional Writing in the United States 1870–1910," www.dotwebb.com/regional_writing/index.html [accessed March 26, 2007]. In addition, for the South generally, see Claud B. Green, "The Rise and Fall of Local Color in Southern Literature," *Mississippi Quarterly,* vol. 17, no. 1 (Winter 1964–65): 1–6. For Kentucky, see Ward, *A Literary History of Kentucky,* 49–64.

5. Josephine Donovan, *New England Local Color Literature: A Women's Tradition* (New York: Frederick Ungar, 1983), 5, 7, 23–24, 30; ECH, "Why I Wrote 'Sally Ann's Experience,'" 163; Dinah Mulock Craik, *A Brave Lady,* serialized in *Harper's Monthly,* May 1869–April 1870.

6. Donovan, *New England Local Color Literature,* 8–9, 30; Wood, "The Literature of Impoverishment," 16; Merrill Maguire Skaggs, *The Folk of Southern Fiction* (Athens: University of Georgia Press, 1972), 194, 217.

7. Rose Terry Cooke, "Mrs. Flint's Married Experience," *Harper's Monthly,* December 1880, 79–101.

8. Harry Stillwell Edwards, "Sister Todhunter's Heart," *Century Magazine,* July 1887, 335–45.

9. Dugald Campbell to MC, August 7, 1898, CFP; ECH, "Why I Wrote 'Sally Ann's Experience,'" 165; H. W. S. Cleveland to LCO; Philip Lindsley to LCO, n.d., transcripts, OFP.

10. WJ, October 15, 1898, 334, January 21, 1899, 17; Lee sketch; Isabel Garghill Beecher to LCO, August 4, 1899, transcript, OFP.

11. ECH, "Why I Wrote 'Sally Ann's Experience,'" 165, 166. Fifty-six dollars would carry the purchasing power of about $1,240 today. The fifteen-dollar check Lida received from *Scribner's* in 1879 for her two poems, a rate of about thirty-five cents per line, would still have been considered generous for poetry in 1898 and much more than even the best magazines paid for prose; Mott, *History of American Magazines,* 4: 39–40.

12. COR to MC, December 14, 1932, OFP.

9. A Jumble of Quilt Pieces

1. LCO to LC, August 1, 1906, LCP (epigraph); notes on Edward Calvert's military service, n.d.; Katherine S. Bauskett to MC, October 4, 1898, CFP; ECH, "Enlisted," *Truth,* 1898. Lida began another patriotic poem, "At Manila," on May 1, 1898, the day Commodore Dewey defeated the Spanish Navy at Manila Bay. Both are reproduced in Lee, "Elizabeth [*sic*] Calvert Hall."

2. LCO, "Women's Attitude towards War," *WJ*, August 13, 1898, 257; LCO, "Heroism of Cuban Women," *WJ*, August 22, 1896, 266; LCO, "The Latest Thing in 'Patriotism,'" *WJ*, December 31, 1898, 417. See also "No Kansans Kissed Hobson," *WJ*, January 21, 1899, 18, Lida's acknowledgment of a correspondent who denied her claim that "hundreds of Kansas women" had kissed Hobson. The four states with full suffrage were Wyoming (1890), Colorado (1893), Idaho (1896), and Utah (1896). In 1898, Louisiana's constitution gave women taxpayers the right to vote on tax questions submitted to the electorate.

3. LCO, "Women's Attitude towards War"; LCO, "The Philippine War," *WJ*, June 3, 1899, 169; LCO, "The Crisis We Face," *Public*, August 4, 1900, 269–70; Kristin Hoganson, "'As Badly Off as the Filipinos': U.S. Women's Suffragists and the Imperial Issue at the Turn of the Twentieth Century," *Journal of Women's History*, vol. 13, no. 2 (Summer 2001): 9–33. Hoganson writes that by late 1899 the Anti-Imperialist League had some thirty thousand members, compared to the NAWSA's fewer than nine thousand. Most anti-imperialist leaders, unfortunately, declined to incorporate woman suffrage into their cause (an exception was Henry Blackwell, who, since Lucy Stone's death in 1893, had assisted his daughter Alice Stone Blackwell in publishing the *Woman's Journal*). For their part, suffragists remained generally self-serving and racially exclusive in their activism, either supporting colonialism or, where they rejected it on principle, neglecting to build alliances with Filipinas or other disenfranchised women.

4. Wheeler, *New Women of the New South*, 115, 116, 119–20; Fuller, 72, 82–84, 86. Laura Clay's formal title at the NAWSA was auditor, an office she held from 1896 to 1911. From 1902 to 1907, she also headed the NAWSA's Membership Committee, where her promotion of the Kentucky Plan increased the number of national members from 17,000 to 45,000 in the last two years of her chairmanship.

5. ECH, "The New Organ," *Cosmopolitan*, February 1899, 411–19. "The New Organ" was one of only three stories to mention Aunt Jane's surname—Parrish—hinting that, like Sally Ann's, her voice carried some spiritual authority.

6. In her monograph on Bowling Green's Civil War history, Lida wrote of "Mr. James Donaldson, familiarly known as 'Uncle Jim,' an old-time Jackson Democrat and an out-spoken Unionist." When the Confederates quit

Bowling Green and he was released from jail, Uncle Jim ran into the street and greeted the sound of exploding Federal shells with "Music! Music! The sweetest music I ever heard"; ECH, "Bowling Green and the Civil War," 243.

7. Ammons, *Conflicting Stories,* 121.

8. Ibid., 47.

9. ECH, "Aunt Jane's Album," *Cosmopolitan,* February 1900, 385–94.

10. Susan E. Bernick describes the characteristics of "traditional quilt culture" in "A Quilt Is an Art Object When It Stands Up like a Man," in Cheryl B. Torsney and Judy Elsley, eds., *Quilt Culture* (Columbia: University of Missouri Press, 1994), 134–50.

11. Showalter, *Sister's Choice,* 147; Pat Ferrero, Elaine Hedges, and Julie Silber, *Hearts and Hands: The Influence of Women and Quilts on American Society* (San Francisco: Quilt Digest Press, 1987), 94–97; [LCO], "Woman in Politics." Shortly after her marriage, Margaret Younglove's sisters, Jane and Mary, touted her sewing skills to her new husband. "I hope she will complete her quilt," Jane wrote Thomas Calvert, and "if she had our assistance the task would be lighter for her. Mary says she is so particular, perhaps we could not do it good enough we would take just as fine stitches as we could"; Jane Younglove to TCC, August 11, 1855, CFP.

12. For a collection of stories and excerpts therefrom relating to quilts and quilting, see Cecilia Macheski, ed., *Quilt Stories* (Lexington: University Press of Kentucky, 1994); see also Cuesta Benberry and Carol Pinney Crabb, *A Patchwork of Pieces: An Anthology of Early Quilt Stories, 1845–1940* (Paducah, Ky.: American Quilter's Society, 1993); Aldrich and Otto, *This Old Quilt.* For discussions of quilting as a metaphor for female values and literary styles, see Showalter, *Sister's Choice,* 145–75, and Melody Graulich, "Piecing and Reconciling: Eliza Calvert Hall's *Aunt Jane of Kentucky,*" in ECH, *Aunt Jane of Kentucky,* ed. Graulich, xxiii–xxxvi.

13. Col. 2:22. In 1929 Virginia Woolf, remarking on how the anonymity of women's lives made them difficult subjects for a novelist, made a similar observation: "Often nothing tangible remains of a woman's day. The food that has been cooked is eaten; the children that have been nursed have gone out into the world." See "Women and Fiction," *Forum,* March 1929, reprinted in Virginia Woolf, *Women and Writing,* ed. Michèle Barrett (New York: Harcourt Brace, Harvest Books, 1979), 49–50.

14. LCO, "More Despotic than Europe," *WJ,* August 16, 1902, 258.

15. LCO to LC, May 6, 1900, May 25, 1909; LC to LCO, July 31, 1906, LCP; "The Kentucky Report," *WJ,* June 15, 1901, 186.

16. "The Kentucky Report"; Fuller, 89–91; Knott, 226–28.

17. "School Suffrage in Kentucky," *WJ,* March 22, 1902, 96; LC to LCO, September 4, 1906, LCP; Fuller, 93; LCO, "The Philippine War." The KERA's membership gain was the largest of any state for 1901; "Miss Clay's Plan," *Woman's Standard,* December 1902, 2.

18. "The End Comes to Miss Mary Calvert at Her Home Yesterday," unidentified newspaper clipping, [November 10, 1902], CFP; LCO to LC, August 1, September 14, 1906, January 2, 1907, May 25, 1909, LCP. For Lida's newspaper lists, see LCO to Mary Barr Clay, March 11, 1909, LCP.

19. Carol Guethlein, "Women in Louisville: Moving toward Equal Rights," *Filson Club History Quarterly*, vol. 55, no. 2 (April 1981): 157–59; LCO, "The Mother's Congress," *Woman's Tribune*, May 1897, 12; Arthur Krock, ed., *The Editorials of Henry Watterson* (Louisville: Courier-Journal Company, 1923), 365; LCO to LC, August 1, September 14, 1906, LCP.

20. LCO, "An Open Letter to Women," *WJ*, December 8, 1900, 390; LCO, "Clubs and Suffrage Association," *Woman's Standard*, August 1904, 3; LCO, "A Kentucky Woman on Kentucky Politics"; LCO, *A Plea for a Little Bit of Common Sense*, Political Equality Series (Warren, Ohio: National American Woman Suffrage Association, 1900); LCO, "Counting and Voting," *WJ*, December 30, 1905, 209.

21. THO to MC, February 11, 1933; LCO to MC, September 25, 1930; Willy Woodward to "Miss Calvert" [MC or JC], January 7, 1939, OFP.

22. Lee sketch; LCO to LC, August 1, 1906, LCP; LCO, "Hired Girl Problem"; LCO to Alice Stone Blackwell, April 17, 1906, NAWSA records. After "The New Organ" and "Aunt Jane's Album," "Sweet Day of Rest" appeared in *Cosmopolitan*, December 1904, 148–55. "Two Loves," a short piece not featuring Aunt Jane, was published in *Cosmopolitan*, November 1904, 67.

23. LCO to LC, August 1, September 30, December 11, 1906; LC to LCO, July 31, October 1, December 15, 1906, November 18, 1907, LCP. Lida's five-dollar salary was being paid at least as early as 1904, when the KERA authorized salaries for the press superintendent and corresponding secretary as long as they could be funded by donations in excess of dues payments; see *WJ*, January 9, 1904, 15.

24. LCO to LC, August 1, 1906, LCP; Johnson, "The History of Ogden College," 106; Johnson and Harrison, "Ogden College: A Brief History," 104–5; James P. Cornette, "The History of Ogden College," unpublished paper, George Peabody College for Teachers, Nashville, Tenn., 1936, Western Kentucky University Archives, 32.

25. Johnson and Harrison, "Ogden College: A Brief History," 204, 205; LCO to LC, August 1, 1906, LCP.

26. LCO to LC, August 1, November 5, 1906, LCP.

27. LC to LCO, October 1, 1906; LCO to LC, August 1, November 5, December 11, 1906, LCP (emphasis in original); *WJ*, December 8, 1906, 196.

28. LCO to JC, November 7, 1929, OFP; LCO to LC, August 1, 1906, LCP (emphasis in original).

29. *WJ*, December 29, 1906, 212; LCO to LC, January 2, 1907, LCP.

10. Aunt Jane of Kentucky

1. *NYT Saturday Review of Books,* March 30, 1907, 188 (epigraph); Edmund Morris, *The Rise of Theodore Roosevelt* (New York: Modern Library, 2001), xxxii, 14; Herman Hagedorn, ed., *The Works of Theodore Roosevelt,* national ed. (New York: C. Scribner's Sons, 1926), 1:10–11, quoted in Morris, *Rise of Theodore Roosevelt,* 294. For Roosevelt's own astonishing inventory of some of the books he read between 1901 and 1903, see Edmund Morris, *Theodore Rex* (New York: Random House, 2001), 285–88.

2. Morris, *Rise of Theodore Roosevelt,* xxvi; "President Roosevelt Enthusiastic Over 'Aunt Jane of Kentucky,'" unidentified newspaper clipping, [May 1907], OFP. Alice Roosevelt Longworth noted in her memoirs that she visited Lexington and Frankfort as well as Louisville, where she attended the Kentucky Derby on May 6, 1907.

3. *Courier-Journal,* June 1, 1907.

4. Morris, *Theodore Rex,* 35; Morris, *Rise of Theodore Roosevelt,* 108.

5. Theodore Roosevelt to Eliza Calvert Obenchain, June 14, 1907, Theodore Roosevelt Papers, Library of Congress; LCO, "Women and Their Ideals." Roosevelt's public praise of *Aunt Jane* gave rise to a story that he actually journeyed to Lida's home to congratulate her personally (see, for example, the *Dallas Daily Times-Herald,* December 23, 1935), but the incident is not well documented, and Lida herself left no record of it. Among the clippings in the Obenchain Family Papers is a local reprint of the *Daily Times-Herald* article, but someone—perhaps Josie or Maggie Calvert—has added a hand-written notation stating that while Roosevelt invited Lida to visit him, they did not meet; see "Woman Author Is Lauded by Paper at Dallas, Texas," unidentified Bowling Green newspaper clipping, February 2, 1936, OFP.

6. *NYT,* June 2, 1907; Little, Brown, and Company, advertising pamphlet for *Aunt Jane of Kentucky,* OFP; Lee, "Elizabeth [*sic*] Calvert Hall"; *Bookman,* June 1907, 444; July 1907, 556; August 1907, 660; LC to LCO, June 10, 1907, Bennett Dep.; *Courier-Journal,* July 6, 1907, May 23, 1908. London's Cassell and Company issued a British edition of *Aunt Jane of Kentucky* in 1909.

7. *WJ,* April 27, 1907, 67; *Courier-Journal,* May 18, 1907; LCO to MC, September 19, 1907, OFP; Lee sketch; ECH, "Sally Ann's Experience," *Cosmopolitan,* July 1908, 167–71; ECH, "Why I Wrote 'Sally Ann's Experience,'" 163. After its first printing of "Sally Ann's Experience," the *Woman's Journal* reprinted it as follows; June 23, 1900, 198–99; December 1, 1900, 382–83 ("Republished by request"); and June 15, 1907, 93–95, with a note about Roosevelt's endorsement. The organ of the Iowa Woman Suffrage Association also printed the story after Roosevelt praised it; see *Woman's Standard,* July 1907, 1–3. "Sally Ann's Experience" appeared in the *Ladies' Home Journal,* October 1907, 17–18.

8. *NYT Saturday Review of Books,* March 30, 1907, 188. More than a decade earlier, referring to the increased tendency to use dialect as an end

in itself rather than as a means of illustration, an editor was convinced that "the public is becoming justly impatient of its excessive and indiscriminate use"; "Too Much Dialect," *Southern Magazine,* July 1894, 647. In a review of John Fox Jr.'s *Hell-fer-Sartin and Other Stories,* George Merriam Hyde also warned that the use of dialect for its own sake created a literature that "inevitably tends downward to the utterly provincial or parochial"; "A New Crop of Dialect," *Bookman,* September 1897, 57.

9. *Syracuse Herald,* n.d., quoted in Little, Brown advertising pamphlet; *Brooklyn Eagle,* March 30, 1907, quoted in Lee, "Elizabeth [*sic*] Calvert Hall"; "Aunt Jane of Kentucky," unidentified Bowling Green newspaper article, OFP. See also (New York) *Evening Telegram,* April 12, 1907, and (Louisville, Ky.) *Post,* April 19, 1907, both quoted in Lee, "Elizabeth [*sic*] Calvert Hall." Learning of warm praise for the book from Pendleton County, Kentucky, the *New York Times* assumed that the book's stories were set in that far northeastern part of the state; *NYT Saturday Review of Books,* November 9, 1907, 715.

10. *Outlook,* May 18, 1907; (New York) *Evening Telegram,* April 12, 1907, both quoted in Lee, "Elizabeth [*sic*] Calvert Hall"; "Aunt Jane of Kentucky," unidentified Bowling Green newspaper article, OFP.

11. ECH, "Why I Wrote 'Sally Ann's Experience,'" 166; *WJ,* April 27, 1907, 67.

12. *Catholic World,* August 1907, 688, quoted in *Book Review Digest,* 1907, 173.

13. ECH, "Why I Wrote 'Sally Ann's Experience,'" 166.

14. Beulah Strong to Clarence Underwood McElroy, May 6, 1907, McElroy Collection.

15. Beulah Strong to LCO, [February 14, 1907], transcript, OFP; *Hartford Courant,* n.d., quoted in Little, Brown advertising pamphlet.

16. "The Author of Aunt Jane," *WJ,* June 15, 1907, 95; *Indianapolis Star,* June 29, 1907; *NYT Saturday Review of Books,* November 9, 1907, 715; *Saturday Evening Post,* n.d., quoted in "The Creator of 'Aunt Jane,'" unidentified newspaper clipping, [1907], OFP. Lida also remembered with affection "the old Scribner with a purple cover when J. G. Holland conducted it"; Lee sketch.

17. *NYT Saturday Review of Books,* August 29, 1908, 478; Galloway "Eliza Calvert Hall Is Seen at Close Range." For Roosevelt's pronouncements on woman suffrage, see Albert Bushnell Hart and Herbert Ronald Ferleger, eds., *Theodore Roosevelt Cyclopedia,* rev. 2nd ed. (Westport, Conn.: Meckler Corp., 1988), 658–59. In his senior thesis at Harvard, Roosevelt had questioned whether the ballot should be given to those who could not fight to defend it, a position which Lida dismissed in her writing about the Philippine War.

18. Warren County, Ky. Deed Book 97, 157, Book 103, 305.

19. LCO to MC, September 19, 1907, OFP.

20. "Aunt Jane of Kentucky," unidentified newspaper article, [1907], OFP; *NYT,* August 29, 1908; Warren County, Ky. Deed Book 103, 305.

21. Galloway, "Eliza Calvert Hall Is Seen at Close Range."

22. Lee sketch. One of the "Gardens of Memory" belonged to Mrs. Nancy
Dunavan, a longtime resident of College Street in Bowling Green; see Mary
Hobson Beard, *Old Homes in and near Bowling Green, Kentucky* (Bowling
Green, Ky.: News Publishing Company, 1964), 18.

11. Seeing Double

1. *Chicago Record-Herald,* [ca. 1909], clipping in OFP (epigraph); *Arena,* December 1907, 687–88; *NYT Saturday Review of Books,* March 30,
1907, 188, June 15, 1907, 381.

2. ECH, "Bowling Green and the Civil War," 248, 250–51; LCO to OR,
August 11, 1915, ORMP.

3. Kentucky "waited until after the civil war to secede"; E. Merton Coulter,
The Civil War and Readjustment in Kentucky (1926; repr., Gloucester, Mass.:
Peter Smith, 1966), vii; Wheeler, *New Women of the New South,* 101, 111; LCO,
"An Educational Campaign," *Womankind,* February 1897, 4; see also LCO, "An
Object Lesson on Political Influence," *Woman's Tribune,* August 3, 1895, 113.

4. Wheeler, *New Women of the New South,* 102, 110, 114, 121, 125;
Fuller, 109; *WJ,* December 8, 1906, 196; XV Club Minutes, April 2, 1896. In
December 1906, Laura Clay lent support to another tactic when she became
president of the Southern Woman's Suffrage Association. Its platform sought
the vote as a specific solution to the "race problem," arguing that the numerical superiority of white women over blacks of both sexes would ensure
white political domination and avoid the necessity for any constitutionally
doubtful measures to minimize the black vote. The organization seemed particularly intent upon use of the ballot to remedy conditions leading to sexual
immorality among black household servants; see "Southern Women's Need,"
Woman's Standard, February 1907, 1. In 1907, however, suffragist Kate Gordon initiated a proposal in Mississippi that candidly sought the vote for white
women only. Although Laura Clay defended this tactic out of sympathy with
the "peculiar problem" of the Deep South states, where blacks were proportionally more numerous than in Kentucky, she did not share Gordon's
extreme enmity toward blacks or support a racial exclusion in her own state
beyond an educational qualification; Fuller, 107–8, 110.

5. LCO, "Captivated Calves," *WJ,* January 19, 1907, 9; LCO, "The 'Unanswerable Argument' against Woman Suffrage," *WJ,* April 11, 1908, 57.

6. LCO, *The "Unanswerable Argument" Answered,* Political Equality Series (Warren, Ohio: National American Woman Suffrage Association,
1908); ECH, "In War Time," *Cosmopolitan,* October 1909, 598–608.

7. "Virginia Heroine, Mrs. E. A. Obenchain," *Confederate Veteran,*
February 1906, 72–73.

8. "Author of the 'Aunt Jane' Books," *Courier-Journal,* July 31, 1909; LC
to LCO, November 18, 1907; LCO to Mary Barr Clay, March 11, 1909, LCP.

9. *WJ*, November 23, 1907, 187, November 28, 1908, 191; LC to LCO, November 18, 1907, January 2, 1909, LCP; Harriet Taylor Upton to LCO, July 29, 1908, SC 261. Carrie Chapman Catt hoped to collect one million signatures for the "Great Petition," as it came to be known, but the NAWSA eventually presented just under 405,000 signatures to the House Speaker in April 1910; Fuller, 119.

10. Knott, 260–61; LC to LCO, January 13, 21, 1909; LCO to LC, February 12, 1909, LCP. The petition to Congress read as follows: "We, the undersigned citizens of the United States, over twenty-one years of age, hereby petition your honorable body to submit to the Legislatures of the several States for ratification an amendment to the National Constitution which shall enable women to vote"; *NYT*, December 6, 1908.

11. Mary M. Mitchell to LCO, January 22, 1909; LCO to LC, February 12, 1909; LCO to Mary Barr Clay, March 11, 1909, LCP.

12. LC to LCO, January 21, 1909; LCO to LC, February 12, May 25, 1909, LCP (emphasis in original); THO to MC, December 14, 1939, OFP; ECH, "Motherhood," *Munsey's Magazine*, February 1906, reproduced in Lee, "Elizabeth [*sic*] Calvert Hall." Lee also quotes part of "Sunday Afternoon," published sometime between 1892 and 1894 in the magazine *Childhood*. Lida, of course, anticipates Virginia Woolf's argument that "a woman must have money and a room of her own if she is to write fiction"; *A Room of One's Own* (New York: Harcourt, Brace and Company, 1929), 4.

13. *Bookman*, November 1909, 307; March 1910, 103; advertisement for *The Land of Long Ago*, *WJ*, December 11, 1909, 203; *NYT Literary Section*, October 22, 1909, pt. 2, 626. A family friend wrote Lida's uncle John Younglove that *The Land of Long Ago* was a "valuable record of real things, too good to have been lost." Seeing both her own experiences and the "well-related ones of my dear grandfather and mother," she praised Lida for making Bowling Green "classic ground—*oblivion-proof*"; Lily Hughes Lucas to JEY, June 11, 1910, YFP (emphasis in original).

14. In "Aunt Jane Goes A-Visiting," a character based on Laura Clay also makes an appearance. Aunt Jane notes with interest that "Miss Laura" is not only free of the stigma that once attached to an "old maid," but in her work "lookin' after" the rights of wives is as busy and contented as any one of them.

15. "More Aunt Jane Stories," *WJ*, September 25, 1909, 154.

16. Wheeler, *New Women of the New South*, 88. Lida was not puritanical about divorce as long as it was the exception and not the rule. "I do not consider divorce a disgrace, necessarily," she wrote a second-time husband, "and one of my best friends is, like yourself, a man who made a mistake in his first marriage"; LCO to JWT, January 15, 1916, JWTC.

17. ECH, "The Sin of Unselfishness," 196. While drunk, Sam Amos commits various irresponsible acts such as trading his fine mare for an old dog. The KERA, of course, had pointed to husbands' misdealings of family as-

sets as evidence of the need for married women's property law reform, not greater feminine virtue. Josephine Henry told the story of a wife who saved money to buy a cow but had no legal recourse when her husband traded it for a gun; "Of Interest to Kentucky Women," *WJ*, July 18, 1891, 227. Lida related a similar anecdote in "Why I Wrote 'Sally Ann's Experience.'"

18. Aunt Jane refers to Luke 20:35: "But they which shall be accounted worthy to obtain that world, and the resurrection from the dead, neither marry, nor are given in marriage."

19. *Bowling Green Messenger*, April 24, 28, 1910; LCO to JC, May 14, 1911, OFP. Margery had spent the past two winter seasons in Dallas as guest of the Major's cousin Harry L. Obenchain and his wife, Josephine, herself a writer and popular reader of dialect stories; *Dallas Morning News*, October 11, 1909.

20. Cecil Calvert Obenchain to JWT, July 7, 1915, JWTC; LCO to JC, May 14, 1911, OFP.

21. Cecil Calvert Obenchain to JWT, June 4, July 4, 1915, JWTC; *Cosmopolitan Magazine* to LCO, June 17, 1908, SC 261; ECH, *Sally Ann's Experience* (Boston: Little, Brown, and Company, 1910), ix–x; Lee sketch; *WJ*, April 8, 1911, 109; *NYT Saturday Review of Books*, August 27, 1910, 474. Another article reported that fifty-five thousand copies of *Sally Ann's Experience* had been printed; Foster, "Distinguished Daughter of Kentucky," 13.

22. ECH, *The Land of Long Ago* (London: Cassell and Company, 1910); LCO to LC, May 25, 1909, LCP; *Bowling Green Messenger*, August 22, 1912; LCO to JC, May 14, 1911, OFP.

23. ECH, *A Book of Hand-Woven Coverlets* (Boston: Little, Brown, and Company, 1912), 3; LCO to JC, May 14, 1911, OFP. *A Book of Hand-Woven Coverlets* was later reported as the product of five years of research, placing its conception around the time *Aunt Jane of Kentucky* was published; Foster, "Eliza Calvert Hall."

24. LCO to Lattie Robertson Coombs, April 4, 1911, SC 77; LCO to LC, August 1, 1906, September 26, 1911, LCP; ECH, "So Fur from the Big Road," 4–5.

25. ECH, *To Love and to Cherish* (Boston: Little, Brown, and Company, 1911), 16–17, 77.

26. Ibid., 9, 10, 39.

27. Ibid., 13, 21–22, 37, 56.

28. Ibid., 53, 69, 76–77.

29. Ibid., 70–71, 202–4.

30. Ibid., 151, 203, 205; *NYT*, August 20, 1911, sect. 6, 508. Three unidentified reviews, including one that is probably a local paper's reprint of the *Louisville Post* review, are in the OFP.

31. ECH, *To Love and to Cherish*, 70. In "So Fur from the Big Road," Lida had argued that a man's duty to "love, cherish and protect" his wife included "warding off from her the deterioration of mind and soul that men-

aces every loving woman who takes upon herself the burdens of housekeeping and child bearing." She advised husbands to return home in the evening prepared to engage their wives intellectually about the day's events and to take an interest in domestic concerns. She seemed to take for granted, however, that such mental stimulation would not undermine a wife's willingness to remain in her traditional role as homemaker.

32. ECH, *To Love and to Cherish*, 56.

12. A Woman Spinning and Weaving

1. May Stanley, "To Eliza Calvert Hall on Her 'Book of Hand-Woven Coverlets,'" *Duluth (Minn.) News-Tribune*, [ca. 1912], clipping in CFP (epigraph); LC to Louise Southgate, June 16, 1909, LCP; *WJ*, May 14, 1910, 78; Report of Kentucky Equal Rights Association, November 10, 1911, LCP. By the time of the 1911 report, Margaret Weissinger had become Margaret (Mrs. Samuel T.) Castleman. May Stanley's poem was included in her book *A Minnesota Christmas and Other Verses* (Duluth, Minn.: O. F. Collier Press, 1914).

2. Forderhase, "The Clear Call of Thoroughbred Women," 31, 34.

3. *Ky. Acts* 1910, ch. 35; Report of Kentucky Equal Rights Association for year 1911–12, LCP; Forderhase, "The Clear Call of Thoroughbred Women," 35; *NYT*, May 22, 1910; Salme Harju Steinberg, *Reformer in the Marketplace: Edward W. Bok and "The Ladies' Home Journal"* (Baton Rouge: Louisiana State University Press, 1979), 68–69. Five years earlier, the *Woman's Standard* had wryly described the *Ladies' Home Journal* as "a periodical which frequently has conniption fits on the subject of woman suffrage, and tries to convey the idea that woman is sort of an ethereal effervescence with little interest in this world other than is claimed by pink teas, chiffon frills and nervous invalidism"; "The *Ladies' Home Journal* and Woman Suffrage," *Woman's Standard*, June 1905, 1. Even though he published many anti-suffrage articles, editor Bok claimed to be neutral on the question until the March 1912 issue, when he confirmed his opposition.

4. LCO to LC, September 26, 1911; LC to LCO, October 7, 1911, LCP. For a fuller description of the feuds within the NAWSA leading up to the 1911 convention, see Fuller, 113–23.

5. LCO to LC, September 26, 1911, LCP.

6. LCO to LC, October 31, 1911; LC to LCO, November 3, 1911, Bennett Dep.; Fuller, 125–27. Before departing for a career at the University of Chicago, in 1892 Sophonisba Breckinridge had passed the Kentucky bar examination and in 1897 had qualified for practice before the state's highest court.

7. Melba Dean Porter, "Madeline McDowell Breckinridge: Her Role in the Kentucky Woman Suffrage Movement, 1908–1920," *Register of the Kentucky Historical Society*, vol. 72, no. 4 (October 1974): 343; Forderhase, "The Clear Call of Thoroughbred Women," 21; Fuller, 128–31; Marjorie Julian Spruill, "Race, Reform, and Reaction at the Turn of the Century: South-

ern Suffragists, the NAWSA, and the 'Southern Strategy' in Context," in Jean H. Baker, ed., *Votes for Women: The Struggle for Suffrage Revisited* (New York: Oxford University Press, 2002), 110–11.

8. LCO to LC, October 31, November 9, December 31, 1911 (emphasis in originals); LC to LCO, November 3, 1911, Bennett Dep. The male teacher was Macon A. Leiper, an English professor. Though Lida does not name her, the Virginia teacher was probably Nellie W. Birdsong of Richmond, a fifth-grade teacher in the Normal training school.

9. LCO to LC, December 31, 1911, Bennett Dep.

10. *Ky. Acts* 1912, ch. 47; Porter, "Madeline McDowell Breckinridge," 348; Report of Kentucky Equal Rights Association for year 1911–12, LCP.

11. LCO to LC, April 1, September 26, October 23, 1912, LCP; *Bowling Green Messenger,* April 21, August 11, 1912; LCO, "As to School Suffrage," *Bowling Green Messenger,* [1912], clipping in LCP. The *Messenger* had endorsed school suffrage in its editorial of March 14, 1912.

12. LC to LCO, February 16, 1912, LCP; ECH, *Book of Hand-Woven Coverlets,* 104, 267–69; Foster, "Eliza Calvert Hall."

13. ECH, *Book of Hand-Woven Coverlets,* 7, 8, 139. Lida had been friends with Wade since at least 1907; when she purchased her house, he had promised to give her a desk as soon as she secured a room to herself; LCO to MC, September 19, 1907, OFP.

14. ECH, *Book of Hand-Woven Coverlets,* 7–8, 266.

15. LCO to LC, December 31, 1911, Bennett Dep.; ECH, *Book of Hand-Woven Coverlets,* 267.

16. ECH, *Book of Hand-Woven Coverlets,* 123–24, 166–67, 268–69.

17. Ibid., 91, 167–68, 199, 220–21. Despite Lida's criticism of the Daughters of the American Revolution, the orthodoxies of local society, together with her undeniable pride in her colonial ancestors, prompted her own (successful) application for DAR membership in 1914.

18. Ibid., 32, 242.

19. LCO to LC, September 26, 1912, LCP; ECH, "The Romance of Your Grandmother's Quilt," *McCall's,* February 1913, 18; *Literary Digest,* December 14, 1912, 1143; *Outlook,* December 14, 1912, 818; *Nation,* February 6, 1913, 138; *Craftsman,* December 1912, 365–67. Given their greater consistency in bearing the same name for the same design rather than "innumerable aliases," Lida described quilts in her *McCall's* article as "far more orderly and law-abiding" than coverlets.

20. *NYT Review of Books,* December 8, 1912, 757; *NYT,* March 24, 1912, May 31, July 19, 1913, July 11, 1915; Alice Van Leer Carrick, *Collector's Luck, or A Repository of Pleasant and Profitable Discourses Descriptive of the Household Furniture and Ornaments of Olden Times* (Boston: Atlantic Monthly Press, 1919), 47 (emphasis in original).

21. LCO to LC, September 26, October 23, 1912, LCP; *NYT,* September 6, 1912.

22. Fuller, 129, 133; *Lexington (Ky.) Herald,* May 26, 1913, quoted in Melba Porter Hay, "Suffragist Triumphant: Madeline McDowell Breckinridge and the Nineteenth Amendment," *Register of the Kentucky Historical Society,* vol. 93, no. 1 (Winter 1995): 33; Porter, "Madeline McDowell Breckinridge," 349–50. A Louisville organizing committee invited suffragists to participate in the centennial celebration of Commodore Oliver Hazard Perry's defeat of the British on Lake Erie during the War of 1812 ("We have met the enemy and they are ours"). Their parade through the city on October 2, 1913, the first of its kind in the South, was impressive: a float, seventy-five women on horseback, college women in academic garb, and others dressed in white with yellow sashes. Following behind individual marchers representing the states where women had gained the vote was "Miss Kentucky," her face veiled to symbolize her ongoing bondage; see Guethlein, "Women in Louisville," 168–69.

23. LCO to Henry Hardin Cherry, March 18, 1913; Henry Hardin Cherry to Madeline McDowell Breckinridge, March 20, 1913; Madeline McDowell Breckinridge to Henry Hardin Cherry, January 3, 1908, March 25, 1913, Henry Hardin Cherry Papers, Western Kentucky University Archives. Whether the Normal School procured a suffrage speaker that spring is unknown, but on May 21, 1913, as part of its yearlong Lyceum Course, a reader presented selections from *Aunt Jane of Kentucky* after being introduced by Lida herself; see (Western Kentucky State Normal School) *Elevator,* June 1913, 277–78.

24. Kentucky Equal Rights Association Board Minutes, March 29, 1916, copy in LCP; LC to LCO, April 9, May 6, 1913; LCO to LC, March 28, 1913, [May 1913], LCP. The Kentucky and Illinois associations became the first two to meet the goal of subscribing $100 for stock in the *Journal;* "Kentucky and Illinois Lead," *WJ,* May 3, 1913, 141.

25. Porter, "Madeline McDowell Breckinridge," 350; LCO to LC, August 1, 1913, LCP; *Courier-Journal,* November 22, 23, 1913. Lida was disappointed that her state was not better represented when a delegation of women "stormed the Capital," according to the *Courier-Journal,* to deliver the suffrage petitions. Kentucky's petition comprised only four signers from Hawesville in addition to the sixteen from Bowling Green. The Major, nevertheless, had tapped prominent locals including Mayor Gilson E. Townsend, Henry Hardin Cherry of the Normal School, J. Lewie Harman and Joseph Stone Dickey of the Bowling Green Business University, Dr. Joseph N. McCormack, secretary of the State Board of Health, and Dr. Lillian H. South, the state bacteriologist; *Courier-Journal,* August 1, 1913.

26. Melba Porter Hay, "Madeline McDowell Breckinridge: Kentucky Suffragist and Progressive Reformer" (PhD diss., University of Kentucky, 1980), 149, 152–53; *Courier-Journal,* November 22, 23, 1913; Fuller, 132. Among the more substantial contributions to the KERA were $1,000 from Mrs. Sallie Hubbard, a doctor's wife from Hickman, Kentucky, and $200 from Alva Belmont of New York.

27. Ida Husted Harper, ed., *History of Woman Suffrage* (New York: Source Book Press, 1970), 6:208; List of Presidents and Chairmen of County Leagues in Kentucky, January 4, 1915; LC to LCO, April 9, May 6, 1913, LCP. The House vote on the suffrage amendment was fifty-one to twenty-nine. As Madge Breckinridge and others looked on from the gallery, opponents derided the extent of support for the bill among Kentucky's women; one snidely attributed it to "the old maids and childless women of Lexington and Frankfort aristocracy," and another to the leisured "members of whist clubs"; *Courier-Journal*, March 13, 1914.

13. Riding to Town

1. *Hartford (Ky.) Herald*, October 12, 1904 (epigraph); "Aunt Jane Goes A-Visiting," in ECH, *Land of Long Ago*, 114, 141.

2. LCO to JC, May 14, 1911, OFP.

3. LCO to JC, September 23, 1904, OFP.

4. Ward, *A Literary History of Kentucky*, 138–41; LCO to MYC, February 12, 1913, OFP; *NYT*, February 13, 1913; "Some New Lamps for Some Old."

5. *Cosmopolitan* magazine to LCO, June 17, 1908, SC 261; LCO to LC, September 26, 1911, LCP; LCO to LC, October 31, 1911, Bennett Dep.; LCO to JC, May 14, 1911, OFP; Cecil Calvert Obenchain to JWT, July 7, 1915, JWTC. How "Courtship" first came to Belasco's attention is not known, but he maintained a "bureau of playwriting" at his theater on West Forty-fourth Street, which received thousands of manuscripts—none of which, he said later, he ever found acceptable; *NYT*, May 15, 1931.

6. LCO to MYC, January 31, 1909, August 2, 26, 1914, OFP.

7. LCO to MYC, August 30, 1914, OFP; *Dallas Morning News*, October 7, December 9, 1914.

8. Cecil Calvert Obenchain to JWT, July 7, September 4, 1915, JWTC.

9. ECH, "How Parson Page Went to the Circus," *Cosmopolitan*, July 1910, 173–82; *NYT*, August 27, 1916; Foster, "Eliza Calvert Hall"; ECH, *Book of Hand-Woven Coverlets*, 20–21 (emphasis in original).

10. Foster, "Eliza Calvert Hall"; Cecil Calvert Obenchain to JWT, October 6, 25, 1915, JWTC; *Dayton (Ohio) Journal*, October 24, 1915.

11. ECH, *Book of Hand-Woven Coverlets*, 5; Cecil Calvert Obenchain to JWT, July 7, August 18, 1915; LCO to JWT, September 15, 1915, JWTC. "Sally Ann's Experience" and "Aunt Jane Goes A-Visiting" both refer to June in Kentucky as the time of "clover and blue-grass."

12. JWT, *Kentucky in American Letters 1784–1912* (Cedar Rapids, Iowa: Torch Press, 1913), xxiii; LCO to [JWT], [ca. 1907], JWTC; News Bureau Release, Eastern Kentucky University, December 7 [n.y.], JWT Vertical File, Eastern Kentucky University Library Special Collections.

13. JWT, *Kentucky in American Letters*, xxiii; News Bureau Release,

Eastern Kentucky University; LCO to JWT, May 13, June 19, August 22 (postmark), September 15, 1915, JWTC.

14. LCO to JWT, August 22, 1915 (postmark), [ca. November 1915], January 15, 1916; Cecil Calvert Obenchain to JWT, August 18, 1915, JWTC; LCO to OR, November 19, 1915, ORP.

15. Cecil Calvert Obenchain to JWT, June 13, July 7, August 18, September 4, October 6, 1915, JWTC.

16. Cecil Calvert Obenchain to JWT, May 30, June 4, 13, July 4, 1915, JWTC.

17. LCO to JWT, September 15, 1915, JWTC.

18. OR to LCO, August 15, 1915, Otto Arthur Rothert Manuscripts Small Collection 716, Ky. Lib.; OR, "Local History in Kentucky Literature," paper read before the Louisville Literary Club, September 27, 1915, Ky. Lib., 4.

19. LCO to OR, August 11, 17, 1915, ORMP; OR, *A History of Muhlenberg County* (Louisville, Ky.: John P. Morton and Company, 1913; repr., Louisville, Ky.: Standard Printing Company, 1964), 203; Galloway, "Eliza Calvert Hall Is Seen at Close Range"; ECH, "The House That Was a Wedding Fee," 17–27; LCO to OR, December 23, 1915, ORP. Lida also learned from her uncle John that the authority for the Lapsley story was Mrs. Nancy Dunavan, the real-life owner of one of Lida's "Gardens of Memory."

20. Lee sketch; LCO to OR, August 11, 1915, ORMP. The threads of fact for "Wedding Fee" were indeed slender. James Rumsey Skiles married his wife near Nashville in 1820, and the deed, not given until 1822, records that Lapsley paid $1,500 for the land. Although Lapsley was a Virginian, he was born thirty-six years after Jefferson and had left the state by age sixteen; Warren County, Ky. Deed Book 10, 276; Fitts and Moody, *Joseph B. Lapsley*, 5.

21. LCO to OR, September 20, 1915, OMP; LCO to OR, November 19, 1915, January 26, 1916, ORP; LCO to OR, August 11, 1915, ORMP. Lida gave another photograph of the house, showing its avenue of trees "as long as the love that knows no turning," to "my beloved" William Wade, to whom she had dedicated *A Book of Hand-Woven Coverlets;* LCO to OR, September 20, 1915, ORMP.

22. LCO to OR, January 26, 1916, ORP.

23. LCO to LC, [1915]; LC to LCO, July 2, 1915 (postmark), LCP; LCO to OR, October 24, 1915, January 26, 1916, ORP.

24. Fuller, 135; *Courier-Journal*, November 9, 11, 1915; Porter, "Madeline McDowell Breckinridge," 356.

25. *Courier-Journal*, March 27, 1916; LCO to Mrs. William A. Lee, March 14, 1916, SC 792. The NAWSA's failure to prioritize either federal or state suffrage amendments had already fractured the movement during the presidency of Anna Howard Shaw. In 1913 two new organizations had formed: the Congressional Union (later National Woman's Party) and the Southern States Woman Suffrage Conference, the former committed to a federal amendment and the latter to state campaigns.

26. *Courier-Journal,* March 28, 29, 1916; LC to LCO, April 23, 1920, Bennett Dep. First introduced in Congress in 1878, the Anthony amendment stated simply: "The right of citizens of the United States to vote shall not be denied or abridged by the United States or by any State on account of sex." A variation of the elections bill had long been advocated by Laura's sister, Sallie Clay Bennett; Fuller, 142–43.

27. LCO to JWT, April 10, 1916, JWTC.

28. LCO to OR, May 5, 1916, ORP (emphasis in original).

29. LCO to Mrs. William A. Lee, July 5, 1916, SC 792; LCO to OR, August 15, 1916, ORP.

14. "Be Glad You Are Not a Woman"

1. LCO to OR, August 15, 1916, ORP; XV Club Minutes, May 12, 1910; *Confederate Veteran,* November 1916, 515.

2. *Bowling Green Messenger,* August 17, 1916; XV Club Minutes, October 19, 1916; *Ogden College Bulletin,* 1916–17, 3. An edited version of Lida's tribute appeared in the Ogden College *Cardinal* for 1917.

3. Warren County, Ky. Will Book 6, 281; LCO to OR, September 6, 13, 23, October 6, 1916, ORP.

4. LCO to JWT, August 22, 1915 (postmark), JWTC; *NYT Book Review,* November 12, 1916, 484. *Bookman,* December 1916, 438, showed *Clover and Blue Grass* ranking sixth among the most popular books sold in Louisville the previous October.

5. In her book on coverlets, Lida had written of the power of inanimate objects to evoke memories and emotions. A room furnished in "old mahogany," she had observed, was a "haunted place"; ECH, *Book of Hand-Woven Coverlets,* 19.

6. Foster, "Distinguished Daughter of Kentucky," 53.

7. Wood, "The Literature of Impoverishment," 5, 11, 24. For an interesting discussion of the traits of the heroines of sentimental literature as distinguished from the women of local color literature, see ibid., 10–12, 18–25.

8. LCO to JWT, June 19, 1915, April 10, 1916, JWTC; "Kentucky Women Poets"; "Lida Calvert Obenchain," *WJ,* October 14, 1899, 326; Foster, "Eliza Calvert Hall"; LCO to OR, June 14, 1921, ORP; Ward, *A Literary History of Kentucky,* 96–97; ECH, "Madison Cawein, Southern Poet, Believed That Form, Rhythm and Music Are Necessary to Poetry," *Dallas Daily Times-Herald,* December 10, 1922. Lida herself had written at least two essays with metaphysical themes; ECH, "The Evolution of Mental Science," *Metaphysical Magazine,* March 1901, 173–82, and, by mid-1899, a contribution to the periodical *Mind* (mentioned in *WJ,* October 14, 1899, 326).

9. LCO to H. L. Mencken, November 28, 1916; H. L. Mencken to LCO, December 8, 1916; LCO to Theodore Dreiser, December 11, 1916,

Theodore Dreiser Papers, Annenberg Rare Book and Manuscript Library, University of Pennsylvania, Philadelphia. Lida's essay itself is, unfortunately, lost.

10. "Aunt Jane Goes A-Visiting," in ECH, *Land of Long Ago;* LCO to OR, October 6, 1916, ORP.

11. LCO to OR, April 30, 1917, ORP.

12. LCO to MYC, May 1917, OFP.

13. LCO to MYC, July 5, 1917; COR to JC, September 25, 1917, OFP.

14. COR to JC, September 25, 1917; LCO to JC, October 11, 1917; LCO to MC, October 6, 1918; LCO to MYC, November 15, 1917, OFP; LCO to LC, April 11, 1920, Bennett Dep. One can only speculate whether, in her travels around Washington late in 1917, Lida saw the National Woman's Party pickets in front of the White House demanding that President Wilson endorse a suffrage amendment to the Constitution.

15. LCO to OR, January 4, 1918, ORP; LCO to MYC, July 5, 1917, February 1, April 30, 1918; LCO to MC, July 3, 1918 (postmark); LCO to MC and JC, July 29, 1918; LCO to JC, June 2, August 20, 1918, OFP (emphasis in original).

16. LCO to JC, February 24, 1918 (postmark); LCO to MC, February 24, (postmark), July 3, October 6, December 7, 1918 (postmark), OFP; Margery Obenchain Winston to MC, July 1918 (postmark), transcript, CFP.

17. COR to JC, September 25, 1917; LCO to JC, February 24, 1918 (postmark), OFP.

18. LCO to MC and JC, July 29, 1918, OFP.

19. Fuller, 146–47.

20. Hay, "Suffragist Triumphant," 35; Paul E. Fuller, "Suffragist Vanquished: Laura Clay and the Nineteenth Amendment," *Register of the Kentucky Historical Society,* vol. 93, no. 1 (Winter 1995): 6–7. Mrs. Catt based her argument for suspending Kentucky's state campaign on the probability that voter fraud would ensure the defeat of suffrage in a referendum; the irregularities behind recent losses in West Virginia, Iowa, and South Dakota had convinced her that the prospects were no better in a "whisky state" like Kentucky. She also warned that in some states, opponents were actually engineering badly organized referenda in order to undermine suffragists' claims of public support. Lastly, Mrs. Catt informed the KERA that it could expect no help from the NAWSA, which was backing only a few state campaigns where success was more likely; see Fuller, 148–49.

21. Lee, "Elizabeth [sic] Calvert Hall"; LCO to JC, August 6, 1918, October 19, 1919; LCO to MC, July 3, October 6, November 7, 1918, OFP; notes on Edward Calvert's military service, CFP.

22. LCO to MYC, April 30, 1918; LCO to JC, June 2, August 20, 1918, December 26, 1920, OFP.

23. Warren County, Ky. Deed Book 125, 380; LCO to MYC, January 12, 1919; LCO to JC, February 5, 1919, OFP.

24. LCO to JC, April 29, 1919 (postmark), OFP (emphasis in original).

25. LCO to MYC, June 5, 1919 (postmark), OFP.

15. Grandmother's Debut

1. LCO to MC and JC, July 29, 1918, OFP; ECH, "Grandmother's Début," *Woman's Home Companion*, December 1919, 14.

2. *NYT*, June 4, 1919.

3. Porter, "Madeline McDowell Breckinridge," 360; Fuller, 153, 155; Knott, 286.

4. LCO to JC, April 29 (postmark), July 21, October 19, 1919; LCO to MYC, June 25, 1919 (postmark), OFP.

5. LCO to JC, October 19, 1919, February 11, 1920; LCO to MYC, December 20, 1919, OFP.

6. Lucinda Calvert to MC and JC, February 16, 1920 (postmark); LCO to MC, May 13, 1933, OFP; Heilbrun, *Writing a Woman's Life*, 12; "Mrs. T. C. Calvert," *Bowling Green (Ky.) Daily Times-Journal*, [1920], typescript, "C" Biography File, Ky. Lib.

7. "Aunt Jane's Album," in ECH, *Aunt Jane of Kentucky*, 79. The Kentucky Museum at Western Kentucky University possesses a "Tumbling Blocks" (cross variation) quilt attributed to Margaret Younglove Calvert. In spring 2005, as part of a cultural exchange organized at the request of the U.S. ambassador, the "Tumbling Blocks" quilt was one of seven loaned for exhibition at the Museum of Decorative and Applied Arts in Riga, Latvia. "But la! the way things turn around," as Aunt Jane would say.

8. LCO to LC, September 26, 1911, LCP; LCO to LC, April 11, 1920, Bennett Dep. The NAWSA leadership wrestled with the question of whether Laura herself should be awarded a service certificate. When Carrie Chapman Catt asked Madge Breckinridge for her opinion, she replied, "It beats me! I could not bear for you not to honor Miss Laura, and I think you will have to do it with a foot-note that in the latter days she dissented from the policy of the National"; Madeline McDowell Breckinridge to Carrie Chapman Catt, December 15, 1919, Breckinridge Family Papers, Manuscript Division, Library of Congress, quoted in Hay, "Suffragist Triumphant," 39.

9. Fuller, "Suffragist Vanquished," 20; LCO to LC, April 11, 1920, Bennett Dep. Fuller argues that Laura Clay was unfairly branded as a "Negrophobe" during Kentucky's ratification campaign and then as a "poor loser" afterward. Ironically, on March 28, 1920, after reportedly waiting until the last day possible in the hope that the Anthony amendment would by then have become law, Governor Edwin P. Morrow approved state legislation (*Ky. Acts* 1920, ch. 101) allowing women to vote for electors in the upcoming presidential election; *NYT*, March 31, 1920. In Texas, suffragists had discounted the result of their state's May 1919 referendum by arguing that the question was improperly packaged with another voting measure imposing

a citizenship requirement, prompting aliens who were enfranchised under existing law to turn out in large numbers to defeat it.

10. LC to LCO, April 23, 1920; LCO to LC, April 11, 1920, Bennett Dep. In her letter to Lida, Laura reported that Eugenia Farmer, who had moved to Minnesota in 1898, had just passed her eighty-fifth birthday and was still working for suffrage.

11. LCO to LC, April 11, 1920, Bennett Dep.

12. Ibid.; Warren County, Ky. Deed Book 139, 67; LCO to JC, March 30, 1920, OFP.

13. LCO to JC, April 23, (postmark), May 12, 1920 (postmark), OFP. Such was Josie's loyalty that years later she made an injudicious claim that a mutual friend had "cheated" Lida in the sale of one of her lots. An embarrassed Lida called upon her to apologize, and the misunderstanding led to a sharp exchange of letters between the sisters; see LCO to JC, October 26, November 1, 1933; JC to LCO, October 31, 1933, OFP.

14. LCO to JC, April 29, 1919 (postmark), OFP; LCO to LC, April 11, 1920, Bennett Dep.; EC to MC, [ca. June 1920], CFP. Maggie replied to Ed in June 1920, noting on the envelope of Ed's letter her opinion that he was ignoring his old friends and neglecting to "give us a call" when he was in the vicinity of Bowling Green.

15. LCO to JC, December 26, 1920, February 3, 1921 (postmark); LCO to MC, February 25, 1921 (postmark), OFP. After Texas and ahead of Kentucky, Arkansas had ratified the Nineteenth Amendment on July 28, 1919.

16. LCO to JC, April 28, July 2, 1921; LCO to MC, November 22, 1921; COR to MC and JC, December 1, 1921, OFP.

17. LCO to Alice Stone Blackwell, December 28, 1921, March 28, 1923, NAWSA records. The letterhead of the *Woman's Journal* at one time listed Eliza Calvert Hall as contributing editor; see, for example, a letter dated June 12, 1915, Bennett Dep.

18. LCO to OR, June 14, 1921, ORP; *Dallas Morning News*, November 7, 1920. Originally untitled, the poem appeared in the *New York Independent*, December 1896, but was reprinted in the *Dallas Morning News* and elsewhere under the title "My Enemy"; see Lee, "Elizabeth [sic] Calvert Hall"; LCO Miscellaneous Poems, OFP. The poem's origin is described in an unidentified Bowling Green newspaper clipping, [post-1916], Daisy Aldridge Scrapbook, Ky. Lib.

19. LCO to JWT, April 10, 1916, JWTC; LCO to OR, May 5, 1916, ORP; ECH, "The Horoscope," *Woman's Home Companion*, January 1922, 17.

20. COR to MC, April 7, 1922; LCO to JC, April 28, 1921, March 27, August 4, 23, 1922 (postmark); LCO to MC, November 13, 1922, OFP. The Major's gravestone in Bowling Green's Fairview Cemetery also notes his Virginia birthplace. Lida's story, "Sarah Preston's Achievement," was apparently neither published nor preserved.

21. LCO to MYC, January 12, 1919; LCO to JC, December 26, 1920,

December 24, 1922, December 30, 1923, OFP; LCO to OR, December 23, 1915, ORP. Like Lida, Elizabeth Cady Stanton complained of the excesses of Christmas; see *WJ*, December 16, 1893, 205.

22. LCO to OR, June 15, 1923, SC 578; LCO to MC, February 28 (postmark), August 27, 1923; LCO to JC, April 22, 1925, March 8, 1927, OFP.

23. LCO to OR, June 14, 1921, ORP; LCO to OR, June 15, 1923, SC 578.

24. LCO to OR, June 15, 1923, SC 578; "Kentucky Women Poets."

16. A Hard Worker All Her Life

1. COR to MC, July 18, 1923 (postmark), December 14, 1932; LCO to JC, May 11, 1925 (postmark), OFP.

2. LCO to JC, April 22, 1925; COR to MC, December 14, 1932, OFP.

3. COR to MC and JC, January 6, 1925, OFP.

4. Ibid.; Willy Woodward to JC, January 27, 1943; LCO to JC, October 19, 1919, April 22, 1925; LCO to MC and JC, December 31, 1924 (postmark); COR to MC, December 14, 1932, OFP; LCO to OR, June 15, 1923, SC 578.

5. LCO to JC, March 8, April 22, May 11, 1925 (postmark); LCO to MC, August 21, 1925; LCO to MC and JC, December 31, 1924 (postmark), OFP; Foster, "Eliza Calvert Hall."

6. *Dallas Morning News,* May 9, 1926, October 30, 1938.

7. ECH, "A Notable Collection of Textiles," *House Beautiful,* January 1927, 54; LCO to JC, January 10, 1926, OFP; Mrs. Carl Medinus, "The Colonial Coverlet Guild of America," *Illinois Clubwoman's World,* November 1929, 5. For its first fifty years, the guild required members to own at least one coverlet and document it with two photographs. Of the nearly one thousand accumulated photographs, one is of a coverlet labeled "Aunt Jane of Kentucky," from Lewis County, Kentucky, contributed by William Wade, to whom Lida dedicated *A Book of Hand-Woven Coverlets;* Steph McGrath, senior curator, DuPage County Historical Museum, Wheaton, Ill., to the author, January 20, 2005. The guild's own coverlet collection, as well as its photographs, minutes, and other historical materials, are now part of the collections of the DuPage County Historical Museum; see www.dupageco.org/museum/generic.cfm?doc_id=267 [accessed January 6, 2005].

8. LCO to JC, September 23, 1904, OFP; Colonial Coverlet Guild of America Minutes, November 6, 1925, DuPage County Historical Museum; EC to Margaret and JC, December 15, 1925, CFP. It seems likely that Lida was also the inspiration for a scholarship fund instituted in 1926 by the Coverlet Guild to benefit the weaving department of the Pine Mountain Settlement School; see Medinus, "Colonial Coverlet Guild of America," 6.

9. LCO to JC, January 10, March 11, 1926, February 26, 1927; LCO to MC, November 6, 1930; LCO to MC and JC, September 9, 1927, OFP.

10. LCO to MC, April 2, 1928 (postmark), October 16, November 19, December 29, 1930; LCO to JC, October 3, 31, 1928; LCO to MC and JC, May 16, 1929, OFP.

11. Lee, "Elizabeth [sic] Calvert Hall"; LCO to MC and JC, May 16, 1929, OFP; Lee sketch; LCO to Sophie Lee, March 20, 1929, SC 792. Sophie Lee was the daughter of Gabriella (Mrs. William A.) Lee of Russellville, with whom Lida corresponded during the National Congressional Campaign Conference of 1916.

12. LCO to Sophie Lee, March 20, 1929, SC 792; LCO to Alice Stone Blackwell, October 9, 1930, NAWSA records.

13. Alice Stone Blackwell, *Lucy Stone: Pioneer of Woman's Rights* (Boston: Little, Brown, and Company, 1930); LCO, "The 'Unanswerable Argument' against Woman Suffrage"; LCO to Alice Stone Blackwell, October 9, 1930, February 7, 1931, NAWSA records. Lida had pressed her views upon Alice at least once before, in a "long rebel letter" referred to in her October 9, 1930, correspondence. The claim of white women's constant vulnerability to rape by "lustful black brutes" as the justification for a coercive culture of white supremacy culminating in lynching is discussed in Jacquelyn Dowd Hall, *Revolt against Chivalry: Jessie Daniel Ames and the Women's Campaign against Lynching* (New York: Columbia University Press, 1979), 129–57. Jessie Daniel Ames, a Texan, established the Association of Southern Women for the Prevention of Lynching in 1930, a year in which nineteen black men were lynched in her home state. One of the most notorious incidents had occurred in Sherman, Texas, in May of that year, after a dispute over wages led to the arrest of a black man on a charge of raping his employer's wife. Lida not only knew of the "Sherman lynching" but, as her February 7, 1931, letter to Alice shows, believed all the lurid rumors that had circulated about the brutality of the alleged attack. As for Alice's reference to "outraged" slave women, Lida was even more adamant, insisting that "no negro woman was ever raped by a white master." Interestingly, her position was more extreme than that of the Major, who noted frankly at one of his club meetings that sex with black women was a "safety valve" for white men in antebellum times; XV Club Minutes, January 2, 1902. Although it seems unlikely that the Major ever discussed interracial sex with Lida, her letters to Alice related his stories of idealistic northerners who had abandoned their sympathy for blacks after a period of residence in the South.

14. LCO to Alice Stone Blackwell, October 9, 1930, February 7, 1931, NAWSA records.

15. COR to JWT, August 27, 1930, JWTC; COR to MC, December 14, 1932; LCO to MC, October 17, 1931; LCO to JC, January 13, 1932, OFP.

16. COR to JWT, July 24, November 19, 1930, June 30, 1931, JWTC.

17. LCO to MC, November 19, 1930, May 18, October 17, 1931; COR to MC, September 8, 1932; LCO to MC and JC, January 14, 1933, OFP; *Dal-*

las Morning News, March 28, May 1, 1931; LCO to Alice Stone Blackwell, December 12, 1932, NAWSA records.

18. COR to MC, September 8, November 14, December 14, 1932; LCO to JC, May 31, 1932, OFP.

19. THO to MC, February 11, 1933, January 28, 1939; COR to MC, December 14, 1932, OFP.

20. LCO to JC, May 19, 1933; LCO to "Patty" [Mrs. William J. Potter], October 5, 1933; LCO to MC and JC, December 5, 1933; THO to MC and JC, December 22, 1933, OFP; Rodes, "First Presbyterian Church," 19–20.

21. LCO to Alice Stone Blackwell, April 29, July 1, 1934, NAWSA records; LCO to JC, December 30, 1923; COR to MC, December 14, 1932, OFP.

22. LCO to MC, September 25, 1930, September 20, November 22, 1934; COR to MC and JC, August 23, 1935; COR to Kate F. (Mrs. Lucien) Graham, September 5, 1935, OFP. Harry Barker may have boarded at Lida's home; on one occasion, Cecil used letterhead with his name and Lida's address engraved at the top; see COR to MC, February 3, 1933, OFP.

23. LCO to Alice Stone Blackwell, April 27, 1935, NAWSA records. On Aunt Jane and work, see "How Sam Amos Rode in the Tournament," 176–77, and "Sweet Day of Rest," 102–3, both in ECH, *Aunt Jane of Kentucky.*

24. COR to MC and JC, August 23, 1935; THO to MC, October 28, 1935; COR to JC, July 23, 1936; THO to EC, MC, JC, and COR, December 22, 1935, OFP.

25. THO to EC, MC, JC, and COR, December 22, 1935, OFP.

Epilogue

1. "Mary Andrews' Dinner Party," in ECH, *Aunt Jane of Kentucky,* 224 (epigraph); THO to EC, MC, JC, and COR, December 22, 1935; COR to MC, July 21, 1936; LCO to MC, June 24, 1930; LCO to JC, May 19, 1933; THO to MC, January 28, 1939, OFP.

2. *Park City Daily News,* December 22, 1935; *Dallas Morning News,* January 19, 1936, June 1, 1941; *Dallas Daily Times-Herald,* December 23, 1935 (clipping in OFP). It is unlikely that the students of Ogden College had any positive influence on Lida's thinking about downtrodden humanity; not only were they all male (except for an occasional handful of special students, including Margery and Cecil Obenchain), but they were regarded as ranking higher on the social scale than students of the nearby Western Kentucky State Normal School.

3. Leontine Fleury to "Miss Calvert" [MC], March 20, [1936]; Willy Woodward to "Miss Calvert" [MC or JC], February 21, 1939, OFP.

4. LCO to Alice Stone Blackwell, April 27, 1935, NAWSA records; COR to JC, July 23, 1936; COR to MC and JC, December 30, 1936, OFP; Lily Hughes Lucas to JC, October 19, 1938; Mrs. Berry M. Stephens to JC,

March 3, 1937, transcript, CFP; *Dallas Morning News,* February 13, 1937. Gossip about Cecil's destructive behavior—a "fast life" in Santa Fe, mental problems, and an earlier suicide attempt—was transmitted by Mrs. Lucas, Lida's childhood friend, after Harry Barker visited her home in Albuquerque. Cecil herself wrote a strange letter to Maggie telling of a car accident she had suffered near Taos and claiming that corrupt state officials, fearing a lawsuit over the bad road, had plotted to put her "out of the way"; COR to MC, July 21, 1936, OFP.

5. Willy Woodward to "Miss Calvert" [MC or JC], January 7, February 21, 1939; Willy Woodward to JC, January 27, 1943, OFP.

6. THO to JC, December 12, 1938; THO to MC, January 28, December 14, 1939, OFP; *Park City Daily News,* December 7, 1938.

7. Willy Woodward to JC, January 27, 1943; THO to JC, December 12, 1938, OFP; Margery Winston Bonnick to MC and JC, October 8, 1944, CFP. Four years after Alex's death, Willy wrote Josie that her family heard from Tom several times a year. She and Josie speculated privately that the married woman with whom Alex had been in love was Tom's wife, Scotta.

8. Margery Winston to MC and JC, March 18, December 26, 1937; Margery Winston to MC, February 11, June 30, 1938; Margery Winston Bonnick to MC and JC, October 8, 1944, CFP. Margery Winston Bonnick died December 14, 2002, preceded by Sydney Bonnick, her husband of more than sixty years. Her obituary noted that she was the granddaughter of "famous Kentucky author and suffragette, Eliza Calvert Obenchain"; *Dallas Morning News,* December 20, 2002.

Selected Bibliography

The following bibliography includes major sources consulted for this biography. See the notes for full citations of sources not listed here.

All published works have been identified as fully as possible, given the limited availability of some of the original periodicals. In a few cases, reprint information has been added to facilitate access.

Works by Lida Calvert Obenchain

Poems

"Prologue to The Queen of the Birds." *Bowling Green (Ky.) Daily Times*, 1886.
"The Linden." *Kentucky Arbor and Bird Day Bulletin*. Compiled by Jennie Graff Crabbe. [Frankfort, Ky.]: J. G. Crabbe, 1910.

Articles, Essays, and Pamphlets

"Why Democratic Women Want the Ballot." *Woman's Tribune,* December 17, 1892, 250.
"Medical Co-Education in Kentucky." *Woman's Journal*, April 21, 1894, 128.
"Edith Thomas's Protest." *Woman's Journal*, August 11, 1894, 254–55.
"The Greek Definition of Idiot." *Woman's Tribune*, August 18, 1894, 141.
"Real Southern Chivalry." *Woman's Journal*, September 15, 1894, 292–93.
"Woman in Politics." *Kentucky Leader,* January 10, 1895.
"A Clerical Defamer of Women." *Woman's Journal*, January 12, 1895, 15.
"Are Political Women Attractive to Men?" *Woman's Journal*, February 9, 1895, 48.
"Charlotte Perkins Stetson: A Poet of Two Reforms." *Louisville (Ky.) Courier-Journal*, March 27, 1895.

"A Point of Honor." *Woman's Journal*, June 22, 1895, 194.

"An Object Lesson on Political Influence." *Woman's Tribune*, August 3, 1895, 113.

"Woman Suffrage a Principle." *Woman's Journal*, February 29, 1896, 72.

"Heroism of Cuban Women." *Woman's Journal*, August 22, 1896, 266.

"The Pioneer Women of Kentucky." *Woman's Journal*, September 5, 1896, 288.

"The Egotistic Sex." *Womankind*, December 1896, 5.

"An Educational Campaign." *Womankind*, February 1897, 4.

"A Higher Physical Life for Women." *Womankind*, May 1897, 5.

"Bits of Theosophy." *Womankind*, May 1897, 6.

"The Passing of the Periodicals." *Womankind*, May 1897, 6.

"A Call and a Response." *Womankind*, May 1897, 11.

"The Mothers' Congress." *Womankind*, May 1897, 12.

"The Evolution of Justice." *Womankind*, August 1897, 8–9; October 1897, 6–7.

"New Domestic Literature." *New York Times*, October 17, 1897.

"The Rights of Wives." *New York Times*, October 24, 1897.

"Women and Their Ideals." *New York Times*, October 31, 1897.

"The Typical Woman's Page." *New York Times*, November 7, 1897.

"Not a Question of Years." *New York Times*, November 14, 1897.

"Extravagance a Virtue." *New York Times*, November 28, 1897.

"Church Wedding Crushes." *New York Times*, December 5, 1897.

"As to Christmas Presents." *New York Times*, December 19, 1897.

"On the Sins of Economy." *New York Times*, December 26, 1897.

"The Art of Hospitality." *New York Times*, December 26, 1897.

"The Myth of Conservatism." *Woman's Journal*, January 15, 1898, 22; January 29, 1898, 38.

"Women and Literature." *New York Times*, January 16, 1898, sect. 2, p. 2.

"Woman's Right to Be Ugly." *New York Times*, January 30, 1898.

"Women's Attitude towards War." *Woman's Journal*, August 13, 1898, 257.

"The Latest Thing in 'Patriotism.'" *Woman's Journal*, December 31, 1898, 417.

"No Kansans Kissed Hobson." *Woman's Journal*, January 21, 1899, 18.

"The Philippine War." *Woman's Journal*, June 3, 1899, 169.

"The Clay Family." *Woman's Journal*, June 3, 1899, 170.

"A Kentucky Woman on Kentucky Politics." *Woman's Journal*, April 21, 1900, 121–22.

A Plea for a Little Bit of Common Sense. Political Equality Series. Warren, Ohio: National American Woman Suffrage Association, 1900.

"The Crisis We Face." *Public*, August 4, 1900, 269–70.

"An Open Letter to Women." *Woman's Journal*, December 8, 1900, 390–91.

"What Fools These Mortals Be!" *Woman's Journal*, February 9, 1901, 44.

"The Emotional Sex." *Woman's Standard*, April 1901, 1.

"The Poetry of Woman Suffrage." *Woman's Standard*, November 1901, 1.

"Mrs. Lida Calvert Obenchain Thinks . . ." *Woman's Tribune*, April 19, 1902, 59.

"A Model Commencement Address." *Woman's Journal*, June 28, 1902, 208.

"More Despotic than Europe." *Woman's Journal*, August 16, 1902, 258.

"A Fool Notion." *Woman's Standard*, August 1903, 1.

"The Climax of Political Corruption." *Woman's Standard*, February 1904, 3.

"Suffrage Work and Other Work." *Woman's Journal*, April 16, 1904, 122–23.

"A Hopeful Sign of the Times." *Woman's Standard*, June 1904, 3.

"Clubs and Suffrage Association." *Woman's Standard*, August 1904, 3.

"The Democratic Convention Recognizes the Rights of Women." *Woman's Standard*, August 1904, 4.

"Louisiana Has Been Having a Local Option Contest . . ." *Woman's Standard*, October 1904, 4.

"A Woman's Home." *Hartford (Ky.) Herald*, October 12, 1904.

"The Seeds of Despotism." *Woman's Standard*, January 1905, 4.

"The Woman on the Pedestal." *Woman's Standard*, September 1905, 4.

"Grover Cleveland's Democracy." *Woman's Standard*, November 1905, 4.

"Interesting Article by Gifted Writer on Subject of 'Hired Girl Problem.'" [Bowling Green, Ky., newspaper], November 1905.

"Counting and Voting." *Woman's Journal*, December 30, 1905, 209.

"Woman's Influence." *Hartford (Ky.) Herald*, November 14, 1906.

"Captivated Calves." *Woman's Journal*, January 19, 1907, 9.

"Sex and Society." *Woman's Journal*, April 20, 1907, 62–63.

"Kentucky." *Woman's Journal*, June 22, 1907, 100.

"Conservatism in India." *Woman's Standard*, March 1908, 3.

"The 'Unanswerable Argument' against Woman Suffrage." *Woman's Journal*, April 11, 1908, 57.

The "Unanswerable Argument" Answered. Political Equality Series. Warren, Ohio: National American Woman Suffrage Association, 1908.

"As to School Suffrage." *Bowling Green (Ky.) Messenger*, [1912].

"William Alexander Obenchain." *Ogden College Bulletin* 4 (April 1917): 4–6.

"Education Does Not Necessarily Mean Mere Completion of School." *Dallas Daily Times-Herald*, December 31, 1922.

"The Aggravating Sex." *Lexington (Ky.) Leader*, n.d.

"In Praise of Curry." [Bowling Green, Ky. newspaper?], n.d.

Works by Eliza Calvert Hall [Lida Calvert Obenchain]

Poems

The Calvert-Obenchain-Younglove Collection, Kentucky Library, Western Kentucky University, includes several of Eliza Calvert Hall's unpublished poems. She also collected many poems, both published and unpublished, in manuscript form under the title "A Wind Harp": see Manuscripts Small Collection No. 284, Kentucky Library, Western Kentucky University.

"Galatea." *Scribner's Monthly,* November 1879, 34.
"A Lesson in Mythology." *Scribner's Monthly,* December 1879, 320.
"An International Episode." *Scribner's Monthly,* April 1880, 952.
"Compensation." *Scribner's Monthly,* October 1880, 852.
"Felicissima." *Atlantic Monthly,* June 1881, 784.
"Her Choice." *Century Magazine,* January 1884, 462.
"One Way of Love." *Century Magazine,* May 1884, 122.
"The Unspoken Word." *Harper's Monthly,* November 1891, 918.
"Sunday Afternoon." *Childhood* [1892–94].
"Queen Bess." *Childhood,* February 1893.
"Song of the Indian Corn." *Arena,* June 1893, 113–14.
"A Forecast." *Kate Field's Washington,* July 26, 1893, 55.
"The White City." *Kate Field's Washington,* October 4, 1893, 215.
"A Modest Request." *Kate Field's Washington,* December 27, 1893, 416.
"Faith." *Kate Field's Washington,* March 7, 1894, 148.
"Hidden Music." *Arena,* July 1894, 255.
"Reasons." *Kate Field's Washington,* September 12, 1894, 167.
"Night-Blooming Cereus." *Kate Field's Washington,* April 13, 1895, 228.
Untitled ["My Enemy"]. *New York Independent,* December 1896. Reprint, *Dallas Morning News,* November 7, 1920.
"A Modern Psyche." In *A Library of the World's Best Literature, Ancient and Modern,* vol. 40, ed. Charles Dudley Warner, 16622. New York: International Society, 1897.
"Enlisted." *Truth* (1898). Reprint, *Wisconsin Memorial Day Annual.* Compiled by O. S. Rice. Madison, Wis.: Democrat Printing Co., 1912.
"The Lombardy Poplar." *Lippincott's Magazine,* June 1899, 830.
"Today." *Arena,* September 1899, 403.
"When Mamma Makes Bread." *Woman's Journal,* October 14, 1899, 323.
"Undecided." *Munsey's Magazine,* July 1905.
"Motherhood." *Munsey's Magazine,* February 1906.
"The Dilemma." *Pearson's Magazine,* December 1908.
"The Pack." Louisville Arts Club, ca. 1920. Reprint, Irene Moss Sumpter, *Our Heritage: An Album of Early Bowling Green Kentucky Landmarks.* Bowling Green, Ky.: American National Bank and Trust Co., 1978.
"The Wind-Harp." Louisville Arts Club, ca. 1920. Reprint, *Louisville (Ky.) Courier-Journal,* August 16, 1931.
"A Cry." Louisville Arts Club, January 29, 1924. Reprint, *Louisville (Ky.) Courier-Journal,* September 25, 1960.
"The Drum." Louisville Arts Club, January 29, 1924.
"A Disciple of Riley." *St. Nicholas,* November 1925, 83.

"My Inspiration." *Intelligencer,* n.d.
"The Prayer of Prayers." *Step Ladder,* n.d.

Articles and Essays

"The Sin of Unselfishness." *Kate Field's Washington,* March 28, 1894, 196–97.
"Woman and Nature." *Kate Field's Washington,* August 1, 1894, 77–78.
"The Omniscience of Ignorance." *Kate Field's Washington,* August 15, 1894, 100–101.
"My Mail Bag." *Kate Field's Washington,* October 17, 1894, 244.
"Second-Hand People." *Kate Field's Washington,* October 24, 1894, 261–63.
"On the Duty of Calling a Spade a Spade." *Kate Field's Washington,* February 9, 1895, 86–87.
"My Mail Bag." *Kate Field's Washington,* March 9, 1895, 148–49.
"The Opinions of 'John.'" *Womankind,* June 1896, 5.
"So Fur from the Big Road." *Womankind,* August 1896, 4–5.
"A Memorial to Henry Timrod." *Womankind,* October 1896, 5.
"A New Club." *Womankind,* October 1896, 6.
"The Evolution of Mental Science." *Metaphysical Magazine,* March 1901, 173–82.
"God, Good and Evil." *Metaphysical Magazine,* June 1906, 238–46.
"Why I Wrote 'Sally Ann's Experience.'" *Cosmopolitan,* July 1908, 163–67.
"The Romance of Your Grandmother's Quilt." *McCall's,* February 1913, 18.
"The Burden of the Ballot." *Woman's Journal,* January 15, 1916, 18.
"Madison Cawein, Southern Poet, Believed That Form, Rhythm and Music Are Necessary to Poetry." *Dallas Daily Times-Herald,* December 10, 1922.
"What Becomes of the Time?" *Dallas Daily Times-Herald,* September 16, 1923.
"Kentucky's Homecoming." *Dallas Daily Times-Herald,* 1924.
"A Notable Collection of Textiles." *House Beautiful,* January 1927, 54.
"Bowling Green and the Civil War." *Filson Club History Quarterly* 11 (October 1937): 241–51.

Short Fiction

"The Look without Words." *Symposium* [1896].
"Sally Ann's Experience." *Cosmopolitan,* July 1898, 283–91.
"The New Organ." *Cosmopolitan,* February 1899, 411–19.
"Aunt Jane's Album." *Cosmopolitan,* February 1900, 385–94.
"Two Loves." *Cosmopolitan,* November 1904, 67.
"Sweet Day of Rest." *Cosmopolitan,* December 1904, 148–55.

"Aunt Jane Goes A-Visiting." *Cosmopolitan,* September 1907, 494–503.
"A Little Story of the Other World, the Men She Had Seen in Her Dreams." *Life,* October 17, 1907.
"A Ride to Town." *Cosmopolitan,* April 1908, 481–91.
"The House That Was a Wedding Fee." *Cosmopolitan,* June 1908, 17–27.
"The Courtship of Miss Amaryllis." *Cosmopolitan,* September 1908, 357–67.
"The Marriage Problem in Goshen." *Cosmopolitan,* November 1908, 588–97.
"The Watch-Meeting." *Cosmopolitan,* January 1909, 167–74.
"An Eye for an Eye." *Cosmopolitan,* April 1909, 526–36.
"The Reformation of Sam Amos." *Cosmopolitan,* June 1909, 42–51.
"In War Time." *Cosmopolitan,* October 1909, 598–608.
"How Parson Page Went to the Circus." *Cosmopolitan,* July 1910, 173–82.
"Grandmother's Début." *Woman's Home Companion,* December 1919, 14.
"The Horoscope." *Woman's Home Companion,* January 1922, 17.

Books

Aunt Jane of Kentucky. Boston: Little, Brown, and Company, 1907.
The Land of Long Ago. Boston: Little, Brown, and Company, 1909.
Sally Ann's Experience. Boston: Little, Brown, and Company, 1910.
To Love and to Cherish. Boston: Little, Brown, and Company, 1911.
A Book of Hand-Woven Coverlets. Boston: Little, Brown, and Company, 1912.
Clover and Blue Grass. Boston: Little, Brown, and Company, 1916.

Books and Articles

Ammons, Elizabeth. *Conflicting Stories: American Women Writers at the Turn into the Twentieth Century.* New York: Oxford University Press, 1991.
"The Author of 'Aunt Jane.'" *Woman's Journal,* June 15, 1907, 95.
Baker, Jean H., ed. *Votes for Women: The Struggle for Suffrage Revisited.* New York: Oxford University Press, 2002.
Beard, Mary Hobson. *Old Homes in and near Bowling Green, Kentucky.* Bowling Green, Ky.: News Publishing Co., 1964.
Carrick, Alice Van Leer. *Collector's Luck, or A Repository of Pleasant and Profitable Discourses Descriptive of the Household Furniture and Ornaments of Olden Times.* Boston: Atlantic Monthly Press, 1919.
Carson, Martha. "The Kentucky Married Women's Property Act: An Early Appeal for Justice." *Border States* 5 (1985): 20–28.
Chused, Richard H. "Married Women's Property Law: 1800–1850." *Georgetown Law Journal* 71 (1983): 1359–1425.

Cooke, Elsie Burmeister. *A History of the Presbyterian Church, Bowling Green, Kentucky.* Bowling Green, Ky.: First Presbyterian Church, 1983.

Coultrap-McQuin, Susan. *Doing Literary Business: American Women Writers in the Nineteenth Century.* Chapel Hill: University of North Carolina Press, 1990.

Crandall, Charles H. *Representative Sonnets by American Poets.* Boston: Houghton, Mifflin and Company, 1890.

Dickenson, Donna. *Margaret Fuller: Writing a Woman's Life.* New York: St. Martin's Press, 1993.

Donovan, Josephine. *New England Local Color Literature: A Women's Tradition.* New York: Frederick Ungar Publishing Co., 1983.

Eakin, Paul John. "Sarah Orne Jewett and the Meaning of Country Life." *American Literature* 38 (January 1967): 508–31.

Elsley, Judy. "Uncovering Eliza Calvert Hall." *Encyclia: The Journal of the Utah Academy of Sciences, Arts, and Letters* 68 (1991): 155–72.

———. "Lack of a Separate Purse: Eliza Calvert Hall's *Aunt Jane of Kentucky.*" *Legacy: A Journal of American Women Writers* 9 (1992): 119–27.

Ferrero, Pat, Elaine Hedges, and Julie Silber. *Hearts and Hands: The Influence of Women and Quilts on American Society.* San Francisco: Quilt Digest Press, 1987.

Fetterley, Judith, and Marjorie Pryse. *American Women Regionalists 1850–1910: A Norton Anthology.* New York: W. W. Norton and Company, 1992.

Fitts, Jere Nelson, and Thomas Newton Moody. *Joseph B. Lapsley: From Rockbridge to Warren.* Bowling Green, Ky.: J. N. Fitts, 1994.

Forderhase, Nancy K. " 'The Clear Call of Thoroughbred Women': The Kentucky Federation of Women's Clubs and the Crusade for Educational Reform, 1903–1909." *Register of the Kentucky Historical Society* 83 (1985): 19–35.

Foster, Fannie Segur. "Eliza Calvert Hall." [Dallas newspaper article, August 1914].

———. "A Distinguished Daughter of Kentucky." *Holland's Magazine,* October 1919, 53.

Fuhrmann, Joseph T. *The Life and Times of Tusculum College.* Greenville, Tenn.: Tusculum College, 1986.

Fuller, Paul E. *Laura Clay and the Woman's Rights Movement.* Lexington: University Press of Kentucky, 1975.

———. "Suffragist Vanquished: Laura Clay and the Nineteenth Amendment." *Register of the Kentucky Historical Society* 93 (Winter 1995): 4–24.

Galloway, Ewing. "Eliza Calvert Hall Is Seen at Close Range." *Henderson (Ky.) Daily Gleaner,* August 30, 1908.

Green, Claud B. "The Rise and Fall of Local Color in Southern Literature." *Mississippi Quarterly* 18 (Winter 1964–65): 1–6.

Guethlein, Carol. "Women in Louisville: Moving toward Equal Rights." *Filson Club History Quarterly* 55 (April 1981): 151–78.

Habegger, Alfred. *My Wars Are Laid Away in Books: The Life of Emily Dickinson.* New York: Modern Library, 2001.

Hall, Eliza Calvert. *Aunt Jane of Kentucky.* Edited by Melody Graulich. Albany, N.Y.: NCUP, Inc., 1992.

———. *A Quilter's Wisdom: Conversations with Aunt Jane.* With an introduction by Roderick Kiracofe. San Francisco: Chronicle Books, 1994.

———. *Aunt Jane of Kentucky.* With a foreword by Bonnie Jean Cox. Lexington: University Press of Kentucky, 1995.

Harris, Sharon M. "'A New Era in Female History': Nineteenth-Century U.S. Women Writers." *American Literature* 74 (2002): 603–18.

Harris, Susan K. "'But Is It Any Good?': Evaluating Nineteenth-Century American Women's Fiction." *American Literature* 63 (1991): 43–61.

Harrison, Lowell H., and James C. Klotter. *A New History of Kentucky.* Lexington: University Press of Kentucky, 1997.

Hart, Albert Bushnell, and Herbert Ronald Ferleger, eds. *Theodore Roosevelt Cyclopedia.* Rev. 2nd ed. Westport, Conn.: Meckler Corp., 1988.

Hay, Melba Porter. "Suffragist Triumphant: Madeline McDowell Breckinridge and the Nineteenth Amendment." *Register of the Kentucky Historical Society* 93 (Winter 1995): 25–42.

Heilbrun, Carolyn G. *Writing a Woman's Life.* New York: Ballantine Books, 1988.

Hoganson, Kristin. "'As Badly Off as the Filipinos': U.S. Women's Suffragists and the Imperial Issue at the Turn of the Twentieth Century." *Journal of Women's History* 13 (Summer 2001): 9–33.

Houchens, Miriam. "Amazing Best Sellers by Kentucky Women Writers." *Filson Club History Quarterly* 41 (October 1967): 353–56.

Jeffrey, Jonathan, and Michael Dowell. *Bittersweet: The Louisville and Nashville Railroad and Warren County.* Bowling Green, Ky.: Landmark Association, 2001.

Johanningsmeier, Charles. "Expanding the Scope of 'Periodical History' for Literary Studies: Irving Bacheller and His Newspaper Fiction Syndicate." *American Periodicals* 5 (1995): 14–39.

John, Arthur W. *The Best Years of the Century: Richard Watson Gilder, "Scribner's Monthly," and the "Century Magazine," 1870–1909.* Urbana: University of Illinois Press, 1981.

Johnson, Jesse B., and Lowell H. Harrison. "Ogden College: A Brief History." *Register of the Kentucky Historical Society* 68 (July 1970): 189–220.

Johnston, John D., Jr. "Sex and Property: The Common Law Tradition, the Law School Curriculum, and Developments toward Equality." *New York University Law Review* 47 (December 1972): 1033–92.

Korda, Michael. *Making the List: A Cultural History of the American Bestseller 1900–1999.* New York: Barnes and Noble Books, 2001.

Kraditor, Aileen S. *The Ideas of the Woman Suffrage Movement, 1890–1920.* New York: Columbia University Press, 1965.

Lebsock, Suzanne D. "Radical Reconstruction and the Property Rights of Southern Women." *Journal of Southern History* 43 (May 1977): 195–216.

Maguire, Roberta S. "Kate Chopin and Anna Julia Cooper: Critiquing Kentucky and the South." *Southern Literary Journal* 35 (2002): 123–37.

McCullough, Kate. *Regions of Identity: The Construction of America in Women's Fiction, 1885–1914*. Stanford, Calif.: Stanford University Press, 1999.

McGill, Anna Blanche. "Kentucky Women Poets: Lida Calvert Obenchain." *Louisville (Ky.) Courier-Journal*, August 16, 1931.

Medinus, Mrs. Carl. "The Colonial Coverlet Guild of America." *Illinois Clubwoman's World*, November 1929, 5.

Moorhead, James H. "The 'Restless Spirit of Radicalism': Old School Fears and the Schism of 1837." *Journal of Presbyterian History* 78 (Spring 2000): 19–34.

Morris, Edmund. *The Rise of Theodore Roosevelt*. New York: Modern Library, 2001.

———. *Theodore Rex*. New York: Random House, 2001.

Mott, Frank Luther. *A History of American Magazines, 1741–1930*. Cambridge, Mass.: Belknap Press, 1957.

Nelson, Narka. *The Western College for Women, 1853–1953*. Oxford, Ohio: Western College, 1954.

Obenchain, Lida Calvert. "Lida Calvert Obenchain." *Woman's Journal*, October 14, 1899, 326.

Porter, Melba Dean. "Madeline McDowell Breckinridge: Her Role in the Kentucky Woman Suffrage Movement, 1908–1920." *Register of the Kentucky Historical Society* 72 (October 1974): 342–63.

Roberts, W. Lewis. "Property Rights of Married Women in Kentucky." *Kentucky Law Journal* 11 (November 1922): 1–9.

Rubin, Louis D., Jr., ed. *The History of Southern Literature*. Baton Rouge: Louisiana State University Press, 1985.

Schneirov, Matthew. *The Dream of a New Social Order: Popular Magazines in America 1893–1914*. New York: Columbia University Press, 1994.

Shammas, Carole. "Re-Assessing the Married Women's Property Acts." *Journal of Women's History* 6 (Spring 1994): 9–30.

Showalter, Elaine. *Sister's Choice: Tradition and Change in American Women's Writing*. Oxford: Clarendon Press, 1991.

Skaggs, Merrill Maguire. *The Folk of Southern Fiction*. Athens: University of Georgia Press, 1972.

Solomon, Martha M., ed. *A Voice of Their Own: The Woman Suffrage Press, 1840–1910*. Tuscaloosa: University of Alabama Press, 1991.

"Some New Lamps for Some Old." [newspaper article, 1913].

Spaas, Lieve, ed. *Paternity and Fatherhood: Myths and Realities*. New York: St. Martin's Press, 1998.

Stanton, Elizabeth Cady, Susan B. Anthony, Matilda Joslyn Gage, and Ida Husted Harper, eds. *History of Woman Suffrage*. New York: Source Book Press, 1970.

Steinberg, Salme Harju. *Reformer in the Marketplace: Edward W. Bok and "The Ladies' Home Journal."* Baton Rouge: Louisiana State University Press, 1979.

Stickles, Arndt M. *Simon Bolivar Buckner: Borderland Knight.* Chapel Hill: University of North Carolina Press, 1940.

Torsney, Cheryl B., and Judy Elsley, eds. *Quilt Culture.* Columbia: University of Missouri Press, 1994.

Townsend, John Wilson. *Kentucky in American Letters 1784–1912.* Cedar Rapids, Iowa: Torch Press, 1913.

"Virginia Heroine, Mrs. E. A. Obenchain." *Confederate Veteran,* February 1906, 72–73.

Ward, William S. *A Literary History of Kentucky.* Knoxville: University of Tennessee Press, 1988.

Webb, Dottie. "Nineteenth-Century Regional Writing in the United States." www.dotwebb.com/regional_writing/index.html [accessed March 26, 2007].

Wheeler, Marjorie Spruill. *New Women of the New South: The Leaders of the Woman Suffrage Movement in the Southern States.* New York: Oxford University Press, 1993.

Wood, Ann Douglas. "The Literature of Impoverishment: The Women Local Colorists in America 1865–1914." *Women's Studies* 1 (1972): 3–45.

Woodress, James, ed. *Essays Mostly on Periodical Publishing in America.* Durham, N.C.: Duke University Press, 1973.

Periodicals

Bowling Green (Ky.) Messenger, 1910–16
Louisville (Ky.) Courier-Journal, 1870–1931
Dallas Daily Times-Herald, 1922–35
Dallas Morning News, 1907–2002
Kate Field's Washington, 1893–95
New York Times, 1897–1931
Park City Daily News (Bowling Green, Ky.), 1935–87
Womankind, 1896–97
Woman's Journal, 1891–1916
Woman's Standard, 1892–1911
Woman's Tribune, 1892–1909

Unpublished Sources

Manuscript Collections

Bennett, Esther. Papers. Deposited with Laura Clay Papers, Margaret I. King Library, University of Kentucky.

Bennett, Mackie E. (Smith), Collection. Kentucky Library, Western Kentucky University.

Blackburn, Luke P. Correspondence. Kentucky Department for Libraries and Archives, Frankfort, Ky.

Calvert-Obenchain-Younglove Collection. Kentucky Library, Western Kentucky University.

Cherry, Henry Hardin. Papers. University Archives, Western Kentucky University.

Clay, Laura. Papers. Margaret I. King Library, University of Kentucky.

Dreiser, Theodore. Papers. Annenberg Rare Book and Manuscript Library, University of Pennsylvania, Philadelphia.

Fisher, Daniel G. Correspondence. Western History Collections, University of Oklahoma, Norman.

McElroy, Clarence Underwood, Collection. Kentucky Library, Western Kentucky University.

National American Woman Suffrage Association Records. Manuscript Division, Library of Congress, Washington, D.C. Microform.

Obenchain, Lida Calvert. Manuscripts Small Collection No. 77. Kentucky Library, Western Kentucky University.

———. Manuscripts Small Collection No. 261. Kentucky Library, Western Kentucky University.

———. Manuscripts Small Collection No. 284. Kentucky Library, Western Kentucky University.

———. Manuscripts Small Collection No. 578. Kentucky Library, Western Kentucky University.

———. Manuscripts Small Collection No. 726. Kentucky Library, Western Kentucky University.

———. Manuscripts Small Collection No. 792. Kentucky Library, Western Kentucky University.

———. Miscellaneous Papers. Filson Historical Society, Louisville, Ky.

Rodes, John B., Collection. Kentucky Library, Western Kentucky University.

Roosevelt, Theodore. Papers. Library of Congress, Washington, D.C. Microform.

Rothert, Otto Arthur. Manuscripts Small Collection No. 716. Kentucky Library, Western Kentucky University.

———. Miscellaneous Papers, 1910–21. Filson Historical Society, Louisville, Ky.

———. Papers. Filson Historical Society, Louisville, Ky.

Townsend, John Wilson, Collection. Library Special Collections, Eastern Kentucky University.

Underwood Collection. Kentucky Library, Western Kentucky University.

Other Unpublished Sources

Colonial Coverlet Guild of America. Minutes. DuPage County Historical Museum, Wheaton, Ill.

Cornette, James P. "The History of Ogden College." Paper, George Peabody
    College for Teachers, 1936. University Archives, Western Kentucky
    University.
Hay, Melba Porter. "Madeline McDowell Breckinridge: Kentucky Suffragist
    and Progressive Reformer." PhD diss., University of Kentucky, 1980.
Johnson, Jesse Butler. "The History of Ogden College." Master's thesis,
    George Peabody College for Teachers, 1929.
Knott, Claudia. "The Woman Suffrage Movement in Kentucky, 1879–1920."
    PhD diss., University of Kentucky, 1989.
Lee, Sophie. "Elizabeth Calvert Hall." Master's thesis, George Peabody Col-
    lege for Teachers, 1929.
Presbyterian Church of Bowling Green. Session Minutes. Kentucky Library,
    Western Kentucky University.
"Reminiscences of the Life and Teachings of Mary K. Jones While a Resi-
    dent of this City." Ca. 1885. Kentucky Library, Western Kentucky Uni-
    versity.
Rothert, Otto. "Local History in Kentucky Literature." Paper read before
    the Louisville Literary Club. September 27, 1915. Kentucky Library,
    Western Kentucky University.
Wilson, Fannie S. "Gleanings from an Old Scrap Book: Green River Female
    Seminary, Bowling Green, Kentucky." 1940. Kentucky Library, Western
    Kentucky University.
XV Club. Minutes. Kentucky Library, Western Kentucky University.

Index

Clay, Sarah (Sallie), 55, 72
Clover and Blue Grass, 165, 170, 172, 175–80
Club, XV. *See* XV Club
Cobb, Irvin S., 162–63
Colby, Clara Bewick, 70
Cole, Grace, 166, 167
Colonial Coverlet Guild of America, 202–3, 208
Comstock, Anthony, 181
Cooke, Rose Terry, 40, 99, 100
Cosmopolitan Magazine, 89, 91–92, 123, 135
Courier-Journal, 114–15, 148
Craftsman, 157
Craik, Dinah Mulock, 99, 100
Crandall, Charles H., 64
Crump, Malcolm H., 41
Curd, Isabella, 17, 18, 24, 29, 31, 47
curtesy, 52, 68, 83, 84

Dallas Kentucky Club, 202, 212
Davis, Jefferson, 42
Descendant, The, (Glasgow), 88
Dickerson, Archer C., 10, 15
Dishman, Mary, 136
Dodge, Mary Mapes, 40
dower, 52, 83, 84
Doyle, Arthur Conan, 92, 143
Dreiser, Theodore, 92, 180–81
Dreiser Protest, 180
Duke, Basil W., 162
Duniway, Abigail Scott, 111

Edwards, Harry Stillwell, 100
Eliot, George, 89, 99, 107

Farmer, Eugenia, 68, 69, 83, 84, 192, 259n10
Fayette County Equal Rights Association, 58
Field, Kate, 75, 77
Filson Club, 168

Fireside Industries, 153
Flexner, Ann Crawford, 162
Fox, John, Jr., 99
Freeman, Mary E. Wilkins, 123

Galloway, Ewing, 127, 129, 135
Garland, Hamlin, 99
Gaskell, Elizabeth, 99, 123
George, Uncle (servant), 17, 32
Gilder, Richard Watson, 40, 45, 180
Gilman, Charlotte Perkins, 80, 88
Glasgow, Ellen, 88
Gooch, Tom C., 213
Green and Barren River Navigation Company, 16
Greeneville College, 5, 6

Hall, Eliza Calvert. *See* Obenchain, Eliza (Lida) Calvert, life of; Obenchain, Eliza (Lida) Calvert, works of
Hall, Thomas James, 4, 7, 17
Harman, J. Lewie, 136
Harper's Monthly, 39
Harris, Joel Chandler, 99, 142
Harris and Ewing, 182
Harte, Bret, 92, 99
Henry, Josephine, 68, 69, 73, 83, 101
Henry, Mathis W., 8, 13
Hindman Settlement School, 153
Hines, Walker, 162
Hobson, Richmond Pearson, 107
Holland, Josiah Gilbert, 40
Holmes, Oliver Wendell, 64
Hopkins, Samuel, 5
Howells, William Dean, 80

International Literary and News Service, 89

Jackson, Helen Hunt, 40
Jackson, Thomas Jonathan (Stonewall), 42, 90